# Śrimad Bhagavad Gītā

## A Vedic Scientific Scripture of Liberation

(Original Sanskrit Text in Devanāgarī script, standard Roman transliteration and English translation)

I0263811

By

**Prof. Ravi Prakash Arya**
Chair Professor
Maharshi Dayanand Saraswati Chair (UGC)
Maharshi Dayanand University, Rohtak

VEDIC SCIENCE
सर्वज्ञानमयो वेदः
Indian Foundation For Vedic Science

AMAZON BOOKS, USA
In association with
INDIAN FOUNDATION FOR VEDIC SCIENCE
H.O.1051, Sector-1, Rohtak, Haryana, India
Delhi Contact Ph. Nos.: 09313033917; 09650183260
Emails: vedicscience@gmail.com; vedicscience@rediffmail.com
Website: https://vedic-sciences.com

# First Edition

Kali era: 5024 (c. 2023)
Kalpa era: 1,97,29,49,124
Brahma era: 15,50,21,97,9,49,124

**ISBN No. 81-87710-57-8**

Dedicated

To

The Sweet and Everlasting Memory of Divine Soul

Of

Late Smt. Prem Vati Prabhakar

The beloved mother of the present author, who was a great source of inspiration for him

# Contents

Introduction ....................................................7

अथ प्रथमोऽध्याय:.................................................. 13

Chapter 1 Arjuna's Dilemma.................................. 13

अथ द्वितीयोऽध्याय:.................................................26

Chapter 2 Sāṅkhya Yoga .......................................26

अथ तृतीयोऽध्याय: .................................................49

Chapter 3 Path of Karma Yoga ..............................49

अथ चतुर्थोऽध्याय:...................................................66

Chapter 4 Jñāna Yoga.............................................66

अथ पंचमोऽध्याय:...................................................82

Chapter 5 Path of Renunciation of acts involving selfish motive and doing acts of altruistic welfare ....82

अथ षष्ठोऽध्याय:......................................................94

Chapter 6 Yoga of Meditation ................................94

अथ सप्तमोऽध्याय:.................................................. 111

Chapter 7 Knowledge or Information and its Realisation ........................................................ 111

अथ अष्टमोऽध्याय: ..................................................121

Chapter 8 Imperishable Brahman .........................121

अथ नवमोऽध्याय: .................................................. 130

Chapter 9 Supreme Knowledge and the Highest Mystery.............................................................. 130

अथ दशमोऽध्याय:................................................... 145

Chapter 10 Expansion of *Ahaṃ*............................ 145

अथैकादशोऽध्याय:.................................................... 162

Chapter 11 Realisation of the Universal Self, i.e. Paramātman.................................................... 162

अथ द्वादशोऽध्याय: .................................................. 184

Chapter 12 Path of Devotion ............................... 184

अथ त्रयोदशोऽध्याय: ................................................ 192

Chapter 13 Division of Body and Soul.................. 192

अथ चतुर्दशोऽध्याय:..................................................205

Chapter 14 Three *Guṇas* of Nature ......................205

अथ पंचदशोऽध्याय:.................................................. 216

Chapter 15 Puruṣottama Yoga.............................. 216

अथ षोडशोऽध्याय:....................................................227

Chapter 16 Spiritualistic &Materialistic Tendencies227

अथ सप्तदशोऽध्याय:..................................................238

Chapter 17 Three Fold Positive Thought..............238

अथाष्टादशोऽध्याय: ..................................................249

Chapter 18 Nirvāṇa ............................................249

# Introduction

Live in the world, but do not get entangled in it. Live in the world, but do not let the world live within you. Remember, it is all a beautiful dream because everything changes and disappears. If you become detached, you will be able to see how people are attached to trivia and how much they are suffering. Moreover, you will laugh at yourself because you were also in the same boat before.

*Doctrine of Śrimad Bhagavad Gītā*

The *Bhagavad Gītā* was first translated into English by Charles Wilkins in 1785 and published by the British East India Company with an introduction by Lord Warren Hastings, the first British Governor-General of India, in which he prophetically wrote: "The writers of the Indian philosophies will survive when the British Dominion in India shall long have ceased to exist, and when the sources which it yielded of wealth and power are lost to remembrance". He further wrote, "I hesitate not to pronounce the Gītā's performance of great originality, of the sublimity of conception, reasoning, and diction almost unequalled and a single exception amongst all the known religions of mankind".

The Gītā deals with day-to-day human problems in a human way. That is why it has a tremendous appeal. It has inspired the human mind in India for centuries, and today, it casts its spell on millions across various parts of the world. Hardly, there is any great personality who was not inspired by its wisdom. Among the great and extraordinary people who were inspired and found their outlook changed by the timeless wisdom of the Gītā are thinkers, writers, scientists and philosophers like Mahatma Gandhi, B.G.Tilak, Sri Aurobindo, Albert Einstein, Dr. Albert Schweitzer, Herman Hesse, Ralph Waldo Emerson, Aldous Huxley, Walt Whitman, Henry David Thoreau, Annie Besant, Robert Oppenheimer, Sir Edwin Arnold and Carlyle to name but a few. It remains the most translated work on the Globe.

Despite enormous popularity, the *Bhagavad Gītā* remains a less understood but better-known text; people know more about it than what it is about. On the analogy of what the *Bhagavad Gītā* says in Chapter 2, Verse 29, some look upon the book as marvellous, a scripture of extraordinary or mysterious value. In contrast, others speak of the book as fantastic. Furthermore, still others, though hearing its teachings, do not comprehend its incredible significance!

'Gita' means a song or poem containing an inspired doctrine, and 'Bhagavat' means a blessed or adorable or venerable or divine One. Hence, *Śrimad Bhagavad Gītā* is variously called as 'The Song of God', 'The Divine Song', 'A Song of Fortune', 'The Lord's Song', 'The Holy Song of God', 'The Song of the Lord', Gūḍārtha Dīpikā, Gītā Rahasya, Jñāneśvarī, Bhavārthadīpikā, Sādhaka Sañjīvanī and so on. The noted English poet, journalist, and a Principal of the Government Sanskrit College at Pune, Sir Edwin Arnold (1832-1904), called his famous poetic version of the *Bhagavad Gītā* as 'The Song of the Celestials'. The Bhagavad Gītā's other title is '*Mokṣa Śāstra*' or 'Scripture of Liberation'. However, it is more popularly known as "The Gītā".

The *Bhagavad Gītā* can be studied from different angles, such as a historical document, a spiritual treatise, a scriptural text for daily chanting and prayer, sublime poetry, an exposition of Grammar and meter, or a management manual, depending on one's outlook and purpose.

The Gītā is not merely a religious book but a spiritual philosophy and ethical doctrine based upon Vedic scientific values. It has its bearing on the practical aspects of applying such principles in our daily lives.

The centuries-old *Bhagavad Gītā* remains the most relevant beacon light for us today. The modern man, like Arjuna, is at a crossroads where the focus is more on improving the Standard of Living rather than the Standard of Life, more on the Stock Exchange Index than on the Human Development Quotient, more on the Cost of Living than on the Quality of Life. It has resulted in his disorientation and imbalance in an environment of shifting values. While science aims to enhance the comfort of human life, spirituality teaches us how to be comfortable with what we have. That is the fundamental difference. In this scenario, the Gītā is the only source of strength for developing an integrated personality, a complete human, within us.

The problem facing us today is that while the world is coming closer physically, it drifts apart mentally and emotionally. Hence, all the conflicts, violence, destruction, and damage across the Globe. The urgent need, therefore, is the reconciliation and reconditioning of the human mindset to inculcate a global vision and bring about the universal brotherhood.

The Gītā is especially suited for the purpose, as it attempts to bring together varied and antithetical forms of consciousness and emphasizes the root conceptions of humanity, which are neither ancient nor modern, belonging neither to the East nor the West but eternal and universal.

Its beauty and sublimity lie in its everlasting relevance to the daily problems of human life, either occidental or oriental. It prescribes the methods which are within the reach of all. It has a message of solace, freedom, salvation, perfection, and peace for all human beings. The more you study it with devotion and faith, the more you will acquire deep knowledge, penetrative insight, and clear thinking. It is indeed a recipe for a sane living for every man and woman in the world.

*Śrimad Bhagavad Gītā* is one of the core texts of Indian philosophy and is considered among the most essential texts in the history of literature and philosophy. It finds a place in the Bhiṣma Parva chapters 23-40 of the *Mahābhārata*. It comprises 18 chapters spread out over 700 verses. Its author is Veda Vyasa, the compiler of the *Mahābhārata* who dictated this epic to Śri Gaṇeśa. Thus, it dates back to 5000 years ago as that of the *Mahābhārata*. *Śrimad Bhagavad Gītā* is a summation of many aspects of the Vedic, Yogic, Vedantic, and Upaniṣadic philosophies.

In India, Ādi Śaṅkara, who lived in 1168 B.C., is credited with revealing the greatness of the Gītā to the world. He retrieved it from the mighty tomes of the epic, the *Mahābhārata*, and wrote a brilliant commentary. It is this commentary that prevails as a classic text even today. However, it may be noted here that we do not come across Ādi Śaṅkarāchārya's commentary on the first chapter and till the 10th śloka of 2nd chapter of *Bhagvad Gītā*. It may have two reasons.

Either this portion was added later to it after Śaṅkarāchārya or he avoided the commentary on this portion for the reasons best known to him. If it was added later, it will be deemed as interpollation. Later, great Ācharyas like Rāmānuja, Madhva, Vallabha, and others came out with their commentaries, which were popular among their followers. In modern times, Sant Jñāneśvara, B.G. Tilak, and Aurobindo contributed their original thinking to the text.

In addition to the above commentaries, several other attempts have been made by scholars from different points of view. Most modern translations have been done purely from the religious point of view, depicting *Śrimad Bhagavad Gītā* as a religious and sacred book of Hindus. This type of attempt has clouded its scientific, spiritual and pragmatic aspect, which is more relevant to today's strife-torn world.

The present translation is first ever translation in English which is most appropriate in many sense. It tries to decode many abstruce concepts of the text in a very easily understandble modern terms. It depicts the Vedic scientific aspect of *Śrimad Bhagavad Gītā*, keeping its spiritual, ethical, and philosophical aspects intact without giving any religious colouring, which is not at all intended by its narrator, the author of the script. It has been attempted that the basic tenets of *Śrimad Bhagavad Gītā* are presented in the most modern suitable terms for learned and laity. Several technical terms in the Bhagavad Gītā don't have their correspondence either in English or other languages of the world. Such terms have been used as it is. Philosophical concepts like life, death, rebirth, etc., have been elaborated scientifically for the benefit of our readers. I hope the learned readers will find this compendium of Vedic philosophy and science most exciting and valuable to determine the future course of their life to reach their cherished goal on the material or spiritual plane.

How to read this translation? There is also a need to address this question. While translating the text, the Sanskrit words that appeared in ślokas have been given in parenthesis (small brackets) in italics, followed by their meanings. So, this translation is also helpful for those who want to know or understand *Bhagavad Gītā* word by word. A further explanation of English words has been given in square brackets like [ ]. So, an explanation in square brackets will be helpful to understand the basic terms and concepts of *Bhagavad Gītā*. I hope this attempt will be appreciated by both the learned and laity.

Prof. Ravi Prakash Arya
Chair Professor
Maharshi Dayanand Saraswati Chair (UGC)
Maharshi Dayanand University, Rohtak

# अथ प्रथमोऽध्याय:

## अर्जुनविषादयोग:

# Chapter 1

[Arjuna's Dilemma]

Let me here point out that-

The very first chapter starts with the dilemma of Arjuna on the battlefield. When Arjuna finds his brothers, relatives as an opponent in the war, he is moved by the massacre of his persons by his persons. He thinks that if this massacre leads to achieving the kingdom of Hastinapur and enables them to be the emperor of the world, this won't be termed an outstanding personal achievement of theirs as they won't be able to celebrate this outstanding achievement because all of their near and dear ones will not be there to witness it. Thus, going by the personal agenda, Arjuna did not find this war as an instrument of happiness; instead, the war would have plunged the entire humanity into chaos. With this idea in mind, Arjuna thinks of withdrawing from the war. However, Krishna is there to guide him on the right path. According to Krishna, he was not fighting the war for his gain or happiness, but he was supposed to fight the war for the safety and security of the nation. The nation was not secure in the hands of Duryodhana, who had not respect for women. A person who was ready to outrage the modesty of his own sister in law, how can he gurantee the safety and security of other women in society. Morover, he wanted to use the power for his own benefit and never applied his mind in making decisions. He was playing as a tool in the hands of anti-social elements like Śakuni. As such, Krishna did not find Arjuna's arguments valid. If a country survives, her citizens survives. If country prospers, her citizen prosper. So, Arjuna needed to fight the war for the sake of the nation, safety and security of women and humanity at large and to exterminate the destructive and anti-social elements having their say in national affairs.

धृतराष्ट्र उवाच

Dhṛtarāṣṭra said

धर्मक्षेत्रे कुरुक्षेत्रे समवेता युयुत्सवः।
मामकाः पाण्डवाश्चैव किमकुर्वत संजय ॥ १.१ ॥

*dharmakṣetre kurukṣetre samavetā yuyutsavaḥ,*
*māmakāḥ pāṇḍavāścaiva kim akurvata Sañjaya. (1.01)*

O Sañjaya, what did my sons and Pāṇḍavas (Pāṇḍu's sons) do when they got together for going to war with each other in Kurukshetra, the land earmarked to fight out the war for Dharma?

संजय उवाच

Sañjaya said

दृष्ट्वा तु पाण्डवानीकं व्यूढं दुर्योधनस्तदा।
आचार्यमुपसंगम्य राजा वचनमब्रवीत्॥ १.२ ॥

*dṛṣṭvā tu pāṇḍvānīkaṁ vyūḍaṁ Duryodhanas tadā,*
*ācāryaṁ upasaṅgamya rājā vacanam abravīta. (1.02)*

Seeing the battle formation of the Pāṇḍava's army, King Duryodhana approached Ācārya Droṇa, and spoke thus:

पश्यैतां पाण्डुपुत्राणामाचार्य महतीं चमूम्।
व्यूढां द्रुपदपुत्रेण तव शिष्येण धीमता॥ १.३ ॥

*paśyaitāṁ pāṇḍuputrāṇām ācārya mahatīṁ camūm,*
*vyūḍāṁ drupadaputreṇa tava śiṣyeṇa dhīmatā. (1.03)*

Behold this mighty army of the sons of Pāṇḍu O Āchārya! This formation has been arranged by your talented disciple, the son of Drupada.

अत्र शूरा महेष्वासा भीमार्जुनसमा युधि।
युयुधानो विराटश्च द्रुपदश्च महारथः॥ १.४॥
*atra śūrā maheṣvāsā bhīmārjuna samā yudhi,*
*yuyudhāno virāṭaṣca drupadaśca mahārathaḥ. (1.04)*

There are warriors armed with mighty weapons equal to Bhīma and Arjuna in war such as Yuyudhāna, Virāṭa and the great warrior, Drupada;

धृष्टकेतुश्चेकितानः काशिराजश्च वीर्यवान्।
पुरुजित्कुन्तिभोजश्च शैब्यश्च नरपुंगवः॥ १.५॥
*dhṛṣṭketuś cekitānaḥ kāśirājaśca vīryavān,*
*purujīt-kuntibhojaśca śaibyaśca narapuṅgavaḥ. (1.05)*

Dhṛṣṭaketu, Chekitāna, and the heroic King of Kāśī; Purujit, Kuntibhoja, and the great, Saibya;

युधामन्युश्च विक्रान्त उत्तमौजाश्च वीर्यवान्।
सौभद्रो द्रौपदेयाश्च सर्व एव महारथाः॥ १.६॥
*yudhāmanyuśca vikrānta uttamaujāśca vīryavān,*
*saubhadro draupadeyāśca sarva eva mahārathāḥ. (1.06)*

The valiant Yudhāmanyu, the formidable Uttamaujā, the son of Subhadrā (Abhimanyu), and the sons of Draupadī; all of them are great warriors.

अस्माकं तु विशिष्टा ये तान्निबोध द्विजोत्तम।
नायका मम सैन्यस्य संज्ञार्थं तान्ब्रवीमि ते॥ १.७॥
*asmākaṁ tu viśiṣṭā ye tannibodha dvijottama,*
*nāyakā mama sainyasya saṁjñārthaṁ tān bravīmi te (1.07)*

You should also know, O great scholar! the distinguished commanders manning my army.

भवान्भीष्मश्च कर्णश्च कृपश्च समितिंजयः।
अश्वत्थामा विकर्णश्च सौमदत्तिस्तथैव च॥ १.८॥
*bhavān bhīṣmaṣca karṇaśca kṛpaśca samitiñjaya,*

*aśvathāmā vikarṇaśca saumadattistathaiva ca. (1.08)*

Yourself, Bhīṣma, Karṇa, and the victorious Kṛpa; Aśvatthāmā, Vikarṇa, and the son of Somadatta.

अन्ये च बहवः शूरा मदर्थे त्यक्तजीविताः ।
नानाशस्त्रप्रहरणाः सर्वे युद्धविशारदाः ॥ १.९ ॥
*anye ca bahavaḥ śūrā madarthe tyakta-jīvitāḥ,*
*nānā- śastra- praharaṇāḥ sarve yuddha-viśāradāḥ. (1.09)*

And many other heroes who are ready to stake their lives for me. They are skilled in operating various weapons and missiles in warfare.

अपर्याप्तं तदस्माकं बलं भीष्माभिरक्षितम् ।
पर्याप्तं त्विदमेतेषां बलं भीमाभिरक्षितम् ॥ १.१० ॥
*aparyāptaṁ tad asmākaṁ balaṁ bhīṣmābhirakṣitam,*
*paryāptaṁ tvidam eteṣāṁ balaṁ bhīmābhirakṣitam. (1.10)*

Our army is invincible in the command of Bhīṣma; while their army commanded by Bhīma is easy to conquer.

अयनेषु च सर्वेषु यथाभागमवस्थिताः ।
भीष्ममेवाभिरक्षन्तु भवन्तः सर्व एव हि ॥ १.११ ॥
*ayaneṣu ca sarveṣu yathā bhāgam avasthitāḥ,*
*bhīṣmam evābhirakṣantu bhavantaḥ sarva eva hi. (1.11)*

Therefore all of you, occupying your respective positions on all fronts, protect just Bhīṣma only.

तस्य संजनयन्हर्षं कुरुवृद्धः पितामहः ।
सिंहनादं विनद्योच्चैः शङ्खं दध्मौ प्रतापवान् ॥ १.१२ ॥
*tasya sañjanayan harṣaṁ kuruvṛddhaḥ pitāmahaḥ,*
*siṁhanādaṁ vinadyoccaiḥ śaṅkhaṁ dadhmau pratāpavān. (1.12)*

The mighty Bhīṣma, the eldest man of the Kuru dynasty, roared like a lion and blew his conch loudly bringing joy to Duryodhana.

ततः शङ्खाश्च भेर्यश्च पणवानकगोमुखाः ।
सहसैवाभ्यहन्यन्त स शब्दस्तुमुलोऽभवत् ॥ १.१३ ॥
*tataḥ śaṅkhāśca bheryaśca paṇavānaka- gomukhāḥ,*
*sahasaivābhyahanyanta sa śabdas tumulo'bhavat. (1.13)*

After that, all of sudden, conches, kettle-drums, cymbals, drums, and trumpets were sounded together. The commotion was tremendous.

ततः श्वेतैर्हयैर्युक्ते महति स्यन्दने स्थितौ ।
माधवः पाण्डवश्चैव दिव्यौ शङ्खौ प्रदध्मतुः ॥ १.१४ ॥
*tataḥ śvetair-hayair-yukte mahati syandane sthitau,*
*mādhavaḥ pāṇḍavaś caiva divyau śaṅkhau pradadhmatuḥ. (1.14)*

Then Krishna, the eliminator of enemies, and Arjuna, seated in a grand chariot yoked with white horses, blew their divine conches.

पांचजन्यं हृषीकेशो देवदत्तं धनंजयः ।
पौण्ड्रं दध्मौ महाशङ्खं भीमकर्मा वृकोदरः ॥ १.१५ ॥
*pāñcajanyaṁ hṛṣikeśo devadattaṁ dhanañjayaḥ,*
*pauṇḍraṁ dadhmau mahāśaṅkhaṁ bhīmakarmā*
*vṛkodaraḥ. (1.15)*

Krishna blew his conch named Pāñcajanya; Arjuna blew his conch named Devadatta; and Bhīma, the performer of formidable deeds and extra-ordinary eater blew (his) great conch named Pauṇḍra.

अनंतविजयं राजा कुन्तीपुत्रो युधिष्ठिरः ।
नकुलः सहदेवश्च सुघोषमणिपुष्पकौ ॥ १.१६ ॥
*anantavijayaṁ rājākuntīputro yudhiṣṭhiraḥ,*
*nakulaḥ sahadevaśca sughoṣmaṇipuṣpakau. (1.16)*

King Yudhiṣṭhira, the son of Kunti, blew the conch called Anantavijaya, while Nakula and Sahadeva blew their conches Sughoṣa and Maṇipuṣpaka.

काश्यश्च परमेष्वासः शिखण्डी च महारथः ।

धृष्टद्युम्नो विराटश्च सात्यकिश्चापराजितः ॥ १.१७ ॥
*kāśyaśca parameṣvāsaḥ śikhaṇḍī ca mahārathaḥ,*
*dhṛṣṭadyumno virāṭaś ca sātyakiś cāparājitaḥ. (1.17)*

The King of Kāśī, the mighty armour; Śikhaṇḍī, the great warrior; Dhṛṣṭdyumna, Virāṭa, and the invincible Sātyaki;

द्रुपदो द्रौपदेयाश्च सर्वशः पृथिवीपते ।
सौभद्रश्च महाबाहुः शङ्खान्दध्मुः पृथक्पृथक् ॥ १.१८ ॥
*drupado draupadeyāś ca sarvaśaḥ pṛthivīpate,*
*saubhadraś ca mahābāhuḥ śaṅkhān dadhmuḥ pṛthak-pṛthak.(1.18)*

King Drupada, and the sons of Draupadi; the mighty son of Subhadrā; all of them blew their respective conches, O Emperor!

स घोषो धार्तराष्ट्राणां हृदयानि व्यदारयत् ।
नभश्च पृथिवीं चैव तुमुलोऽभ्यनुनादयन् ॥ १.१९ ॥
*sa ghoṣo dhārtarāṣṭrāṇāṁ hṛdayāni vyadārayat,*
*nabhaśca pṛthivīṁ caiva tumulo vyanunādayan. (1.19)*

The tumultuous uproar of the conches of the commanders of the army led by Pāṇḍavas, pierced the hearts of the Kauravas and resounded through earth and sky.

अथ व्यवस्थितान्दृष्ट्वा धार्तराष्ट्रान् कपिध्वजः ।
प्रवृत्ते शस्त्रसंपाते धनुरुद्यम्य पाण्डवः ॥ १.२० ॥
*atha vyavasthitān dṛṣṭvā dhārtarāṣṭrān kapi-dhvajaḥ,*
*pravṛtte śastra-sampāte dhanur udyamya pāṇḍavaḥ. (1.20)*

When the sons of Dhṛtarāṣṭra occupied their positions and the war broke out, Arjuna, whose flag bore the sign of Hanuman, took up his bow and spoke these words to Śri Krishna:

अर्जुन उवाच

Arjuna said

हृषीकेशं तदा वाक्यमिदमाह महीपते।
सेनयोरुभयोर्मध्ये रथं स्थापय मेऽच्युत॥ १.२१॥
यावदेतान्निरीक्षेऽहं योद्धुकामानवस्थितान्।
कैर्मया सह योद्धव्यमस्मिन्रणसमुद्यमे॥ १.२२॥

*hṛṣīkeśaṁ tadā vākyam idam āha mahīpate,*
*senayor ubhayor madhye rathaṁ sthāpaya me'cyuta. (1.21)*
*yāvad etānnirīkṣe'haṁ yoddhukāmān avasthitān,*
*kair mayā saha yoddhavyam asmin raṇa-samudyame.(1.22)*

O Achyuta, (Infallible one) park my chariot between the two armies, so that I may have a look at those who stand on the battlefield to fight out war with us.

योत्स्यमानानवीक्षेऽहं य एतेऽत्र समागताः।
धार्तराष्टरस्य दुर्बुद्धेर्युद्धे प्रियचिकीर्षवः॥ १.२३॥

*yotsyamānān avekṣe'haṁ ya ete'tra samāgatāḥ,*
*dhārtarāṣṭrasya durbuddher yuddhe priyacikīrṣavaḥ. (1.23)*

I would like to see those who would fight here with the view to favour the crooked Duryodhana in this war.

संजय उवाच

Sañjaya said

एवमुक्तो हृषीकेशो गुडाकेशेन भारत।
सेनयोरुभयोर्मध्ये स्थापयित्वा रथोत्तमम्॥ १.२४॥

*evamukto hṛṣikeśo guḍākeśena bhārata,*
*senayor ubhayor madhye sthāpayitvā rathottamam. (1.24)*

O King, on the request of Arjuna [the Guḍākeśa, i.e. a person who wins over his sleep], Krishna, [the Hṛṣikeśa, i.e. who keeps the people happy] parked that excellent chariot amid the two armies.

भीष्मद्रोणप्रमुखतः सर्वेषां च महीक्षिताम्।
उवाच पार्थ पश्यैतान्समवेतान्कुरूनिति॥ १.२५॥

*bhiṣma-droṇa-pramukhataḥ sarveṣāṁ ca mahīkṣitām,*
*uvāca pārtha paśyaitān samavetān kurūniti. (1.25)*

Facing Bhīṣma, Droṇa, and all other Kings; Krishna said to Arjuna: Behold these assembled Kurus!

तत्रापश्यत्स्थितान्पार्थः पितृनथ पितामहान्।
आचार्यान्मातुलान्भ्रातृन्पुत्रान्पौत्रान्सखींस्तथा श्वशुरान्सुहृदश्चैव
सेनयोरुभयोरपि ॥१.२६
*tatrāpaśyat sthitān pārthaḥ pitṛnatha pitāmahān,*
*ācāryān mātulān bhrātṛn putrān pautrān sakhīnstathā*
*śvaśurān suhṛdaścaiva senayor ubhayor api.*

There Arjuna came across his elders, grandfathers, teachers, maternal uncles, brothers, sons, grandsons, and friends.

तान्समीक्ष्य स कौन्तेयः सर्वान्बन्धूनवस्थितान्।
कृपया परयाविष्टो विषीदन्निदमब्रवीत् ॥ १.२७ ॥
*tān samikṣya sa kaunteyaḥ sarvān bandhūn avasthitān.*
*kṛpayā parayāviṣṭo viṣīdannidamabravīt (1.27)*

He found his fathers-in-law, kinsmen, and other dear ones standing in the ranks of the two armies.

अर्जुन उवाच
Arjuna said

कृपया परयाविष्टो विषीदन्निदमब्रवीत्।
दृष्ट्वेमं स्वजनं कृष्ण युयुत्सुं समुपस्थितम्॥ १.२८ ॥
*kṛpayā parayāviṣṭoviṣīdan idam abravīt,*
*dṛṣṭvemaṁ svajanaṁ Kṛṣṇa yuyutsuṁ samupasthitam.(1.28)*

Overcome with great compassion and sorrow Arjuna said— O Krishna, seeing these kinsmen standing with a desire to fight,

सीदन्ति मम गात्राणि मुखं च परिशुष्यति।
वेपथुश्च शरीरे मे रोमहर्षश्च जायते॥ १.२९ ॥
*sidanti mama gātrāṇi mukhaṁ ca pariśuṣyati,*
*vepathuśca śarīre me romaharṣaśca jāyate. (1.29)*

My limbs are failing and my mouth is becoming dry.

My body is trembling and I am feeling frightened.

गाण्डीवं स्रंसते हस्तात्त्वक्चैव परिदह्यते।
न च शक्नोम्यवस्थातुं भ्रमतीव च मे मनः॥ १.३०॥
*gāṇḍivaṁ sransate hastāt tvak caiva paridahyate,*
*na ca śaknomi avasthātuṁ bhramatīva ca me manaḥ. (1.30)*

The bow, Gāṇḍīva, is slipping from my hands and my skin is burning. I am not able to stabilize myself and I am feeling giddy.

निमित्तानि च पश्यामि विपरीतानि केशव।
न च श्रेयोऽनुपश्यामि हत्वा स्वजनमाहवे॥ १.३१॥
*nimittāni ca paśyāmi viparītāni Keśvaḥ.*
*na ca śreyo'nupaśyāmi hatvā svajanam āhave. (1.31)*

O Krishna, I see bad omens and I won't find emancipation by killing my kinsmen in battle.

न काङ्क्षे विजयं कृष्ण न च राज्यं सुखानि च।
किं नो राज्येन गोविन्द किं भोगैर्जीवितेन वा॥ १.३२॥
*na kāṅkṣe vijayaṁ Kṛṣṇa na ca rājayaṁ sukhāni ca,*
*kiṁ no rājyena Govinda kiṁ bhogair jīvitena vā. (1.32)*

I desire neither victory nor pleasure nor kingdom, O Krishna. What is the use of kingdom, or enjoyment, or even life, O Govinda?

येषामर्थे काङ्क्षितं नो राज्यं भोगाः सुखानि च।
त इमेऽवस्थिता युद्धे प्राणांस्त्यक्त्वा धनानि च॥ १.३३॥
*yeṣām arthe kāṅkṣitaṁ no rajyaṁ bhogāḥ sukhāni ca,*
*ta ime avasthitā yuddhe prāṇāns tyaktvā dhanāni ca. (1.33)*

For whom we desire kingdom, enjoyment, and pleasure, they are standing here for the battle, giving up the desire for their lives and wealth.

आचार्याः पितरः पुत्रास्तथैव च पितामहाः।
मातुलाः श्वशुराः पौत्राः श्यालाः सम्बन्धिनस्तथा॥ १.३४॥

*ācāryāḥ pitaraḥ putrāstathaiva ca pitāmahāḥ,*
*mātulāḥ śvaśurāḥ pautrāḥ śyālāḥ sambandhinastathā. (1.34)*

Teachers, elders, sons and grandfathers, maternal uncles, fathers-in-law, grandsons, brothers-in-law, and other relatives.

एतान्न हन्तुमिच्छामि घ्नतोऽपि मधुसूदन।
अपि त्रैलोक्यराज्यस्य हेतोः किं नु महीकृते॥ १.३५॥
*etānna hantum icchāmi ghnato'pi Madhusūdana,*
*api trailokyarājyasya hetoḥ kiṁ nu mahīkṛte. (1.35)*

I do not wish to kill them all, even if they are going to kill me or even if I get the sovereignship of the three worlds, what to say of this earthly rulership, O Madhusudana (the killer of foes).

निहत्य धार्तराष्ट्रान्नः का प्रीतिः स्याज्जनार्दन।
पापमेवाश्रयेदस्मान्हत्वैतानाततायिनः॥ १.३६॥
*nihatya dhṛtarāṭrān naḥ kā prītiḥ syājjanārdana,*
*papam eva-āśrayed asmān hatvaitān ātatāyinaḥ. (1.36)*

O Janardana, what pleasure shall we find by killing the sons of Dhṛtarāṣṭra? We shall only incur pāpa (downgradation) upon killing these foes.

तस्मान्नार्हा वयं हन्तुं धार्तराष्ट्रान्स्वबान्धवान्।
स्वजनं हि कथं हत्वा सुखिनः स्याम माधव॥ १.३७॥
*tasmānnārhā vayaṁ hantuṁ dhṛtarāṣṭrān svabāndhavān,*
*svajanaṁ hi kathaṁ hatvā sukhinaḥ syām Mādhava. (1.37)*

Therefore, we are not able to kill our kinsmen, the sons of Dhṛtarāṣṭra. How can we be happy after killing them, O Mādhava?

यद्यप्येते न पश्यन्ति लोभोपहतचेतसः।
कुलक्षयकृतं दोषं मित्रद्रोहे च पातकम्॥ १.३८॥
*yadyapyete na paśyanti lobhopahata-cetasaḥ,*
*kulakṣyakṛtaṁ doṣaṁ mitradrohe ca pātakaṁ. (1.38)*

Though they, blinded by greed, do not see any evil or harm in the destruction of the family and in revolting with friends.

कथं न ज्ञेयमस्माभिः पापादस्मान्निवर्तितुम् ।
कुलक्षयकृतं दोषं प्रपश्यद्भिर्जनार्दन ॥ १.३९ ॥

*katham na jñeyam asmābhiḥ pāpād asmān nivartitum,
kulakṣaya-kṛtaṁ doṣaṁ prapaśyadbhir Janārdana. (1.39)*

Why shouldn't we, knowing harm and evil in the devastation of the family, think about saving us from this pāpa (act of downfall), O Janārdana (Krishna)?

कुलक्षये प्रणश्यन्ति कुलधर्माः सनातनाः ।
धर्मे नष्टे कुलं कृत्स्नमधर्मोऽभिभवत्युत ॥ १.४० ॥

*kulakṣaye praṇasyanti kuladharmaḥ sanātanāḥ,
dharme naṣṭe kulaṁ kṛtsnam adharmo'bhibhavatyuta. (1.40)*

With the destruction of the family, the eternal family values will disappear, and with the eradication of family values, the vice will take over the entire family.

अधर्माभिभवात्कृष्ण प्रदुष्यन्ति कुलस्त्रियः ।
स्त्रीषु दुष्टासु वार्ष्णेय जायते वर्णसङ्करः ॥ १.४१ ॥

*adharmābhibhavāt Kṛṣṇa praduṣyanti kulastriyaḥ,
striṣu duṣṭāsu Vārṣṇeya jāyate varṇasaṅkaraḥ. (1.41)*

O Krishna, with the preponderance of vice, the women in society will be humiliated by corrupt persons and there will be an admixture good and bad values in persons.

सङ्करो नरकायैव कुलघ्नानां कुलस्य च ।
पतन्ति पितरो ह्येषां लुप्तपिण्डोदकक्रियाः ॥ १.४२ ॥

*saṅkaro narakāyaiva kulaghnānāṁ kulasya ca,
patanti pitaro hyeṣāṁ luptapiṇḍodaka kriyāḥ. (1.42)*

The admixture will lead to the downfall of the family lines and its destructors. For want of proper care by estranged family members, family elders will also see their downfall from Vānaprastha or Saṁnyāsa Āśramas.

Note: In ancient times, it was the responsibility of families and society to look after the elderly persons of family and society. It was not the responsibility of state.

दोषैरेतैः कुलघ्नानां वर्णसङ्करकारकैः ।
उत्साद्यन्ते जातिधर्माः कुलधर्माश्च शाश्वताः ॥ १.४३ ॥
*doṣair etaiḥ kulaghnānāṁ varṇasaṅkara-kārakaiḥ,*
*utsādyante jātidharmāḥ kuladharmāś ca śāśvatāḥ. (1.43)*

Due to the mistakes of destructive forces, eternal human values and family values will be wiped out.

उत्सन्नकुलधर्माणां मनुष्याणां जनार्दन ।
नरके नियतं वासो भवतीत्यनुशुश्रुम ॥ १.४४ ॥
*utsanna kuladharmāṇāṁ manuṣyāṇāṁ Janārdana,*
*Narake'niyataṁ vāso bhavati ityanuśuśruma. (1.44)*

It is heard, O Janārdana, that people whose family values are eroded, are liable to witness downfall hereafter [next life] in lower species.

अहो बत महत्पापं कर्तुं व्यवसिता वयम् ।
यद्राज्यसुखलोभेन हन्तुं स्वजनमुद्यताः ॥ १.४५ ॥
*aho bata mahatpāpaṁ kartuṁ vyavasitā vayam,*
*yadrājyasukhalobhena hantuṁ svajanam udyatā. (1.45)*

Alas! we are bent upon committing a great pāpa by slaying our kinsmen just for the sake of greed for the crown.

यदि मामप्रतीकारमशस्त्रं शस्त्रपाणयः ।
धार्तराष्ट्रा रणे हन्युस्तन्मे क्षेमतरं भवेत् ॥ १.४६ ॥
*yadi mām aprtikāram aśastra śastra-pāṇayaḥ,*
*dhārtarāṣṭrā raṇe hanyustanme kṣemataraṁ bhaveta. (1.46)*

It would be far better for me if the sons of Dhṛtarāṣṭra

should kill me with their weapons in battle, while I am unarmed and unresisting.

संजय उवाच

Sañjaya said

एवमुक्त्वार्जुनः सङ्ख्ये रथोपस्थ उपाविशत्।
विसृज्य सशरं चापं शोकसंविग्नमानसः॥ १.४७॥
*evamuktvārjunaḥ saṅkhye rathopastha upāviśat,*
*visṛjya saśaraṁ cāpaṁ śokasaṁvignamānasaḥ. (1.47)*

Having expressed his views thus in the battlefield, Arjuna occupied the back seat of the chariot. He left his arms and became bemoaned.

ॐ तत्सदिति श्रीमद् भगवद्गीतासूपनिषत्सु ब्रह्मविद्यायां योगशास्त्रे श्रीकृष्णार्जुनसंवादे अर्जुनविषादयोगो नाम प्रथमोऽध्यायः॥ १॥

Here ends the first chapter in the *Bhagvad Gītā*, named Sāṅkhya yoga, dealing with the Brahmavidyā as propounded in the Upaniṣad and Yogaśāstra in the form of dialogue between Śri Krishna and Arjuna.

# अथ द्वितीयोऽध्यायः

## साङ्ख्ययोगः

# Chapter 2

(Sāṅkhya Yoga)

The present chapter deals with knowledge of Śāṅkhya. It teaches us how the soul gets embodied. Its embodiment is called bondage and disembodiment Mokṣa. There is nothing such as can be called life and death. Since the ātman is ever-existing, it neither dies nor takes birth. So, Arjuna's worry for his near and dear ones was unfounded. Krishna argues there is no reason to mourn the death if one believes that ātman neither takes birth nor dies. The other way around, if one thinks that it dies and takes birth, that also gives no rationale to mourn the death since whoever dies takes birth, and whoever takes birth indeed dies. On these points of argument, he wins over Arjuna. Here, Arjuna is a layman unaware of his past and future.

On the other hand, Krishna is a Brahma-realized Yogī who is well aware of the past and providence. So, it was natural for Arjuna to undergo such a dilemma, and the greatness of Śri Krishna brought him out of the blue. This chapter of Gītā is very relevant for every human being. Each person is bound to face such situations in his or her life. Veda Vyasa wrote these teachings of Krishna with a broader perspective of achieving highest goal of life. Knowing right and wrong, ethical and non-ethical, helps people deal with situations. It is often said: ऋते ज्ञानात् न मुक्तिः *ṛte jñānāt na muktiḥ* - there can be no liberation either from suffering or from mundane life without proper knowledge (proper information of the phenomenon).

In this chapter, Śri Krishna wants to tell Arjuna that if something is unavoidable, do it happily and boldly without looking into its pros and cons. The war was unavoidable. Had Arjuna avoided fighting the war, the enemy would not let him go scot-free. So, all the arguments given by Arjuna during the wartime were baseless. His withdrawal from the war at that time would have benefited the enemies of society. Śri Krishna tried to make him understand the situation and justified fighting the war with beautiful arguments.

संजय उवाच।

Sañjaya said

तं तथा कृपयाविष्टमश्रुपूर्णाकुलेक्षणम्।
विषीदन्तमिदं वाक्यमुवाच मधुसूदनः ॥ २.१ ॥
*tam tathā kṛpayāviṣṭam aśrupūrṇākulekṣaṇam,*
*viṣidantam idam vākyam uvāca madhusūdanaḥ. (2.1)*

Sañjaya Said— The slayer of ultras (Śri Krishna) said these words to Arjuna who was overwhelmed with compassion and despair and whose eyes were tearful and downcast.

श्री कृष्ण उवाच

Krishna said

कुतस्त्वा कश्मलमिदं विषमे समुपस्थितम्।
अनार्यजुष्टमस्वर्ग्यमकीर्तिकरमर्जुन ॥ २.२ ॥
*kutas tvā kasmalam idam viṣame samupasthitam,*
*anāryajuṣṭam asvargyam akīrtikaram Arjuna. (2.2)*

Śri Krishna Said— O Arjuna! where has this dejection come from to you on the battle-field? This is not fit for an Arya (the person of noble mind and deeds). It is disgraceful, does not lead one to happiness and bliss.

क्लैब्यं मा स्म गमः पार्थ नैतत्त्वय्युपपद्यते।
क्षुद्रं हृदयदौर्बल्यं त्यक्त्वोत्तिष्ठ परंतप॥ २.३॥
*klaibyam mā sma gamaḥ pārtha naitat tavyyupapadyate,*
*kṣudram hṛdaya daurbalyam tyaktvottiṣṭha parantapa. (2.3)*

Don't be overpowered by cowardice, O son of Pṛthā [Kuntī], because it doesn't behove you. Shake off this weakness of poor heart and get up, O slayer of foes [terrorists].

अर्जुन उवाच।
Arjuna said

कथं भीष्ममहं सङ्ख्ये द्रोणं च मधुसूदन।
इषुभिः प्रतियोत्स्यामि पूजार्हावरिसूदन॥ २.४॥
*kathaṁ bhiṣmam ahaṁ saṁkhye droṇam ca Madhusūdana,*
*iṣubhiḥ prati yotsyāmi pujārhav arisudana. (2.4)*

Arjuna Said— How shall I strike Bhīṣma and Droṇa with arrows on the battle-field, since, both of them are respectable, O slayer of ultras?

गुरूनहत्वा हि महानुभावान्
श्रेयो भोक्तुं भैक्ष्यमपीह लोके।
हत्वार्थकामांस्तु गुरुनिहैव
भुञ्जीय भोगान् रुधिरप्रदिग्धान्॥ २.५॥
*gurūn ahatvā hi mahānubhāvān,*
*śreyo bhoktum bhaikṣyam apīha loke,*
*hatvārthakāmāns tu gurūnihaiva,*
*bhuñjīya bhogān rudhirapradigdhān. (2.05)*

It would be better to live on alms in this world than to slay these highly respectable gurus, because if I like to achieve my goal by killing them, I would, indeed, enjoy pleasures stained with their blood.

न चैतद्विद्मः कतरन्नो गरीयो
यद्वा जयेम यदि वा नो जयेयुः।

यानेव हत्वा न जिजीविषामः
तेऽवस्थिताः प्रमुखे धार्तराष्ट्राः ॥२.६ ॥

*na caitad vidmaḥ kataran no gariyo,*
*yad vā jayema yadi vā no jayeyuḥ,*
*yān eva hatvā na jijivişāmas,*
*te'vasthitāḥ pramukhe Dhārtarāṣṭrāḥ. (2.6)*

Neither do we know which alternative [to beg or bury] is better for us, nor do we know whether we shall conquer them or they will conquer us. The sons of Dhṛtarāṣṭra, killing whom we don't even wish to live, are standing in front of us. [Arjuna expresses here his intention that he doesn't intend to kill his cousins].

कार्पण्यदोषोपहतस्वभावः
पृच्छामि त्वां धर्मसंमूढचेताः ।
यच्छ्रेयः स्यान्निश्चितं ब्रूहि तन्मे
शिष्यस्तेऽहं शाधि मां त्वां प्रपन्नम् ॥ २.७ ॥

*kārpaṇyadoṣopahata svabhāvaḥ,*
*pṛccāmi tvāṁ dharma sammuḍhacetāḥ,*
*yacchreyaḥ syān niścitaṁ brūhi tan me,*
*śiṣyas te'haṁ śādhi māṁ tvāṁ prapannam. (2.7)*

Overcome by the weakness of compassion and confusion about Dharma [duty], I request you to tell me decisively what is in the larger interest of society and humankind. I am your disciple and need your expert guidance.

Note: Dharma may be defined as the eternal law governing, upholding, and supporting the creation and the world order. It also means duty, righteousness, ideal conduct, moral values, and truth. Adharma is an antonym for Dharma. Expert guidance is necessary during the moment of crisis.

न हि प्रपश्यामि ममापनुद्याद्

यच्छोकमुच्छोषणमिन्द्रियाणाम् ।
अवाप्य भूमावसपत्नमृद्धं
राज्यं सुराणामपि चाधिपत्यम् ॥ २.८ ॥

*na hi prapaśyāmi mamāpanudyād,*
*yacchokam ucchoṣaṇamindriyāṇām,*
*avāpya bhūmāv asapatnam ṛddhaṁ rājyam,*
*surāṇampi cādhipatyam. (2.8)*

I do not perceive anything that can remove my desensitizing sorrow. This sorrow can't even be removed by attaining an unrivalled and prosperous kingdom on this earth, or even lordship over the divine people.

संजय उवाच

Sañjaya said

एवमुक्त्वा हृषीकेशं गुडाकेशः परंतपः ।
न योत्स्य इति गोविन्दमुक्त्वा तूष्णीं बभूव ह ॥ २.९ ॥

*evaṁ uktvā Hṛṣikeśaṁ Guḍākeśaḥ parantapa,*
*na yotsya iti Govindam uktvā tūṣṇiṁ babhūva ha. (2.09)*

Sañjaya said—O slayer of ultras (Dhṛtarāṣṭra), after speaking this to Śri Krishna, the controller of the sleep (Guḍākeṣa Arjuna) said to Krishna: I shall not fight war, and became silent.

तमुवाच हृषीकेशः प्रहसन्निव भारत ।
सेनयोरुभयोर्मध्ये विषीदन्तमिदं वचः ॥ २.१० ॥

*tamuvāca Hṛṣikeśa prahasanniva Bhārata,*
*senayor ubhayor madhye viṣidantam idaṁ vacaḥ. (2.10)*

O descendant of Bharats, Śri Krishna smiled and spoke these words to the despondent Arjuna amid the two armies.

श्री कृष्ण उवाच

Śri Krishna said

अशोच्यानन्वशोचस्त्वं प्रज्ञावादांश्च भाषसे ।

गतासूनगतासूंश्च नानुशोचन्ति पण्डिता: ॥ २·११ ॥
*aśocyānanvaśocas tvaṁ prajñāvādāñśca bhāṣase,*
*gatāsūn agatāsūñśca nānuśocanti paṇḍitāḥ. (2.11)*

You grieve for those who are not worthy of grief, and yet speak the words of wisdom. The wise grieves neither for the living nor for the dead.

नत्वेवाहं जातु नासं न त्वं नेमे जनाधिपा: ।
न चैव न भविष्याम: सर्वे वयमत: परम् ॥ २.१२ ॥
*na tvevāhaṁ jātu nāsaṁ na tvaṁ neme janādhipāḥ,*
*na caiva na bhaviṣyāmaḥ sarve vayam ataḥ param. (2.12)*

There was never a time when I, you, or these kings did not exist; nor shall we ever cease to exist in the future.

देहिनोऽस्मिन्यथा देहे कौमारं यौवनं जरा ।
तथा देहान्तरप्राप्तिर्धीरस्तत्र न मुह्यति ॥ २.१३ ॥
*dehino'smin yathā dehe kaumāraṁ yauvanaṁ jarā.*
*tathā dehāntara prāptir dhiras tatra na muhyati. (2.13)*

Just as this body of Ātmā acquires a childhood, youth, and adulthood, similarly Ātmā acquires another body after death. The wise are not deluded by this. (See also 15.08)

Note: Ātmā or Ātmān means individuated soul.

मात्रास्पर्शास्तु कौन्तेय शीतोष्णसुखदु:खदा: ।
आगमापायिनोऽनित्यास्तांस्तितीक्षस्व भारत ॥ २.१४ ॥
*mātrā sparśāstu Kaunteya śitoṣṇasukha duḥkhadāḥ,*
*āgamāpāyino'nityātāns titikṣasva Bhārata. (2.14)*

The (*sparśa*) contacts of the (*mātrā*) senses with the stimuli lead to feelings of heat, cold, pain, and pleasure. They come and go. Therefore, [learn to] endure them, O Arjuna, the descendant of Bharatas.

यं हि न व्यथ्यन्त्येते पुरुषं पुरुषर्षभ।
समदुःखसुखं धीरं सोऽमृतत्वाय कल्पते॥ २.१५॥
*yaṁ hi na vyathyantyete puruṣaṁ puruṣarṣbha,*
*sama duḥkhasukhaṁ dhīraṁ so' mṛtatvāya kalpate. (2.15)*

O best of persons [Arjuna]! A person endowed with patience and who is indifferent to the feelings of pain and pleasure becomes worthy of emancipation.

नासतो विद्यते भावो नाभावो विद्यते सतः।
उभयोरपि दृष्टोऽन्तस्त्वनयोस्तत्त्वदर्शिभिः॥ २.१६॥
*nāsato vidyate bhāvo nābhāvo vidyate sataḥ.*
*ubhayor api dṛṣṭo'ntastvanayos tattvadarśibhiḥ. (2.16)*

There can not be absence of the sat [eternal Ātmā] and presence of the asat [perishable objects]. The seekers of truth indeed realise the difference between these two.

Note: Perishable objects continue to change every movement.

अविनाशि तु तद्विद्धि येन सर्वमिदं ततम्।
विनाशमव्ययस्यास्य न कश्चित्कर्तुमर्हति॥ २.१७॥
*avināśi tu tadviddhi yena sarvam idaṁ tatam,*
*vināśam avyayasyāsya na kaścit kartum arhati. (2.17)*

Know that Ātmā who is pervading this entire body is indestructible. No one can destroy this indestructible (Ātmā).

अन्तवन्त इमे देहा नित्यस्योक्ताः शरीरिणः।
अनाशिनोऽप्रमेयस्य तस्माद्युध्यस्व भारत॥ २.१८॥
*antavanta ime dehā nityasyoktāḥ śarīriṇaḥ,*
*anāśino'prameyasya tasmādyudhyasva Bhārata. (2.18)*

Bodies of the eternal, imperishable, and incomprehensible souls are said to be perishable. Therefore, fight war, O Arjuna, the descendant of Bharatas.

य एनं वेत्ति हन्तारं यश्चैनं मन्यते हतम्
उभौ तौ न विजानीतो नायं हन्ति न हन्यते ॥ २.१९ ॥
*ya enaṁ vetti hantāraṁ yaścainaṁ manyate hatam,*
*ubhau tau na vijānito nāyaṁ hanti na hanyate. (2.19)*

The one who thinks that this Ātmā is a slayer and the one who thinks that Ātmā is slain, both are ignorant because this Ātmā neither slays [is not the doer] nor is slain.

न जायते म्रियते वा कदाचिन्
नायं भूत्वा भविता वा न भूयः ।
अजो नित्यः शाश्वतोऽयं पुराणो
न हन्यते हन्यमाने शरीरे ॥ २.२० ॥
*na jāyatemriyate vā kadācin,*
*nāyaṁ bhūtvā bhavitā vā bhūyaḥ,*
*ajo nitya śāśvato'yaṁ purāṇo,*
*na hanyate hanyamāne śarire. (2.20)*

The Ātmā is neither born nor does it die at any time, nor having been died it will cease to exist again. It is unborn, eternal, primeval. It is not destroyed even when the physical body is destroyed.

वेदाविनाशिनं नित्यं य एनमजमव्ययम् ।
कथं स पुरुषः पार्थ कं घातयति हन्ति कम् ॥ २.२१ ॥
*vedavināśinaṁ nityaṁ ya enam ajam avyayam,*
*kathaṁ sa puruṣaḥ Pārtha kaṁ ghātayati hanti kam. (2.21)*

O son of Pṛthā (Kuntī), how can a person who knows that the Ātmā is indestructible, eternal, unborn, and imperishable, kill anyone or cause anyone to be killed?

वासांसि जीर्णानि यथा विहाय
नवानि गृह्णाति नरोऽपराणि ।
तथा शरीराणि विहाय जीर्णानि
अन्यानि संयाति नवानि देही ॥ २.२२ ॥

*vāsānsi jīrṇāni yathā vihāya,*
*navāni gṛhṇāti naro'parāṇi,*
*tathā śarīrāṇi vihāya jīrṇāni,*
*anyāni sañyāti navāni dehi. (2.22)*

Just as a person puts on new garments after discarding the old ones, similarly Ātmā acquires new bodies after casting away the old bodies [as per its sanskāras] .

नैनं छिन्दन्ति शस्त्राणि नैनं दहति पावकः ।
न चैनं क्लेदयन्त्यापो न शोषयति मारुतः ॥ २.२३ ॥
*nainaṁ chindanti śastrāṇi nainaṁ dahati pāvakaḥ,*
*na cainaṁ kledayantyāpo na śoṣayati mārutaḥ. (2.23)*

Weapons do not cut this Ātmā, fire does not burn it, water does not dampen it, and the wind does not dry it.

अच्छेद्योऽयमदाह्योऽयमक्लेद्योऽशोष्य एव च ।
नित्यः सर्वगतः स्थाणुरचलोऽयं सनातनः ॥ २.२४ ॥
*acchedyo'yam adāhyo'yam akledyo'śoṣya eva ca,*
*nityaḥ sarvagataḥ sthāṇur acalo'yaṁ sanātanaḥ. (2.24)*

This Ātmā cannot be cut, burned, dampened, or dried up. It is eternal. It pervades all the bodies of [humans, animals, plants]. It is unchanging, immovable, and eternal or permanent.

अव्यक्तोऽयमचिन्त्योऽयमविकार्योऽयमुच्यते ।
तस्मादेवं विदित्वैनं नानुशोचितुमर्हसि ॥ २.२५ ॥
*avyakto'yam acintyo'yamvikāryo'yam ucyate,*
*tasmādevaṁ viditvainaṁ nānuśocitum arhasi. (2.25)*

The Ātmā is said to be un-manifest, unthinkable, and unchanging. Realising this significance of Ātmā, you should abandon your grief.

अथ चैनं नित्यजातं नित्यं वा मन्यसे मृतम् ।
तथापि त्वं महाबाहो नैवं शोचितुमर्हसि ॥ २.२६ ॥
*atha cainaṁ nityajātaṁ nityaṁ vā manyase mṛtam,*

*tathāpi tvaṁ mahābāho naivam śocitum arhasi. (2.26)*

If you think that this Ātmā takes birth and dies perpetually, even then, O long-armed Arjuna, you should not have any reason to grieve.

जातस्य हि ध्रुवो मृत्युर्ध्रुवं जन्म मृतस्य च।
तस्मादपरिहार्येऽर्थे न त्वं शोचितुमर्हसि॥ २.२७॥
*jātasya hi dhruvo mṛtyurdhruvam janma mṛtasya ca,*
*tasmād apariharye'rthe na tvaṁ śocitum arhasi. (2.27)*

Because, if we go by that philosophy, everyone who takes birth is going to die definitely, and whoever dies is going to take birth without fail. Therefore, you should not lament over the inevitable.

अव्यक्तादीनि भूतानि व्यक्तमध्यानि भारत।
अव्यक्तनिधनान्येव तत्र का परिदेवना॥ २.२८॥
*avyaktādīni bhūtāni vyaktamadhyāni Bhārata,*
*ayakta-nidhanānyeva tatra kā paridevanā. (2.28)*

All beings, O Arjuna belonging to the line of Bharatas, are un-manifest before birth. They are manifest between birth and death only. They are un-manifest even after death. So, what is there to grieve about?

आश्चर्यवत्पश्यति कश्चिदेनम्
आश्चर्यवद्वदति तथैव चान्यः।
आश्चर्यवच्चैनमन्यः श्रृणोति
श्रुत्वाऽप्येनं वेद न चैव कश्चित्॥ २.२९॥
*āścaryavat paśyati kaścidenam,*
*āścaryavad vadati tathaiva cānyaḥ,*
*āścaryavaccainam anyaḥ śṛṇoti,*
*śrutvāpyenaṁ veda na kaścit. (2.29)*

Some look upon this Ātmā as a wonder, another describes it as wonderful thing, and others hear of it [from the learned scholars] as if it's a wonder. Even after hearing about it no one actually knows it.

देही नित्यमवध्योऽयं देहे सर्वस्य भारत।
तस्मात्सर्वाणि भूतानि न त्वं शोचितुमर्हसि॥ २.३०॥
*dehī nityam avadhyo'yaṁ dehe sarvasya Bhārata,*
*tasmāt sarvāṇi bhūtāni na tvaṁ śocitum arhasi. (2.30)*

O Arjuna from the line of Bharatas, this Ātmā that dwells in various kinds of bodies is eternal and indestructible. Therefore, you should not mourn for all these beings.

स्वधर्ममपि चावेक्ष्य न विकम्पितुमर्हसि।
धर्म्याद्धि युद्धाच्छ्रेयोऽन्यत्क्षत्रियस्य न विद्यते॥ २.३१॥
*svadharmamapi cāvekṣya na vikampitum arhasi.*
*dharmyāddhi yuddhācchreyo'nyat kṣatriyasya na vidyate. (2.31)*

Considering also your duty as a kṣatriya [warrior], you should not waver. Because there is nothing better for a kṣatriya than to fight out the war to protect public and establish dharma.

यदृच्छया चोपपन्नं स्वर्गद्वारमपावृतम्।
सुखिनः क्षत्रियाः पार्थ लभन्ते युद्धमीदृशम्॥ २.३२॥
*yadṛcchayā copapannaṁ svargadvāram apāvṛtam,*
*sukhinaḥ kṣatriyāḥ Pārtha labhante yuddham īdṛśam.(2.32)*

Only the fortunate kṣatriyas, O Pārtha [son of Pṛthā], get such an opportunity for an unsought war that is like an open door to immortality in history.

अथ चेत्त्वमिमं धर्म्यं संग्रामं न करिष्यसि।
ततः स्वधर्मं कीर्तिं च हित्वा पापमवाप्स्यसि॥ २.३३॥
*atha cettvamiṁ dharmyaṁ saṅgrāmaṁ na kariṣyasi,*
*tataḥ svadharmaṁ kīrtiṁ ca hitvā pāpam avāpsyasi. (2.33)*

If you will not perform your duty in the war to protect dharma and public, then failing in your duty you will lose reputation and incur pāpa [held liable for the spread of adharma and destruction of public].

अकीर्तिं चापि भूतानि कथयिष्यन्ति तेऽव्ययाम्।
संभावितस्य चाकीर्तिर्मरणादतिरिच्यते॥ २.३४॥
*akīrtiṁ cāpi bhūtāni kathayiṣyanti te'vyayām,*
*sambhāvitasya cākīrtir marṇādatiricyate. (2.34)*

People will talk about you in a disgraceful manner forever. Dishonour to the honoured one is worse than death.

भयाद्रणादुपरतं मंस्यन्ते त्वां महारथाः।
येषां च त्वं बहुमतो भूत्वा यास्यसि लाघवम्॥ २.३५॥
*akīrtiṁ cāpi bhūtāni kathayiṣyanti te'vyayām,*
*sambhāvitasya cākīrtir marṇādatiricyate. (2.35)*

Here the great warriors will think that you have retreated from the battle out of fear [and not because of compassion that you are overwhelmed with]. Those who have great regard for you will lose the same.

अवाच्यवादांश्च बहून्वदिष्यन्ति तवाहिताः।
निन्दन्तस्तव सामर्थ्यं ततो दुःखतरं नु किम्॥ २.३६॥
*avācyavādāñśca bahūn vadiṣyanti tavāhitāḥ,*
*nindantastava sāmarthyaṁ tato duḥkhataraṁ nu kim.(2.36)*

The people will give disgusting remarks against you and ridicule your ability. What could be more outlandish than that?

हतो वा प्राप्स्यसि स्वर्गं जित्वा वा भोक्ष्यसे महीम्।
तस्मादुत्तिष्ठ कौन्तेय युद्धाय कृतनिश्चयः॥ २.३७॥
*hato vā prāpsyasi svargaṁ jitvā vā bhokṣyase mahīm,*
*tasmāduttiṣṭha Kaunteya yuddhāya kṛtaniścaya. (2.37)*

You will rise to divinity and become immortal in history if killed, or you will rule the earth if emerge victorious. Therefore, get up and get going with the determination to fight, O son of Kunti.

सुखदुःखे समे कृत्वा लाभालाभौ जयाजयौ।
ततो युद्धाय युज्यस्व नैवं पापमवाप्स्यसि॥ २.३८॥
*sukhaduḥkhe same kṛtvā lābhālābhau jayājayau,*
*tato yuddhāya yujyasva naivaṁ pāpam avāpsyasi. (2.38)*

Keeping yourself indifference to pleasure and pain, gain and loss, victory and defeat alike, engage yourself in war as your duty. By doing so you won't be held responsible for pāpa.

एषा तेऽभिहिता साङ्ख्ये बुद्धिर्योगे त्विमां शृणु।
बुद्ध्या युक्तो यया पार्थ कर्मबन्धं प्रहास्यसि॥ २.३९॥
*eṣā te abhihitā sāṅkhye buddhir yoge tvimāṁ śṛṇu,*
*buddhayā yukto yayā Pārtha karmabandhaṁ prahāsyasi.* (2.39)

You have been told here from the point of Sāṅkhya [the nature of embodiment of soul in the matter of life and death]. Now listen to it from the point of yoga [practical method causing disembodiment or liberation]. Endowed with the wisdom of Yoga, you will free yourself from the bondage of kārmika sanskāras.

Note: The Sāṅkhya describes the process of embodiment of the soul. The Yoga describes the method of disembodiment.

नेहाभिक्रमनाशोऽस्ति प्रत्यवायो न विद्यते।
स्वल्पमप्यस्य धर्मस्य त्रायते महतो भयात्॥ २.४०॥
*nehābhikramanāśo'sti pratyavāyo na vidyate,*
*svalpam apyasya dharmasya trāyate mahato bhayāt. (2.40)*

In the yoga, no effort goes futile, and there is no chance of getting results contrary to the efforts we have made. Even a little practice of this protects one from great fear of what to do and what not.

व्यवसायात्मिका बुद्धिरेकेह कुरुनन्दन।
बहुशाखा ह्यनन्ताश्च बुद्धयोऽव्यवसायिनाम्॥ २.४१॥

*vyavasāyātmikā buddhir ekeha kurunandana,*
*bahuśākhā hyanantāśca buddhayo'vyavasāyinām. (2.41)*

Those who are sure of their goal, have only one mind, but those who are unsure of their goal have many or wavering minds, O son of Kurus.

यामिमां पुष्पितां वाचं प्रवदन्त्यविपश्चित: ।
वेदवादरता: पार्थ नान्यदस्तीति वादिन: ॥ २.४२ ॥
*yām imāṁ puṣpitāṁ vācaṁ pravadantyavipaścitaḥ,*
*veda vādaratāḥ pārtha nānyadastīti vādinaḥ. (2.42)*

Those unwise, who indulge into jugglery of words and talk about material prosperity by Vedas and say that there is nothing else [except this enjoyment].

कामात्मान: स्वर्गपरा जन्मकर्मफलप्रदाम् ।
क्रियाविशेषबहुलां भोगैश्वर्यगतिं प्रति ॥ २.४३ ॥
*kāmātmanaḥ svarga parā janmakarmaphalapradām,*
*kriyāviśeṣabahulāṁ bhogaiśvaryagatiṁ prati. (2.43)*

They believe that (*svarga-parāḥ*) material enjoyment is the highest goal of life, and the life of enjoyment is the reward of good karmas; they prescribe various specific rituals for the attainment of material enjoyment and prosperity.

भोगैश्वर्यप्रसक्तानां तयापहृतचेतसाम् ।
व्यवसायात्मिका बुद्धि: समाधौ न विधीयते ॥ २.४४ ॥
*bhogaiśvaryaprasaktānāṁ tayāpahṛtacetasāṁ,*
*vyavasāyātmikā buddhiḥ samādhau na vidhīyate. (2.44)*

They are totally taken in by the allurement of material enjoyment and attached to it. Their mind fails to establish in Samādhi.

त्रैगुण्यविषया वेदा निस्त्रैगुण्यो भवार्जुन ।
निर्द्वन्द्वो नित्यसत्त्वस्थो निर्योगक्षेम आत्मवान् ॥ २.४५ ॥
*traiguṇyaviṣayā vedā nistraiguṇyo bhavārjuna,*

*nirdvandvo nityasattvastho niryogakṣema ātmavān. (2.45)*

The Vedas deal with the worldly creation involving the three Guṇas [sattva, rajas, and tamas]. O Arjuna, you rise above the allurements of worldly things made up of the three Guṇas. Become free from duality [combination of soul and body], be ever dominated by sattva Guṇa and unconcerned with the thoughts of acquisition and preservation of material things. Know your true nature [that you are only a spiritual element].

यावानर्थ उदपाने सर्वत: संप्लुतोदके।
तावान्सर्वेषु वेदेषु ब्राह्मणस्य विजानत: ॥ २.४६ ॥
*yāvānarthaḥ udapāne sarvataḥ samplutodake,*
*tāvān sarveṣu vedeṣu brāhmaṇasya vijānataḥ. (2.46)*

To a person who has realised Brahman, the Vedas become uselsess for him [called Vedānta, end of knowledge], just as a glass of water or a reservoir loses its importance for a thirsty person when all the places are inundated with waters.

कर्मण्येवाधिकारस्ते मा फलेषु कदाचन।
मा कर्मफलहेतुर्भूर्मा ते सङ्गोऽस्त्वकर्मणि ॥ २.४७ ॥
*karmaṇyevādhikāraste mā phaleṣu kadācana,*
*mā karmaphala heturbhūr mā te saṅgo'stvakarmaṇi. (2.47)*

You have jurisdiction over your nitya karma [obligatory duty] only, and not over the results/fruits. The fruits of work should not be your motive. You should never be inactive or refrain from your duty [solely because you have no control over fruit].

योगस्थ: कुरु कर्माणि सङ्गं त्यक्त्वा धनंजय।
सिद्ध्यसिद्ध्यो: समो भूत्वा समत्वं योग उच्यते ॥ २.४८ ॥
*yogasthaḥ kuru karmāṇi saṅgaṁ tyaktvā Dhanañjaya,*
*siddhyasiddhyoḥ samo bhūtvā samatvaṁ yoga ucyate. (2.48)*

Do your duty in a yogic state of mind, O Dhanañjaya [winner of the material and spiritual wealth], with your mind committed to God and unconcerned about material gain or loss. Be indifferent to success and failure which is called the yogic state of mind or indifferent mind.

दूरेण ह्यवरं कर्म बुद्धियोगाद्धनंजय ।
बुद्धौ शरणमन्विच्छ कृपणाः फलहेतवः ॥ २.४९ ॥
*dūreṇa hyavaraṁ karma buddhiyogāddhanañjaya,*
*buddhau śaraṇam anviccha kṛpaṇā phalahetavaḥ. (2.49)*

Kāmya karma [karma done with the desire for material gain] is far inferior to buddhi-yoga [mind unconcerned about material gain or loss]. Therefore, go to the shelter of buddhi-yoga [or try to develop a state of indifferent mind], O Dhanañjaya [the winner of material and spiritual wealth]. Kāmya karmas [or karmas done with the desire for material gain, makes a man pitiable and fearful [and the person who never takes into account the material gain and loss, lives a life of boldness].

बुद्धियुक्तो जहातीह उभे सुकृतदुष्कृते ।
तस्माद्योगाय युज्यस्व योगः कर्मसु कौशलम् ॥ २.५० ॥
*buddhiyukto jahātīha ubhe sukṛtaduṣkṛte,*
*tasmādyogāya yujyasva yogaḥ karmasu kauśalam. (2.50)*

A person equipped with buddhi-yoga [mind unconcerned about material gain] becomes free from the notion of good or bad acts in his/her lifetime itself. Therefore, strive for a buddhi-yoga [mind unconcerned about material gain or loss] as in 2.48. Buddhi-yoga [the development of an indifferent mind or when the mind becomes unconcerned about gain or loss] enhances work efficiency.

कर्मजं बुद्धियुक्ता हि फलं त्यक्त्वा मनीषिणः ।

जन्मबन्धविनिर्मुक्ता: पदं गच्छन्त्यनामयम्॥ २.५१॥
*karmajaṁ buddhiyuktā hi phalaṁ tyaktvā manīṣiṇaḥ,*
*janmabandhavinirmuktāḥ padaṁ gacchantyanāmayam. (2.51)*

The wise men, possessed with buddhi-yoga [an indifferent mind] remain unconcerned about fruits of the work done by them. They are freed from the bondage of rebirth and attain the blissful divine state.

यदा ते मोहकलिलं बुद्धिर्व्यतितरिष्यति।
तदा गन्तासि निर्वेदं श्रोतव्यस्य श्रुतस्य च॥ २.५२॥
*yadā te mohakalilaṁ buddhir vyatitariṣyati,*
*tadā gantāsi nirvedaṁ śrotavyasya śrutasya ca. (2.52)*

(*yadā*) When (*te buddhi*) your mind (*mohakalilaṁ*) stained by attachment (*vyatitariṣyati*) is purifed, then you will not worry about what has been heard and what is to be heard.

श्रुतिविप्रतिपन्ना ते यदा स्थास्यति निश्चला।
समाधावचला बुद्धिस्तदा योगमवाप्स्यसि॥ २.५३॥
*śrutivipratipannā te yadā sthāsyati niścalā,*
*samādhāvacalā buddhis tadā yogam avāpsyasi. (2.53)*

When your mind is not confused by the conflicting views, it will become calm and stay firm in samādhi, then you are supposed to have attained the state of indifferent mind (*buddhi-yoga*).

अर्जुन उवाच।
Arjuna said

स्थितप्रज्ञस्य का भाषा समाधिस्थस्य केशव।
स्थितधी: किं प्रभाषेत किमासीत व्रजेत किम्॥ २.५४॥
*sthitaprajñsya kā bhāṣā samādhisthasya keśavaḥ,*
*sthitdhiḥ kiṁ prabhāṣeta kimāsīta vrajeta kim. (2.54)*

O Keśava, what is the sign of a person whose mind is established in one's own self and stay firm in samādhi?

How does a person with a steady mind behave? How does he speak, sit, and walk?

श्री कृष्ण उवाच

Śri Krishna said

प्रजहाति यदा कामान्सर्वान्पार्थ मनोगतान्।
आत्मन्येवात्मना तुष्टः स्थितप्रज्ञस्तदोच्यते॥ २.५५॥
*prajahāti yadā kāmān sarvān pārtha manogatān,*
*ātmanyevātmanā tuṣṭaḥ sthitaprajñastadocyate. (2.55)*

When one shuns all desires completely and is satisfied within one's own self, then one is called a person of steady mind, O son of Pṛthā.

दुःखेष्वनुद्विग्नमनाः सुखेषु विगतस्पृहः।
वीतरागभयक्रोधः स्थितधीर्मुनिरुच्यते॥ २.५६॥
*duḥkheṣvanudvignamanā sukheṣu vigataspṛhaḥ,*
*vītarāga-bhaya-krodhaḥ sthitadhīr munirucyate. (2.56)*

A person whose mind is unperturbed by sorrow, who does not crave for pleasures, and who is free from attachment, fear, and anger; such a person is called a Muni [sage] and a person of unwavering mind.

यः सर्वत्रानभिस्नेहस्तत्तत्प्राप्य शुभाशुभम्।
नाभिनन्दति न द्वेष्टि तस्य प्रज्ञा प्रतिष्ठिता॥ २.५७॥
*yaḥ sarvatrānabhisnehas tat tat prāpya śubhāśubham,*
*nābhinandati na dveṣṭi tasya prajñā pratiṣṭhitā. (2.57)*

Those who stay unconcerned about anything, who feel neither elated at attaining what they think good or auspicious nor desolate at the achievement of what they think bad or unauspicious, their prajñā (mind) is deemed unwavering.

यदा संहरते चायं कूर्मोऽङ्गानीव सर्वशः।
इन्द्रियाणीन्द्रियार्थेऽभ्यस्तस्य प्रज्ञा प्रतिष्ठिता॥ २.५८॥
*yadā saṁharate cāyaṁ kūrmo'ṅgānīva sarvaśaḥ,*

*indriyāṇīndriyārthebhyas tasya prajñā pratiṣṭhitā. (2.58)*

When one can completely withdraw the senses from their stimuli, like a tortoise withdraws its limbs [into the shell], then the prajñā [mind] of such a person is considered steady. (2.58)

Note: The various stimuli of various sense organs are as follows: Sight is the stimulus for eyes, audition for ears, olfaction for nose, skin sensation for skin and food for tongue.

How to withdraw senses from their stimuli? Śri Krishna tells this secret to Arjuna as follows:

विषया विनिवर्तन्ते निराहारस्य देहिनः ।
रसवर्जं रसोऽप्यस्य परं दृष्ट्वा निवर्तते ॥ २.५९ ॥
*viṣayā vinivartante nirāhārasya dehinaḥ,*
*rasavarjaṁ raso'pyasya paraṁ dṛṣṭvā nivartate. (2.59)*

All senses, except the tongue, can be withdrawn from their stimuli if one observes fasting. The craving for food also disappears from the one who has realised the Supreme.

यततो ह्यपि कौन्तेय पुरुषस्य विपश्चितः ।
इन्द्रियाणि प्रमाथीनि हरन्ति प्रसभं मनः ॥ २.६० ॥
*yatato hyapi kaunteya puruṣasya vipaścitaḥ,*
*indriayāṇi pramāthīni haranti prasabhaṁ manaḥ. (2.60)*

These powerful senses, O son of Kunti, forcibly deflect the mind of even a wise person striving for restraint.

तानि सर्वाणि संयम्य युक्त आसीत मत्परः ।
वशे हि यस्येन्द्रियाणि तस्य प्रज्ञा प्रतिष्ठिता ॥ २.६१ ॥
*tāni sarvāṇi sañyamya yukta āsīta matparaḥ,*
*vaśe hi yasyendriyāṇi tasya prajñā pratiṣṭhitā. (2.61)*

Having withdrawn all these senses from their stimuli, listen to me attentively. Who has control over his senses, he endows with a steady state of mind *(prajñā)*.

ध्यायतो विषयान्पुंसः सङ्गस्तेषूपजायते ।
सङ्गात्संजायते कामः कामात्क्रोधोऽभिजायते ॥ २.६२ ॥
*dhyāyato viṣayān punsaḥ saṅgas teṣūpajāyate,*
*saṅgātsañjāyate kāmaḥ kāmāt krodho'bhijāyate. (2.62)*

One develops an attachment to stimuli by thinking about them. The attachment develops into the desire for achieving them, and the failure to achieve them invites frustration.

क्रोधाद्भवति संमोहः संमोहात्स्मृतिविभ्रमः ।
स्मृतिभ्रंशाद् बुद्धिनाशो बुद्धिनाशात्प्रणश्यति ॥ २.६३ ॥
*krodhādbhavati sammohaḥ sammohāt smṛti-vibhramaḥ,*
*smṛtibhrañśād buddhināśo buddhināśāt praṇaśyati. (2.63)*

Frustration translates into a fixing state where one is not able to decide what to do and what not. The fixing state of mind leads to the memory loss. Loss of memory results in the loss of reasoning and the loss of reasoning proves ruinous.

रागद्वेषविमुक्तैस्तु विषयानिन्द्रियैश्चरन् ।
आत्मवश्यैर्विधेयात्मा प्रसादमधिगच्छति ॥ २.६४ ॥
*rāgadveṣaviyuktais tu viṣayān indriyaiś caran,*
*ātmavaśyair vidheyātmā prasādam adhigacchati. (2.64)*

A disciplined person, if allows his senses under his/her control to be attracted to their stimuli with the indifferent mind without any like or dislike, love or hatred, he attains tranquillity.

प्रसादे सर्वदुःखानां हानिरस्योपजायते ।
प्रसन्नचेतसो ह्याशु बुद्धिः पर्यवतिष्ठते ॥ २.६५ ॥
*prasāde sarvaduḥkhānāṁ hānir asyopajāyate,*

*prasannacetaso hyāśu buddhiḥ paryavatiṣṭhate. (2.65)*

All sorrows are dissipated upon the attainment of tranquillity. The mind of such a tranquil person stabilises soon.

नास्ति बुद्धिरयुक्तस्य न चायुक्तस्य भावना।
न चाभावयतः शान्तिरशान्तस्य कुतः सुखम्॥ २.६६॥
*nāsti buddhir ayuktasya na cāyuktasya bhāvanā,*
*na cābhāvayataḥ śāntir aśāntasya kutaḥ sukham. (2.66)*

An unsteady person neither has a mind established in himself/herself nor do positive attitude. Without positive attitude there is no peace; and without peace, there can be no happiness.

इन्द्रियाणां हि चरतां यन्मनोऽनुविधीयते।
तदस्य हरति प्रज्ञां वायुर्नावमिवाम्भसि॥ २.६७॥
*indriyāṇāṁ hi caratāṁ yanmano'nuvidhīyate,*
*tadasya harati prajñāṁ vāyur nāvam ivāmbhasi. (2.67)*

When the mind starts following senses, roving to their stimuli, it steals away the prajñā (mindfulness of true nature of soul) like a storm that takes away a boat on the sea from its destination.

तस्माद्यस्य महाबाहो निगृहीतानि सर्वशः।
इन्द्रियाणीन्द्रियार्थेभ्यस्तस्य प्रज्ञा प्रतिष्ठिता॥ २.६८॥
*tasmādyasya mahābāho nigṛhītāni sarvaśaḥ,*
*indriyāṇīndriyārthebhyas tasya prajñā pratiṣṭhitā. (2.68)*

Therefore, O big-armed Arjuna, prajñā (mind) becomes steady when one's senses are completely withdrawn from their stimuli.

या निशा सर्वभूतानां तस्यां जागर्ति संयमी।
यस्यां जाग्रति भूतानि सा निशा पश्यतो मुनेः॥ २.६९॥
*yā niśā sarvabhūtānāṁ tasyāṁ jāgarti saṅyamī,*
*yasyāṁ jāgrati bhūtāni sā niśā paśyato muneḥ. (2.69)*

So far as the question of self-realisation is concerned, a yogī with restrained mind remains active while all others are inactive. On the other hand, in the matter of sensory pleasures, he is inactive while others are active.

आपूर्यमाणमचलप्रतिष्ठं समुद्रमापः प्रविशन्ति यद्वत्।
तद्वत्कामा यं प्रविशन्ति सर्वे स शान्तिमाप्नोति न कामकामी॥ २.७०॥
*āpūryamāṇam acalapratiṣṭhaṁ,*
*samudramāpaḥ praviśanti yadvat,*
*tadvat kāmā yaṁ praviśanti sarve,*
*sa śāntim āpnoti na kāmakāmī. (2.70)*

Just as the waters of the rivers merge into the full and calm ocean without any ripples, similarly if all desires merge into one's mind without creating any disturbance, he attains peace and not he who hankers after material gains or objects.

विहाय कामान्यः सर्वान्पुमांश्चरति निःस्पृहः।
निर्ममो निरहङ्कारः स शान्तिमधिगच्छति॥ २.७१॥
*vihāya kāmān yaḥ sarvān pumāñś carati niḥspṛhaḥ,*
*nirmamo nirahaṅkāraḥ sa śāntim adhigacchati. (2.71)*

One who abandons all desires and becomes free from all longing and the feeling of 'I' and 'my' attains peace.

एषा ब्राह्मी स्थितिः पार्थ नैनां प्राप्य विमुह्यति।
स्थित्वास्यामन्तकालेऽपि ब्रह्मनिर्वाणमृच्छति॥ २.७२॥
*eṣā brāhmī sthitiḥ Pārtha naināṁ prāpya vimuhyati,*
*sthitvāsyām antakāle'pi brahma-nirvāṇam ṛcchati. (2.72)*

O son of Pṛthā, this is the Brāhmī state or Turīya [state of mind suitable to self-realisation]. Attaining this [state], one no longer remains fixed. Maintaining this state, even at the end of one's life, a person attains oneness with the Supreme.

ॐ तत्सदिति श्रीमद् भगवद्गीतासूपनिषत्सु ब्रह्मविद्यायां योगशास्त्रे

श्रीकृष्णार्जुनसंवादे साङ्ख्ययोगो नाम द्वितीयोऽध्यायः ॥ २ ॥

Here ends the second chapter in the *Bhagvadgitā* named as Sāṅkhya yoga dealing with the Brahmavidyā as propounded in the Upaniṣad and Yogaśāstra in the form of dialogue between Śri Krishna and Arjuna.

# अथ तृतीयोऽध्यायः

## कर्मयोगः

# Chapter 3

(Method of doing Nitya Karmas)

There are three types of karmas—nitya, kāmya and niṣiddha. Nitya karmas are those karmas that are obligatory to sustain life for a dehabhṛt [a human being who takes his body for the soul] and inculcate dharma [knowledge by the study of Śāstras, moral, ethical and spiritual values, yajñā-an obligation towards nature, dāna-a social obligation and tapa-a personal obligation]. Kāmya karmas are those that are done for the fulfilment of some personal desires. Naimittika karmas are those that are done on account of some particular occasion. Niṣiddha karmas are those that the Śāstras prohibit. The present chapter deals with Karma Yoga [What sorts of karmas are to be performed and how]. In this chapter, Śri Krishna tells Arjuna that a dehabhṛt [a human being who considers his body a soul] cannot completely abandon all karmas. So what type of action is to be done and how? It is the main mind-boggling question for every human being. According to Śri Krishna, kāmya and niṣiddha karmas are the cause of bondage, so they are not required to be done. Yes, nitya karmas, which are obligatory duties towards nature, society, for personal sustenance and spiritual upliftment can be done. Since every human being exploits nature for his well-being and sustenance, it is obligatory on the part of everybody to protect the environment. Our actions should be such as to protect the environment. We always exploit nature for our use, so it becomes our moral duty to contribute to its protection. The best way to protect natural forces and the environment is performing Yajña. Yajña is described as the best service to nature. Through Yajña, one can help precipitation to take place, which causes the growth of vegetation and grains. Yajña is only an environmental friendly action of ours. One who does not perform Yajña is described as a thief in the real sense of terms.

However, while doing nitya karmas, one should not do them out of some self-interest or motive. The nitya karmas, done for self-interest, are described as actions with attachment [sakāma or kāmya] and actions without any personal motive behind them or attachment to them are said as 'actions without attachment' or '*niṣkāma karma*'. According to Śri Krishna, niṣkāma nitya karma leads one to self-realisation, and sakāma nitya karma again becomes the cause of bondage like kāmya, naimittika and niṣiddha karmas that deters human beings from achieving their real goal of self-realisation.

अर्जुन उवाच ।

Arjuna said

ज्यायसी चेत्कर्मणस्ते मता बुद्धिर्जनार्दन ।
तत्किं कर्मणि घोरे मां नियोजयसि केशव ॥ ३.१ ॥
*jyāyasī cetakarmaṇas te matā buddhir Janārdana,*
*tatkiṁ karmaṇi ghore māṁ niyojayasi Keśavaḥ. (3.01)*

Arjuna Said— If you consider that buddhi-yoga [mind unconcerned about material gain or loss] is better than kāmya karma [action done with the desire of material gain], then why do you want me to drag in this horrible war, O Keśava?

व्यामिश्रेणेव वाक्येन बुद्धिं मोहयसीव मे ।
तदेकं वद निश्चित्य येन श्रेयोऽहमाप्नुयाम् ॥ ३.२ ॥
*vyāmiśreṇeva vākyena buddhiṁ mohayasīva me,*

*tadekaṁ vada niścitya yena śreyo'hamāpnuyām. (3.02)*

You seem to confuse my mind by apparently mixed statements. Tell me, decisively, one thing through which I may attain the emancipation.

श्री कृष्ण उवाच
Śri Krishna said

लोकेऽस्मिन् द्विविधा निष्ठा पुरा प्रोक्ता मयानघ।
ज्ञानयोगेन साङ्ख्यानां कर्मयोगेन योगिनाम्॥ ३.३॥
*loke'smin dvividhā niṣṭhā purā proktā mayānagha,*
*jñānayogena sāṁkhyānāṁ karmayogena yogināṁ. (3.03)*

Śri Krishna Said— In this world, O Arjuna, two types of *(niṣṭhā)* knowledge are in practice, as already told by me—theoretical knowledge as ordained in Sāṅkhya and practical knowledge as ordained in Yoga.

[Jñāna-yoga is also called Sāṅkhya-yoga, Saṁnyāsa-yoga, and yoga of knowledge. The word Jñāna means knowledge].

न कर्मणामनारम्भान्नैष्कर्म्यं पुरुषोऽश्नुते।
न च संन्यसनादेव सिद्धिं समधिगच्छति॥ ३.४॥
*na karmaṇām anārambhānnaiṣkarmyaṁ puruṣo'śnute,*
*na ca saṁnyasanādeva siddhiṁ samadhigacchati. (3.04)*

One cannot achieve the state of niṣkāma karma yoga either by not taking an initiative or by renunciating nitya karmas [obligatory actions].

न हि कश्चित्क्षणमपि जातु तिष्ठत्यकर्मकृत्।
कार्यते ह्यवशः कर्म सर्वः प्रकृतिजैर्गुणैः॥ ३.५॥
*na hi kaścit kṣaṇamapi jātu tiṣṭhaty akarmakṛt,*
*kāryate hyavaśaḥ karma sarvaḥ prakṛtijair guṇaiḥ. (3.05)*

Because no embodied soul can remain actionless even for a moment. Everyone is bound to do action due to sattva, rajas and tamas the guṇas born of prakṛti.

कर्मेन्द्रियाणि संयम्य य आस्ते मनसा स्मरन्।
इन्द्रियार्थान्विमूढात्मा मिथ्याचारः स उच्यते॥ ३.६॥
*karmendriyāṇi sañymya ya āste manasā smaran,*
*indriyārthān vimuḍhātmā mithyācāraḥ sa ucyate. (3.06)*

Who restrains his motor organs, but keep thinking of sensory enjoyment, he is deluded one [not understaning reality] and called a hypocrite.

यस्त्विन्द्रियाणि मनसा नियम्यारभतेऽर्जुन।
कर्मेन्द्रियैः कर्मयोगमसक्तः स विशिष्यते॥ ३.७॥
*yas tvindriyāṇi manasā niyamyārabhate'rjuna,*
*karmendriyaiḥ karmayogam asaktaḥ sa viśiṣyate. (3.07)*

The one who controls the senses organs mentally, and engages the motor organs to karma-yoga [for doing nitya karmas] (*asaktaḥ*) without any attachment, is superior than that hypocrite, O Arjuna.

नियतं कुरु कर्म त्वं कर्म ज्यायो ह्यकर्मणः।
शरीरयात्रापि च ते न प्रसिद्ध्येदकर्मणः॥ ३.८॥
*niyataṁ kuru karma tvaṁ karma jyāyo hyakarmaṇaḥ,*
*śarirayātrāpi ca te na prasiddhyed akarmaṇaḥ. (3.08)*

Perform nitya karma regularly, because action is indeed better than inaction. Even the life cannot be sustained without doing nitya karma.

Note: The same principle applies to the matter, starting from the minutest atoms to the heaviest heavenly bodies. They can also not sustain or survive without karma (motion).

यज्ञार्थात्कर्मणोऽन्यत्र लोकोऽयं कर्मबन्धनः।
तदर्थं कर्म कौन्तेय मुक्तसङ्गः समाचर॥ ३.९॥
*yajñārthāt karmaṇo'nyatra loko'yaṁ karmbandhanaḥ,*
*tadarthaṁ karma kaunteya muktasaṅgaḥ samācara. (3.09)*

Other than performed for yajñā [self-realisation],

karmas can also cause bondage. Therefore, O Arjuna, do other nitya karmas without attachment to them and any personal motive or self-interest behind them.

सहयज्ञाः प्रजाः सृष्ट्वा पुरोवाच प्रजापतिः ।
अनेन प्रसविष्यध्वमेष वोऽस्त्विष्टकामधुक् ॥ ३.१० ॥
*sahayajñāḥ prajāḥ sṛṣṭvā purovāca prajāpatīḥ,*
*anena prasaviṣyadhvam eṣa vo'stviṣṭkāmadhuk. (3.10)*

Prajāpati, the Almighty Creator, at the beginning of creation, created living beings with the technique of yajña and said— May you all (*prasviṣyadhvam*) prosper by this yajña and may this yajña fulfil your [material and spiritual] desires.

देवान्भावयतानेन ते देवा भावयन्तु वः ।
परस्परं भावयन्तः श्रेयः परमवाप्स्यथ ॥ ३.११ ॥
*devānbhāvayatānena te devā bhāvayantu vaḥ,*
*parasparaṁ bhāvayantaḥ śreyaḥ paramavāpsyatha. (3.11)*

Nourish the deities [natural forces] by performing yajña/havana and eco-friendly activities on the earth, and the natural forces will nourish you. Thus, by nourishing one another, you may attain the supreme good.

How can one attain supreme good by bhoga of natural resources? The answer is— First, a jīva will enjoy the natural resources. Afterwards, he would get fed up with it and realise that bhoga of material resources is ultimately painful, and so he would tread the path of self-realisation.

Note: Deva means a celestial body, a natural force constituting an environment like water, light, heat, vapours, clouds, lightning, etc., known in the Vedas by various names of Indra, Agni, Parjanya, Āpaḥ, Vṛtra, etc.

इष्टान्भोगान्हि वो देवा दास्यन्ते यज्ञभाविताः ।

तैर्दत्तानप्रदायैभ्यो यो भुङ्क्ते स्तेन एव सः ॥ ३.१२ ॥
*iṣṭān bhogān hi vo devā dāsyante yajñabhāvitāḥ,*
*tairdattān apradāya-aibhyo yo bhuṅkte stena eva saḥ. (3.12)*

The natural forces nourished by yajña/havana, will give you the desired gifts like rain, etc. One who enjoys natural gifts like the pure air, water, rain, light, heat, etc. provided by nature without nourishing nature (in return) is, indeed, a thief who wants to exploit natural resources for his benefit.

Here, Śri Krishna wants to convey that we should not always go on exploiting natural resources until and unless we do something to regenerate them through our activities. Such activities are called yajña in addition to Nitya Agnihotra. A person who always exploits natural resources and never cares for its regeneration is a thief. It shows the awareness of preserving the environment and natural resources. Yajña/havana performed in the terrestrial fire at our homes has been called a great source of nourishing the environment. That is why Śri Krishna emphasizes performing yajña or havan daily. After Krishna, Swami Dayananda Saraswati in the modern days emphasized performing yajñas daily. According to Swami Dayananda Saraswati, we are polluting the environment through our activities, so it becomes the moral duty of every human being to nourish nature daily with yajña.

यज्ञशिष्टाशीनः सन्तो मुच्यन्ते सर्व किल्बिषैः
भुञ्जते ते त्वघं पापा ये पचन्त्यात्मकारणात् ॥ ३.१३ ॥
*yajñaśiṣṭāśinaḥ santo mucyante sarvakilbiṣaiḥ,*
*buñjate tvaghaṁ pāpā ye pacantyātmakāraṇāt. (3.13)*

Good people eat after performing yajña/havana (or, say, exploit nature or the environment after its due nourishment or preservation). They are freed from all obligations towards nature and five types of pāpas like (*peṣaṇaṁ*) grinding, (*kaṇḍanam*) winnowing [separating the chaff from grain], (*chulli*) cooking on fireplace, (*udkumbha*) storing water and *(mārjani)* brooming while doing household work. [If nature sustains us, it is our obligatory duty to preserve it]. Nevertheless, wicked people who cook food only to sustain their own lives [exploit the environment for their interest without nourishing it] eat evil and are evildoers since they fail in their obligatory duty towards preserving nature and the environment.

अन्नाद्भवन्ति भूतानि पर्जन्यादन्नसंभवः।
यज्ञाद्भवति पर्जन्यो यज्ञः कर्मसमुद्भवः॥ ३.१४॥
*annādbhavanti bhūtāni parjnyādannsambhavaḥ,*
*yajñādbhavati parjanyo yajñaḥ karmasamudbhavaḥ. (3.14)*

Meaning 1: Food, which is the life force for the living beings, is produced by rain, rain is induced by yajña, and yajña is the the outcome of the nitya actions of human beings.

Scientific Meaning 2: The material and immaterial things are the product of active energy [called vikṛti]. Active energy [vikṛti] is the product of Parjanya [inactive energy or prakṛti/āpaḥ/salila, a homogenous state of sattva, rajas and tamas guṇas]. The motion causes the process of creation.

कर्म ब्रह्मोद्भवं विद्धि ब्रह्माक्षरसमुद्भवम्।
तस्मात्सर्वगतं ब्रह्म नित्यं यज्ञे प्रतिष्ठितम्॥ ३.१५॥
*karma brhmodbhavaṁ viddhi brahmākṣarasamudbhavam,*
*tasmātsarvagataṁ brahma nityaṁ yajñe pratiṣṭhitam. (3.15)*

Meaning 1: Yajña and eco-friendly activities are prescribed in the Vedas. The Vedas are the product of Almighty Brahman. Thus, the all-pervading Brahman

(Almighty God) is ever-present in yajña (or process of creation).

Meaning 2: Motion is produced by Brahman and Brahman is Akṣara (imperishable). So all pervading Brahman is behind the process of creation.

एवं प्रवर्तितं चक्रं नानुवर्तयतीह यः ।
अघायुरिन्द्रियारामो मोघं पार्थ स जीवति ॥ ३.१६ ॥
*evaṁ pravartitaṁ cakraṁ nānuvartayatīha yaḥ,*
*aghāyur indriyārāmo moghaṁ pārtha sa jīvati. (3.16)*

The one who does not perform study of Vedas and cycle of yajña started by Iśvara, and who rejoices in sensuous pleasures, he is committing a great sin and lives in vain, O Arjuna.

यस्त्वात्मरतिरेव स्यादात्मतृप्तश्च मानवः ।
आत्मन्येव च संतुष्टस्तस्य कार्यं न विद्यते ॥ ३.१७ ॥
*yastvātmaratireva syād ātma-tṛptaśca mānavaḥ,*
*ātmanyeva ca santuṣṭas tasya kāryaṁ na vidyate. (3.17)*

The one who dwells in the Self only, who is satisfied with the Self, who is content in the Self alone, for such a (Self-realized) person, there is no duty towards nature and environment. Because such a person is not exploiting natural resources for his/her sustenance, he/she needs not to perform his/her obligatory duty towards nourishing and preserving nature and the environment.

नैव तस्य कृतेनार्थो नाकृतेनेह कश्चन ।
न चास्य सर्वभूतेषु कश्चिदर्थव्यपाश्रयः ॥ ३.१८ ॥
*naiva tasya kṛtenārtho nākṛteneha kaścana,*
*na cāsya sarvabhūteṣu kaścid-artha-vypāśrayaḥ. (3.18)*

A person who has settled in Brahman has left with no objective for which he has to undertake an action. If he does not act, it will not adversely affect his routine life. He does not need help from anybody to achieve anything in his life. He becomes self-sustained.

Note: Artha-vypāśraya means help of other persons or creatures for achieving some objective.

तस्मादसक्त: सततं कार्यं कर्म समाचर।
असक्तो ह्याचरन्कर्म परमाप्नोति पूरुष: ॥ ३.१९ ॥
*tasmād asktaḥ satataṁ kāryaṁ karma samācara,*
*asakto hyācaran karma paramāpnoti pūruṣaḥ. (3.19)*

Therefore, always perform your nitya karma efficiently without involvement (any selfish interest) because doing nitya karma without selfish interest helps in the attainment of the Supreme.

कर्मणैव हि संसिद्धिमास्थिता जनकादय: ।
लोकसंग्रहमेवापि संपश्यन्कर्तुमर्हसि ॥ ३.२० ॥
*karmaṇaiva hi sansiddhimāsthitā janakādayaḥ,*
*loka-saṅgraham evāpi sampaśyan kartum arhasi. (3.20)*

King Janaka and others attained perfection (or Self-realisation) by doing nitya karmas without selfish interest. Keeping in view of altruistic welfare, you should perform your duty.

Note: Here lokasaṅgrah means altruistic welfare activities. The duty of a kṣatriya [king] is also his nitya karma.

यद्यदाचरति श्रेष्ठस्तत्तदेवेतरो जन: ।
स यत्प्रमाणं कुरुते लोकस्तदनुवर्तते ॥ ३.२१ ॥
*yad yad ācarati śreṣṭhas tat tad evetaro janaḥ,*
*sa yat pramāṇaṁ kurute lokastad anuvartate. (3.21)*

Great leaders are always followed by others. Whatever standard they set, the world follows.

न मे पार्थास्ति कर्तव्यं त्रिषु लोकेषु किंचन।
नानवाप्तमवाप्तव्यं वर्त एव च कर्मणि ॥ ३.२२ ॥
*na me Pārtha asti kartavyaṁ triṣu lokeṣu kiṁcana.*
*na anavāptam avāptavyaṁ varta eva ca karmaṇi. (3.22)*

O son of Pṛthā (Arjuna), there is nothing left to be done by me in the three worlds, nor is there anything unattained that I should obtain, yet I engage in action.

Note : The only reason is altruistic welfare. If one has a selfish motive behind an action, he is said to be attached, but if the same action is performed for altruistic welfare, one is said to be unattached.

यदि ह्यहं न वर्तेयं जातु कर्मण्यतन्द्रितः।
मम वर्त्मानुवर्तन्ते मनुष्याः पार्थ सर्वशः ॥ ३.२३ ॥
*yadi hy ahaṁ na varteyaṁ jātu karmaṇy atandritaḥ.*
*mama vartmānuvartante manuṣyāḥ Pārtha sarvaśaḥ. (3.23)*

If I do not engage in action simply because I am not going to be benefited by it, O son of Pṛthā [Arjuna], people would follow me. That is, they will avoid doing any such action as is not going to benefit them [serve their self-interests].

उत्सीदेयुरिमे लोका न कुर्यां कर्म चेदहम्।
सङ्करस्य च कर्ता स्यामुपहन्यामिमाः प्रजाः ॥ ३.२४ ॥
*utsīdeyurime lokā na kuryāṁ karma ced aham.*
*saṅkarasya ca kartā syām upahanyām imāḥ prajāḥ. (3.24)*

If people like me abandon nitya karmas and duties, the world order will break for want of actions necessary for its sustenance. Because, if leading people like me abandon nitya karmas, it will create a (*saṅkara*) confusion among others also and they will also abstain from doing their obligatory duties and karmas. This will be fatal for the sustenance of human life on this earth

सक्ताः कर्मण्यविद्वांसो यथा कुर्वन्ति भारत।
कुर्याद्विद्वांस्तथाऽसक्तश्चिकीर्षुर्लोकसंग्रहम्॥ ३.२५॥
*saktāḥ karmaṇy avidvānso yathā kurvanti Bhārat,*
*kuryād vidvānstathā'saktaścikīrṣurlokasaṅgraham. (3.25)*

O Arjuna, from the line of Bharatas, while the layman acts with attachment [only because of selfish interest], the wise performs without attachment, i.e. for altruistic welfare to maintain world order.

न बुद्धिभेदं जनयेदज्ञानां कर्मसङ्गिनाम्।
जोषयेत्सर्वकर्माणि विद्वान्युक्तः समाचरन्॥ ३.२६॥
*na buddhibhedaṁ janayed ajñānāṁ karmasaṅginām.*
*joṣayet sarvakarmāṇi vidvānyuktaḥ samācaran. (3.26)*

The wise should not deter or deviate the mind of the layperson who acts according to some selfish motives [with attachment]. However, the enlightened one should work himself without attachment or sustenance of the world to inspire others to follow suit.

प्रकृतेः क्रियमाणानि गुणैः कर्माणि सर्वशः।
अहङ्कारविमूढात्मा कर्ताहमिति मन्यते॥ ३.२७॥
*prakṛteḥ kriyamāṇāni guṇaiḥ karmāṇi sarvaśaḥ.*
*ahaṅkāra vimūḍhātmā kartāham iti manyate. (3.27)*

All actions are performed by three guṇas of prakṛti [physical body is made of the sattva, rajas and tamas guṇas], but a person deluded by the notion that he is the body assumes himself to be the doer. (See also 5.09, 13.29, and 14.19).

Note: Here Śri Krishna wants to say that the real nature of a human being is not the body or mind but soul.

तत्त्ववित्तु महाबाहो गुणकर्मविभागयोः।
गुणा गुणेषु वर्तन्त इति मत्वा न सज्जते॥ ३.२८॥

*tattava vittu mahābāho guṇa-karma-vibhāgayoḥ,*
*guṇā guṇeṣu vartanta iti matvā na sajjate. (3.28)*

The one who knows, O Long-Armed Arjuna, about the the guṇas [body including sense organs and motor organs made of three guṇas] and actions done by it, does not associate himself/heself to them knowing the fact that actions are being done by the body under the dominance of sattva, rajas or tamas guṇas, and that the sattva, rajas or tamas guṇas are associated with stimuli made of these guṇās and not with soul.

प्रकृतेर्गुणसंमूढा: सज्जन्ते गुणकर्मसु।
तानकृत्स्नविदो मन्दान्कृत्स्नविन्न विचालयेत्॥ ३.२९॥
*prakṛter guṇsammūḍhāḥ sajjante guṇakarmasu,*
*tānakṛtsnavido mandān kṛtsnavinna vicālayet. (3.29)*

Those who, under delusion, identify their soul with the body constituted of guṇas, associate them with the actions done by body. The wise who knows the complete truth should not confuse himself following those who are unaware of the truth. (See also 3.26)

मयि सर्वाणि कर्माणि संन्यस्याध्यात्मचेतसा।
निराशीर्निर्ममो भूत्वा युध्यस्व विगतज्वर:॥ ३.३०॥
*mayi sarvāṇi karmāṇi saṁnyasy ādhyātma-cetasā,*
*nirāśīrmamo bhūtvā yudhyasva vigata-jvaraḥ. (3.30)*

Leaving all actions unto Parameśvara and (*adhyātma-chetasā*) making your mind as if you are doing all actions as the servant to Iśvara, engage yourself [your body] into war (*nirāśī*) without any expectations and (*nir-mama*) notion of I, my and me.

Note: Adhyātma-chetasā here means to make one's mind as if he is the servant of God.

ये मे मतमिदं नित्यमनुतिष्ठन्ति मानवा:।

श्रद्धावन्तोऽनसूयन्तो मुच्यन्ते तेऽपि कर्मभिः ॥ ३.३१ ॥
*ye me matam idaṁ nityam anutiṣṭhanti mānavāḥ,*
*śraddhāvanto'nasūyanto mucyante te'pi karmabhiḥ. (3.31)*

Those who always follow my view faithfully with a positive frame of mind, will be able to free themselves from the moral and ethical issues associated with actions.

ये त्वेतदभ्यसूयन्तो नानुतिष्ठन्ति मे मतम् ।
सर्वज्ञानविमूढांस्तान्विद्धि नष्टानचेतसः ॥ ३.३२ ॥
*ye tvetadabhyasūyanto nānutiṣṭhanti me matam,*
*sarvajñāna vimūḍhāns tān viddhi naṣṭān acetasaḥ. (3.32)*

But, those who do not follow my view and find fault with it, know them ignorant of this knowledge, devoid of wisdom and ruined.

सदृशं चेष्टते स्वस्याः प्रकृतेर्ज्ञानवानपि ।
प्रकृतिं यान्ति भूतानि निग्रहः किं करिष्यति ॥ ३.३३ ॥
*sadṛśaṁ ceṣṭate svasyāḥ prakṛter jñānavānapi,*
*prakṛtiṁ yānti bhūtāni nigraḥ kiṁ kariṣyati. (3.33)*

Even wise men act according to their (*prakṛti*) the past life sanskāras manifesting in the present life. So, all living beings are led by their prakṛtis (*sanskāras*). How can, my or your (*nigrahaḥ*) instructions will help?

इन्द्रियस्येन्द्रियस्यार्थे रागद्वेषौ व्यवस्थितौ ।
तयोर्न वशमागच्छेत्तौ ह्यस्य परिपन्थिनौ ॥ ३.३४ ॥
*indriyasyendriyasyārthe rāgadveṣau vyavasthitau,*
*tayor na vaśamāgacchetau hyasya paripanthinau. (3.34)*

Rāga [attachment] and dveśa [aversion] are the characteristics of sense organs and their stimuli. A seeker should not be overpowered by this rāga [attachment] and dveśa [aversion], because they are stumbling blocks, indeed, on seeker's path to (*śreya*) wellbeing.

श्रेयान्स्वधर्मो विगुणः परधर्मात्स्वनुष्ठितात् ।

स्वधर्मे निधनं श्रेय: परधर्मो भयावह: ॥ ३.३५ ॥
*śreyān svadharmo viguṇaḥ paradharmāt svanuṣṭhitāt,*
*svadharme nidhanaṁ śreyaḥ paradharmo bhayāvahaḥ.(3.35)*

(*svadharmaḥ*) Living one's own dharma [*sanskāras*] (*viguṇaḥ*), howsoever inferior [causing downfall] it is, is (*śreyān*) far better than (*su+anuśṭhitāt*) beautifully living other's dharma [*sanskāras*]. (*śreyaḥ*) It is better (*nidhanam*) to die (*svadharme*) while living one's own dharma [*sanskāras*], as (*paradharmaḥ*) living other's sanskāras and disregarding your own sanskāras (*bhayāvahaḥ*) may result into dreadful consequences [of your downfall to lower species, for want of exhaustion of your own sanskāras].

Note: So long as you do not live the sanskāras accumulated by you in your past life, they will not last. So, inexhausted sanskāras will cause your downfall in the next life.

अर्जुन उवाच

Arjuna said

अथ केन प्रयुक्तोऽयं पापं चरति पूरुष: ।
अनिच्छन्नपि वार्ष्णेय बलादिव नियोजित: ॥ ३.३६ ॥
*atha kena prayukto'yaṁ pāpaṁ carati pūruṣaḥ,*
*anicchannapi vārṣṇeya balādivaniyojitaḥ. (3.36)*

Arjuna said— O Krishna, descendant of Vṛṣṇis, what impels one to commit pāpa unwillingly as if forced by a king?

श्री कृष्ण उवाच

Śri Krishan said

काम एष क्रोध एष रजोगुणसमुद्भव: ।
महाशनो महापाप्मा विद्ध्येनमिह वैरिणम् ॥ ३.३७ ॥
*kāma eṣa krodha eṣa rajoguṇa-samudbhavaḥ,*

*mahāśano mahāpāpmā viddhyenam iha vairiṇam. (3.37)*

Śri Krishna said that (*kāma*) desire turns into anger when not fulfilled due to some reasons. This desire is the product of rajoguṇa or, say, due to desire, rajoguṇa becomes active and forces one into action. Desires [kāma] are insatiable and a great devil. Know them as the enemy.

धूमेनाव्रियते वह्निर्यथादर्शो मलेन च।
यथोल्बेनावृतो गर्भस्तथा तेनेदमावृतम्॥ ३.३८॥
*dhūmenāvriyate vahnir yathādarśo malena ca.*
*yatholbenāvṛto garbhastathā tenedam āvṛtam. (3.38)*

As the fire is enveloped by smoke, and mirror by dust, as the placenta envelops an embryo, so also wisdom is enveloped by (kāma) the passionate desire for all sensual and material pleasures.

आवृतं ज्ञानमेतेन ज्ञानिनो नित्यवैरिणा।
कामरूपेण कौन्तेय दुष्पूरेणानलेन च॥ ३.३९॥
*āvṛtaṁ jñānam etena jñānino nityavairiṇā,*
*kāmarūpeṇa kaunteya duṣpūreṇānalena ca. (3.39)*

O Arjuna, the son of Kunti, the wisdom of a wise man is often covered by the everlasting enemy of desire (kāma), which is (*duṣpūra*) fulfilled with great difficulty and is (*anala*) insatiable like fire.

Note: Desire is everlasting enemy of wise and not the fool. Wise knows that this desire impels him to do wrong things, so he keeps repenting, remains unhappy and distressed.

इन्द्रियाणि मनो बुद्धिरस्याधिष्ठानमुच्यते।
एतैर्विमोहयत्येष ज्ञानमावृत्य देहिनम्॥ ३.४०॥
*indriyāṇi mano buddhir asyādhiṣṭhānam ucyate,*
*etair vimohayatyeṣa jñānam āvṛtya dehinam. (3.40)*

The senses, the mind, and the intellect are said to be the seat of desire [kāma]. Enveloping wisdom in the company of these [senses, mind, and intellect], it deludes the embodied soul.

तस्मात्त्वमिन्द्रियाण्यादौ नियम्य भरतर्षभ।
पाप्मानं प्रजहि ह्येनं ज्ञानविज्ञाननाशनम्॥ ३.४१॥
*tasmāttvam indriyāṇyādau niyamya Bharatarṣabha,*
*pāpmānaṁ prajahi hyenaṁ jñānavijñāna nāśanam. (3.41)*

Therefore, O Best of Bharatas [Arjuna], control your senses at the outset and kill this devil [of material desire] that destroys or hinders the knowledge and experience [realisation] of it.

इन्द्रियाणि पराण्याहुरिन्द्रियेभ्य: परं मन:।
मनसस्तु परा बुद्धिर्यो बुद्धे: परतस्तु स:॥ ३.४२॥
*indriyāṇi prāṇyāhur indriyebhyaḥ paraṁ manaḥ,*
*manasastu parā buddhir yo buddheḥ paratastu saḥ. (3.42)*

The sense organs are said to be more potent than the physical body, the mind is more potent than sense organs, the intellect [discriminatory power] is still more powerful than the mind, and Ātmā is more potent even than the intellect.

एवं बुद्धे: परं बुद्ध्वा संस्तभ्यात्मानमात्मना।
जहि शत्रुं महाबाहो कामरूपं दुरासदम्॥ ३.४३॥
*evaṁ buddheḥ paraṁ buddhvā sanstabhyātmānamatmanā,*
*jahi śatruṁ mahābāho kāmarūpaṁ durāsadam. (3.43)*

Thus, knowing the Ātmā to be powerful than the intellect, one should control one's mind intelligently, and kill this mighty enemy of desire [kāma], O Long-Armed Arjuna.

ॐ तत्सदिति श्रीमद् भगवद्गीतासूपनिषत्सु ब्रह्मविद्यायां योगशास्त्रे श्रीकृष्णार्जुनसंवादे कर्मयोगो नाम तृतीयोऽध्याय:॥ ३॥

Here ends the third chapter in the *Bhagvadgitā* dealing with the Brahmavidyā as propounded in the Upaniṣad and Yogaśāstra in the form of a dialogue between Śri Krishna and Arjuna.

# अथ चतुर्थोऽध्यायः

## ज्ञानयोगः

# Chapter 4

[Self-realisation and Brahma-realisation]

The present chapter deals with Jñāna Yoga. In this chapter, Śri Krishna tells Arjuna the actual meaning of Saṁnyāsa. People think that Saṁnyāsa is the abandonment of karma itself. If one abandons karma, he will not be bound by its fruits. Nevertheless, this is not the proper interpretation of the concept of Saṁnyāsa. According to Śri Krishna, abandonment of karma cannot be Saṁnyāsa. Here, Saṁnyāsa means the abandonment of kāmya karmas. In this chapter, karmas have been divided into three categories—Karma, Vikrama and Akarma. According to Śri Krishna, yajña and efforts are the only ways to achieve success in life. No other means of worship or prayer can help an individual. Many types of yajñas have also been mentioned in this chapter.

श्री कृष्ण उवाच

Śri Krishna said

इमं विवस्वते योगं प्रोक्तवानहमव्ययम्।
विवस्वान्मनवे प्राह मनुरिक्ष्वाकवेऽब्रवीत्॥ ४.१॥

*imaṁ Vivasvate yogaṁ proktavān aham avyayam,*
*Vivasvān Manave prāha Manur Ikṣvākave'bravīt. (4. 1)*

Śri Krishna Said— I taught this imperishable [science of] Jñāna-yoga to Vivasvāna at the beginning of this Manvantara. Vivasvāna taught it to his son Manu. Manu taught it to his son Ikṣavāku.

एवं परम्पराप्राप्तमिमं राजर्षयो विदुः।
स कालेनेह महता योगो नष्टः परंतप॥ ४.२॥

*evaṁ prampаrā prāptam imaṁ rājarṣayo viduḥ,*
*sa kāleneha mahatā yogo naṣṭaḥ parantapa. (4.2)*

Thus, the royal sages received this Jñāna-yoga in succession. For long, this science of Jñāna- yoga got lost from this earth, O destroyer of enemies.

स एवायं मया तेऽद्य योग: प्रोक्त: पुरातन: ।
भक्तोऽसि मे सखा चेति रहस्यं ह्येतदुत्तमम् ॥ ४.३ ॥
*sa evāyaṁ mayā te'dya yogaḥ proktaḥ purātanaḥ,*
*bhakto'si me sakhā ceti rahasyaṁ hyetaduttamam. (4.3)*

Today, I have explained the same old science to you because you are dear to me and my best friend. This science of Jñāna-yoga is the supreme mystery indeed.

अर्जुन उवाच
Arjuna said

अपरं भवतो जन्म परं जन्म विवस्वत: ।
कथमेतद्विजानीयां त्वमादौ प्रोक्तवानिति ॥ ४.४ ॥
*aparaṁ bhavato janma paraṁ janma vivasvataḥ,*
*kathaṁ etad vijānīyāṁ tvamādau proktavān iti. (4.4)*

Arjuna said— You are born now [5000 years ago at the end of 28th Dvāpara], but Vivasvāna was born much before you at the beginning of this [Vaivasvata] Manvantara [12 crores or say 120 million years ago]. How can I understand that you taught this yoga to Vivasvāna at the beginning of this Vaivasvata Manvantara ?

श्री कृष्ण उवाच
Śri Krishan said

बहूनि मे व्यतीतानि जन्मानि तव चार्जुन ।
तान्यहं वेद सर्वाणि न त्वं वेत्थ परंतप ॥ ४.५ ॥
*bahūni me vyatītāni janmāni tava cārjuna,*
*tānyahaṁ veda sarvāṇi na tvaṁ vettha parantapa. (4.05)*

Śri Krishna said— Both you and I have taken many

births. I remember them all, O destroyer of the enemies [Arjuna], but you do not remember them.

अजोऽपि सन्नव्ययात्मा भूतानामीश्वरोऽपि सन्।
प्रकृतिं स्वामधिष्ठाय संभवाम्यात्ममायया ॥ ४.६ ॥
*ajo'pi sannavyayātmā bhūtānāmiśvaro'pi san,*
*prakṛtiṁ svām adhiṣṭhāya saṁbhavāmyātma māyayā. (4.06)*

Though the soul is unborn [eternal], imperishable, and the master of physical bodies; yet it takes birth again and again bound by its Sanskāras. [This is the reason that you and I have taken many births].

यदा यदा हि धर्मस्य ग्लानिर्भवति भारत।
अभ्युत्थानमधर्मस्य तदात्मानं सृजाम्यहम् ॥ ४.७ ॥
*yadā yadā hi dharmasya glānir bhavati bhārata,*
*abhyutthānam adharmasya tadātmānam sṛjāmyaham.(4.07)*

Whenever there is a decline of Dharma [moral and ethical values and rule of natural law in the social and individual sphere] and the rise of Adharma, O Arjuna, from the line of Bharatas, then the people like me take birth to re-establish the Dharma [value system and rule of natural law].

परित्राणाय साधूनां विनाशाय च दुष्कृताम्।
धर्मसंस्थापनार्थाय संभवामि युगे युगे ॥ ४.८ ॥
*paritrāṇāya sādhūnāṁ vināśāya ca duṣkṛtām,*
*dharmasansthāpanārthāya saṁbhavāmi yuge yuge. (4.8)*

To protect the righteous and destroy the wicked and to re-establish the rule of Dharma, people like me take birth in all the ages.

जन्म कर्म च मे दिव्यमेवं यो वेत्ति तत्त्वतः।
त्यक्त्वा देहं पुनर्जन्म नैति मामेति सोऽर्जुन ॥ ४.९ ॥
*janma karma ca me divyam evaṁ yo vetti tatvataḥ.*
*tyaktvā dehaṁ punarjanma naiti mām eti so'rjuna. (4.9)*

The one who truly realises that Iśvara is governing his birth and karmas [actions], he is not born again after leaving this body. He achieves liberation as per my statement.

वीतरागभयक्रोधा मन्मया मामुपाश्रिताः ।
बहवो ज्ञानतपसा पूता मद्भावमागताः ॥ ४.१० ॥
*vītrāgabhayakrodhā manmayā māmupāśritāḥ,*
*bahavo jñāna-tapasā pūtā madbhāvam āgatāḥ. (4.10)*

Many, having been freed from attachment, fear, and anger (*manmāya*), realised Brahman and (*māmupāśritā*) and merged in Him. They, having been (*pūtā*) purified (*jñāna-tapasā*) by the tapaḥ [yoga of Brahma-realisation] attain (*madbhāva*) mokṣa.

ये यथा मां प्रपद्यन्ते तांस्तथैव भजाम्यहम् ।
मम वर्त्मानुवर्तन्ते मनुष्याः पार्थ सर्वशः ॥ ४.११ ॥
*ye yathā māṁ prapadyante tāns tathaiva bhajāmyaham,*
*mama vartmānuvartante manuṣyāḥ pārtha sarvaśaḥ. (4.11)*

With whatever motive people approach Brahman, He (*bhajāmi*) conducts them in the same way. All spiritual beings variously follow the path of Brahman.

काङ्क्षन्तः कर्मणां सिद्धिं यजन्त इह देवताः ।
क्षिप्रं हि मानुषे लोके सिद्धिर्भवति कर्मजा ॥ ४.१२ ॥
*kāṅkṣantaḥ karmaṇāṁ siddhiṁ yajanta iha devatāḥ,*
*kṣipraṁ hi mānuṣe loke siddhir bhavati karmajā. (4.12)*

Those who long to fulfil their desires perform kāmya karmas or kāmya yajñas. The fruition of one's action can be attained in human species quickly through performing kāmya karmas or kāmya yajñas.

Here, Krishna has clearly stated that the fruition of our action can be attained only through kāmya karmas or kāmya yajñas, not through worship or depending upon fate. Kāmya yajña or karma [efforts done in the right direction at the right time] here symbolises yajñas or karmas done for the fulfilment of some desires by a person. So, according to the Gītā, one should do kāmya yajña or karmas to redeem his/her mundane desires or achieve success. The same principle of success was propagated by Swami Dayananda Saraswati later in the 49th century of Kaliyuga (19th century AD), the founder of the Arya Samaj Movement.

चातुर्वर्ण्यं मया सृष्टं गुणकर्मविभागशः ।
तस्य कर्तारमपि मां विद्ध्यकर्तारमव्ययम् ॥ ४.१३ ॥
*cāturvarṇyaṁ mayā sṛṣṭaṁ guṇa-karma-vibhāgaśaḥ,*
*tasya kartāram api māṁ viddhyakartāram avyayam. (4.13)*

I have implemented this system of classification of human beings into four varṇas based upon their karmas born of sattva, rajas and tamas guṇas as described in the Vedas. Know that Brahman, who is imperishable and beyond karmas and their fruits, is the maker of this system. (See also 18.41).

| Sr. No. | Varṇa | Guṇa | Karmas |
|---|---|---|---|
| 1 | Brāhmaṇa | Primary: Sattva | Śama (control of mind), dama (control of senses) and Tapa (yoga practice) |
| 2 | Kṣatriya | Primary: Rajas<br>Seconday: Sattava | Śaurya (bravery), teja (good health) |

| | | | |
|---|---|---|---|
| 3 | Vaiśya | Primary: Rajas<br>Secondary: Tamas | Trading and marketing |
| 4 | Śudra | Primary: Tamas<br>Secondary: Rajas | Production, manufacturing and service sector |

न मां कर्माणि लिम्पन्ति न मे कर्मफले स्पृहा।
इति मां योऽभिजानाति कर्मभिर्न स बध्यते॥ ४.१४॥
*na mam̐ karmāṇi limpanti na me karmaphale spṛhā,*
*iti mām̐ yo'bhijānāti karmabhirna sa badhyate. (4.14)*

As a soul, I am not attached to nitya actions, nor do I desire their fruits. The one who understands this truth [that he is also the soul] cannot be bound by karmas.

एवं ज्ञात्वा कृतं कर्म पूर्वैरपि मुमुक्षुभिः।
कुरु कर्मैव तस्मात्त्वं पूर्वैः पूर्वतरं कृतम्॥ ४.१५॥
*evam̐ jñātvā kṛtam̐ karma pūrvairapi mumukṣubhiḥ,*
*kuru karmaiva tasmāttvam̐ pūrvaiḥ pūrvataram̐ kṛtam.(4.15)*

The ancient seekers of liberation also performed actions with this understanding. Therefore, you should perform an action like the ancients did.

किं कर्म किमकर्मेति कवयोऽप्यत्र मोहिताः।
तत्ते कर्म प्रवक्ष्यामि यज्ज्ञात्वा मोक्ष्यसेऽशुभात्॥ ४.१६॥
*kim̐ karma kimakarmeti kavayo'pyatra mohitāḥ,*
*tatte karma pravakṣyāmi yajjñātvā mokṣyase'śubhāt. 4.16)*

Even the wise are confused about what action is worth doing according to Śāstras and what is not. Therefore, I shall clearly explain the nature of action worth doing according to Śāstras, knowing that one shall (*mokṣyase*) be freed from (*aśubhāt*) this wordly life and birth-death cycle.

कर्मणो ह्यपि बोद्धव्यं बोद्धव्यं च विकर्मण: ।
अकर्मणश्च बोद्धव्यं गहना कर्मणो गति: ॥ ४.१७ ॥
*karmaṇo hyapi boddhavyaṁ boddhavyaṁ ca vikarmaṇaḥ,*
*akarmaṇaśca boddhavyaṁ gahanā karmaṇo gatiḥ. (4.17)*

The true nature of action is very difficult to understand. Therefore, one should know the nature of karma [action worth doing according to the Śāstras], the nature of vikarma [action prohibited in the Śāstras], and also the nature of akarma [inaction].

कर्मण्यकर्म य: पश्येदकर्मणि च कर्म य: ।
स बुद्धिमान्मनुष्येषु स युक्त: कृत्स्नकर्मकृत् ॥ ४.१८ ॥
*karmaṇyakarma yaḥ paśyedakarmaṇi ca karma yaḥ,*
*sa buddhimān manuṣyeṣu sa yuktaḥ kṛtsna karmakṛt. (4.18)*

What is karma? Karma is the effort or activity of the body. The one who sees inaction in action [controls activities of the body if it is a prohibited action] and action in inaction [puts efforts if the body is in inaction with respect to a prescribed action] is a wise person among human beings. Such a person is yogī and is said to be the knower of all actions. (See also 3.05, 3.27, 5.08 and 13.29)

यस्य सर्वे समारम्भा: कामसङ्कल्पवर्जिता: ।
ज्ञानाग्निदग्धकर्माणं तमाहु: पण्डितं बुधा: ॥ ४.१९ ॥
*yasya sarve samārambhāḥ kāmasaṅkalpavarjitāḥ,*
*jñānāgni-dagdha-karmāṇaṁ tamāhuḥ paṇḍitaṁ budhāḥ. (4.19)*

A person whose actions are free from desires caused by (*saṅkalpa*) sanskāras, whose actions are sanctified by the fire of knowledge, is called a Paṇḍita [genius] by the wise. A person who has abandoned all kāmya karmas that a person is forced to do due to his/her sanskāras is defined as a Paṇḍita in Gītā.

So, the persons who call themselves Paṇḍitas should take care that they are not involved in kāmya acts, and their nitya actions should also be free from selfish motives. They may perform acts of social service directed to the upliftment of society. The world's great people have directed their energy into social service without selfish motives. Swami Dayananda, a great social reformer of modern times, once said, "I may postpone my program of attaining mokṣa till all human beings are liberated from misery, superstitions and ignorance. I am worried about the deteriorating social values and increasing ignorance in Indian society and the world. So, my first program is to liberate innocent, ignorant human beings from the bondage of social evils and ignorance."

त्यक्त्वा कर्मफलासङ्गं नित्यतृप्तो निराश्रयः ।
कर्मण्यभिप्रवृत्तोऽपि नैव किंचित्करोति सः ॥ ४.२० ॥
*tyaktvā karmaphalāsaṅgaṁ nityatṛpto nirāśrayaḥ,*
*karmaṇyabhipravṛtto'pi naiva kiñcitkaroti saḥ. (4.20)*

With the help of the above wisdom, having abandoned attachment to the fruits of work by way of doing altruistic welfare work [because when a person does the social work or work that is going to affect the entire humanity or society, he doesn't feel attached to the fruits of works], one who is ever content or free from desire of sensory objects and (*āśraya*) does not engage in actions with the motive to attain success in the goals pertaining life here or hereafter, such a person though remains engaged in work [social and humanitarian activities], is not said to be the doer of any work, as he/she is endowed with self-realisation which does not form the part of action.

Krishna wants to say that social or humanitarian work

never binds a person into the cycle of life and death, as no selfish interest is involved in such activities. Only actions involving selfish interest are said to bind a person into the cycle of life and death. Here, it may be pointed out that if some social or humanitarian activity is carried out by someone to pursue his selfish interest, that is not niṣkāma karma activity. For example, suppose social activity is carried out to make money, for name and fame or for the sake of business. In that case, that is sakāma karma [or action with a selfish motive] that traps us into the cycle of life and death, leading us to lower species of animals, birds, insects, plants, etc.

निराशीर्यतचित्तात्मा त्यक्तसर्वपरिग्रहः।
शारीरं केवलं कर्म कुर्वन्नाप्नोति किल्बिषम्॥ ४.२१॥
*nirāśīryatacittātmā tyakta-sarva-parigrahaḥ,*
*śārīraṁ kevalaṁ karma kurvannāpnoti kilbiṣam. (4.21)*

Free from expectations, exercising (*yat*) control of (*chitta*) mind, (*ātmā*) body and senses, (*tyakta*) renouncing (*sarva-prigraha*) all means of enjoyment, (*śārīram karma*) doing actions for the sustenance of the body, one is not bound by (*kilbiṣam*) actions causing bondage of life.

यदृच्छालाभसंतुष्टो द्वन्द्वातीतो विमत्सरः।
समः सिद्धावसिद्धौ च कृत्वापि न निबध्यते॥ ४.२२॥
*yadṛcchālābhasantuṣṭo dvandvātīto vimatsaraḥ,*
*samaḥ siddhāvasiddhau ca kaṛtvāpi na nibadhyate. (4.22)*

Such a person, even while performing actions for the sustenance of his life, does not come under bondage, as due to attainment of jñāna [right understanding of the facts] he has freed himself from all such actions along with their causes leading to bondage.

गतसङ्गस्य मुक्तस्य ज्ञानावस्थितचेतसः।

यज्ञायाचरतः कर्म समग्रं प्रविलीयते ॥ ४.२३ ॥
*gatasaṅgasya muktasya jñānāvasthitacetasaḥ,*
*yajñāyācarataḥ karma samagraṁ pravilīyate. (4.23)*

Those who are devoid of attachments of all types, (*mukta*) free from the idea of dharma and adharma, whose mind is settled in the realisation of self and Brahman alone, who performs actions for carrying out yajñas, all their karmas with fruits come to an end.

Note: The *Śatapatha Brāhmaṇa* says: यज्ञो वै श्रेष्ठतमं कर्म। All positive karmas are yajña. Here, yajña means Agnihotra and also selfless action since it is directed at the welfare of humanity and purifying the environment that sustains humanity. Other forms of worship are directed to God for the fulfilment of self-interests. That is why Śri Krishna emphasises on yajña as a best tool of worship, prayer, and the welfare of humankind.

ब्रह्मार्पणं ब्रह्म हविः ब्रह्माग्नौ ब्रह्मणा हुतम्।
ब्रह्मैव तेन गन्तव्यं ब्रह्म कर्म समाधिना ॥ ४.२४ ॥
*brahmārpaṇaṁ brahma havirbrahmāgnau brahmaṇā hutam,*
*brahmiva tena gantavyaṁ brahmakarmasamādhinā. (4.24)*

Here the term Brahmārpaṇa (offering to the Almighty) has been defined.

Brahmārpaṇa is (*Brahma-haviḥ*) offering of (*brahma*) *ātman* to the (*Brahmāgnau*) fire of Brahman (God) (*Brahmaṇā hutam*) by the ātmā itself through the (*Brahma karma*) action of *samādhī.* One attains Brahman through the Brahma-act of samādhī. (Also see 9.16)

According to Śri Krishna, spiritual yajña can also be performed like astronomical and material yajñas. In the spiritual yajña, Brahman [Almighty God] acts as fire,

Brahma [individuated soul] acts as an oblation and samādhī acts as means of yajña.

दैवमेवापरे यज्ञं योगिनः पर्युपासते।
ब्रह्माग्नावपरे यज्ञं यज्ञेनैवोपजुह्वति ॥ ४.२५ ॥
*daivamevāpare yajñaṁ yoginaḥ paryupāsate,*
*brahmāgnāvapare yajñaṁ yajñenaivopajuhvati. (4.25)*

Thus there are many categories of yogis— those who perform devayajña [i.e. material yajña performed in the material fire only], others who perform yajña in the fire of Brahman through samādhi yajña as discussed in detail in the earlier śloka [verse].

श्रोत्रादीनीन्द्रियाण्यन्ये संयमाग्निषु जुह्वति।
शब्दादीन्विषयानन्य इन्द्रियाग्निषु जुह्वति ॥ ४.२६ ॥
*śrotrādinīndriyāṇyanye saṁyamāgniṣu juhvati,*
*śabdādīnviṣayānanya indriyāgniṣu juhvati. (4.26)*

There are others who sacrifice their senses organs in the fire of restraint, yet others sacrifice sensory objects in the fire of the sense organs.

सर्वाणीन्द्रियकर्माणि प्राणकर्माणि चापरे।
आत्मसंयमयोगाग्नौ जुह्वति ज्ञानदीपिते ॥ ४.२७ ॥
*sarvāṇīndriyakarmāṇi prāṇakarmāṇi cāpare,*
*ātmasaṁyamayogāgnau juhvati jñānadīpite. (4.27)*

There are still others who offer all the functions of the senses, and the functions of Prāṇa [or the five bio-impulses] as oblation in the fire of the yoga of self-restraint kindled by knowledge.

द्रव्ययज्ञास्तपोयज्ञा योगयज्ञास्तथापरे।
स्वाध्यायज्ञानयज्ञाश्च यतयः संशितव्रताः ॥ ४.२८ ॥
*dravya-yajñāstapoyajñā yogayajñāstathāpare,*
*svādhyāya-jñāna-yajñāśca yatayaḥ saṁśitavratāḥ. (4.28)*

There are others who perform Dravya yajñas

[hoarding of material things], others perform tapo yajña [austerity of mind body and speech], still others practice yoga of yajña, while the ascetics with strict vows do svādhyāya yajña [the study of Vedas and Śāstras —ancient scientific books] and jñāna yajña [right understanding of the Śāstras].

अपाने जुह्वति प्राणं प्राणेऽपानं तथापरे।
प्राणापानगती रुद्ध्वा प्राणायामपरायणाः॥ ४.२९॥
*apāne juhvati prāṇaṁ prāṇe'pānaṁ tathāpare,*
*prāṇāpānagatī ruddhvā prāṇāyāmaparāyaṇāḥ. (4.29)*

Furthermore, others are engaged in the practice of Prāṇāyāma. Some offer oblations of (*prāṇa*) inhalation into (*apāna*) exhalation [that is, they do pūraka prāṇāyāma], and others offer oblation of (*apāna*) exhalation into (*pṛāṇa*) inhalation [that is they do rechaka pṛāṇāyama]. Others do kumbhaka prāṇāyāma by suspending the movement of prāṇa [inhalation] and apāna [exhalation].

अपरे नियताहाराः प्राणान्प्राणेषु जुह्वति।
सर्वेऽप्येते यज्ञविदो यज्ञक्षपितकल्मषाः॥ ४.३०॥
*apare niyatāhārāḥ prāṇānprāṇeṣu juhvati,*
*sarve'pyete yajñavido yajñakṣapitakalmaṣāḥ. (4.30)*

Many others have restricted or regulated their diet and offer oblations of prāṇas [breathings that have not been controlled] into the prāṇas [breathings that have been controlled]. All these are the experts of yajña and have eliminated (*kilbiṣa*) their karmas causing bondage.

यज्ञशिष्टामृतभुजो यान्ति ब्रह्म सनातनम्।
नायं लोकोऽस्त्ययज्ञस्य कुतोऽन्यः कुरुसत्तम॥ ४.३१॥
*yajñaśiṣtāmaṛtabhujo yānti brahma sanātanam,*
*nāyaṁ loko'styayajñasya kuto'nyaḥ kurusattama. (4.31)*

Here, the remains of yajña are called Amṛta (nectar). Those who eat nectar after doing the yajñas mentioned above attain eternal Brahman. (*ayajñasya*) A person who does not perform even a single yajña from the yajñas stated above cannot attain even this human body, what to say of attaining divinity [which requires specific means and efforts].

एवं बहुविधा यज्ञा वितता ब्रह्मणो मुखे।
कर्मजान्विद्धि तान्सर्वानेवं ज्ञात्वा विमोक्षयसे॥ ४.३२॥
*evaṁ bahuvidhā yajñā vitatā brahmaṇo mukhe,*
*karmajānviddhi tānsarvān evaṁ jñātvā vimokṣyase. (4.32)*

Thus, many types of yajñas are explained in the Vedas. All of them require physical, mental and verbal efforts. If you can know this fact, you can attain emancipation. (See also 3.14)

श्रेयान्द्रव्यमयाद्यज्ञाज्ज्ञानयज्ञः परंतप।
सर्वं कर्माखिलं पार्थ ज्ञाने परिसमाप्यते॥ ४.३३॥
*śreyān dravyamayād-yajñāj jñana-yajñaḥ parantapa,*
*sarvaṁ karmākhilaṁ pārtha jñāne parisamāpyate. (4.33)*

Jñāna yajña [self-realisation and realisation of Brahman] is superior to material yajña [yajña performed with the help of material things], O destroyer of the enemies [Arjuna], as the material yajñās lead to the cycle of life and death, but self-realisation do not do so. Moreover, all actions have to culminate in self-realisation.

तद्विद्धि प्रणिपातेन परिप्रश्नेन सेवया।
उपदेक्ष्यन्ति ते ज्ञानं ज्ञानिनस्तत्त्वदर्शिनः॥ ४.३४॥
*tadviddhi praṇipātena paripraśnena sevayā,*
*upadekṣyanti te jñānaṁ jñāninas tattva-darśinaḥ.(4.34)*

So, know how can you acquire that knowledge from

experts [self-realized Āchāryas]? Approach them with humble reverence, by sincere inquiry, and by service. They will teach you that knowledge.

यज्ज्ञात्वा न पुनर्मोहमेवं यास्यसि पाण्डव।
येन भूतान्यशेषेण द्रक्ष्यस्यात्मन्यथो मयि॥ ४.३५॥
*yajjñātvā na punarmohamevaṁ yāsyasi pāṇdava,*
*yena bhūtānyaśeṣeṇa drakṣyasyātmanyatho mayi. (4.35)*

Knowing that O Arjuna, you shall not be confused again like this. By this knowledge, you shall behold the entire creation in your own self or Parameśvara. [That is, you will not differentiate between you and others].

अपि चेदसि पापेभ्यः सर्वेभ्यः पापकृत्तमः।
सर्वं ज्ञानप्लवेनैव वृजिनं संतरिष्यसि॥ ४.३६॥
*yajjñātvā na punarmohamevaṁ yāsyasi pāṇdava,*
*yena bhūtānyaśeṣeṇa drakṣyasyātmanyatho mayi. (4.36)*

Even if you are the greatest pāpa committer [doer of karmas leading to your bondage], you shall cross over the ocean of (*vṛjinaṁ*) pāpa (*plavena eva*) by the raft of knowledge alone.

यथैधांसि समिद्धोऽग्निर्भस्मसात्कुरुतेऽर्जुन।
ज्ञानाग्निः सर्वकर्माणि भस्मसात्कुरुते तथा॥ ४.३७॥
*yathaidhāṁsi samiddho'gnirbhasmasāt kurute'rjuna,*
*jñānāgniḥ sarvakarmāṇi bhasmasāt kurute tathā. (4.37)*

As the (*edhāṁsi*) blazing fire reduces wood to ashes, the fire of knowledge helps eliminate the imprints of sanskāras of all karmas, O Arjuna.

Note: According to Vedānta Darśana, *sanskāra bījāt sṛṣṭi*, i.e. these imprints of sanskāras act as the seed for the next life.

न हि ज्ञानेन सदृशं पवित्रमिह विद्यते।
तत्स्वयं योगसंसिद्धः कालेनात्मनि विन्दति॥ ४.३८॥

*na hi jñānena sadṛśaṁ pavitramiha vidyate,*
*tatsvayaṁ yoga-saṁsiddhaḥ kālenātmani vindati. (4.38)*

Nothing is as pure as (*jñāna*) self-realisation in this world. That knowledge can be achieved by a seeker himself/herself through perfection in yoga. With the passage of time the whole knowledge is revealed in his soul.

श्रद्धावाँल्लभते ज्ञानं तत्परः संयतेन्द्रियः ।
ज्ञानं लब्ध्वा परां शान्तिमचिरेणाधिगच्छति ॥ ४.३९ ॥
*śraddhāvānṁ llabhate jñānaṁ tatparaḥ saṁyatendriyaḥ,*
*jñānaṁ labdhvā parāṁ śāntim acireṇādhigacchati. (4.39)*

The one who maintains a positive attitude, (*tatparaḥ*) doing all efforts to gain this knowledge and has control over the senses, attains this knowledge. Having attained this knowledge, one achieves the supreme peace immediately.

अज्ञश्चाश्रद्दधानश्च संशयात्मा विनश्यति ।
नायं लोकोऽस्ति न परो न सुखं संशयात्मनः ॥ ४.४० ॥
*ajñaścā śraddadhānaśca sañśayātmā vinaśyati,*
*nāyaṁ loko'sti na paro na sukhaṁ sañśayātmanaḥ. (4.40)*

But the one who is (*ajña*) devoid of self-realisation, possessing negative attitude, assailed by doubt is destined to perish. The dubious mind can neither achieve happiness (*ayaṁ lokaḥ*) in this life nor (*paraḥ*) hereafter.

योगसंन्यस्तकर्माणं ज्ञानसंछिन्नसंशयम् ।
आत्मवन्तं न कर्माणि निबध्नन्ति धनंजय ॥ ४.४१ ॥
*yoga-sannyastkarmāṇaṁ jñānasañcchinna-sañśayam,*
*ātmavantaṁ na karmāṇi nibadhnanti dhanañjaya. (4.41)*

The person who can renounce kāmya karmas involving dharma and adharma with the help of jñāna-yoga and whose doubt [whether he is body or soul] is destroyed by self-realisation (*ātmavantaṁ*) and who has become confident about his true nature [that he is soul not body], he can never be bound by karmas [that is karmas cannot leave their imprints upon his mind as sanskāras], O conqueror of wealth.

तस्मादज्ञानसंभूतं हृत्स्थं ज्ञानासिनात्मनः ।
छित्त्वैनं संशयं योगमातिष्ठोत्तिष्ठ भारत ॥ ४.४२ ॥
*tasmād ajñāna sambhūtaṁ hṛtsthaṁ jñānāsinātmanaḥ.*
*chittavainaṁ sañśayaṁ yogam ātiṣṭhottiṣṭha bhārata. (4.42)*

Therefore, O Arjuna, the descendant of Bharatas, (*ātiṣṭha*) resort (*yogaṁ*) to yoga and eliminate the doubt of (*hṛtsthaṁ*) your mind (*ajñāna-saṁbhūtam*) born of the ignorance with the (*jñāna-asi*) sword of knowledge, and rise up [to fight].

ॐ तत्सदिति श्रीमद् भगवद्गीतासूपनिषत्सु ब्रह्मविद्यायां योगशास्त्रे श्रीकृष्णार्जुनसंवादे ज्ञानयोगो नाम चतुर्थोऽध्यायः ॥ ४ ॥

Here ends the fourth chapter, named Jñānayoga in the *Bhagvadgitā*, dealing with the Brahmavidyā as propounded in the Upaniṣad and Yogaśāstra in the form of dialogue between Śri Krishna and Arjuna.

# अथ पंचमोऽध्यायः

## संन्यासयोगः

# Chapter 5

[Renunciation of Kāmya, Naimmittika and Niṣiddha Karmas]

Here in this chapter, Śri Krishna wants to tell deluded Arjuna that he will fight a war in the interest of the nation [altruistic interest] and not in his selfish interest. Arjuna's interest should be the interest of the nation. He has to be a saṁnyāsī [renounciate of kāmya karmas) and a karma-yogī [renounciate of the fruits of even nitya karmas]. Defending his nation from the anti-national forces or enemy is the nitya karma [obligatory duty] of a kṣatriya. Karma-yoga in the war can be applied by fighting the war in the national interest and not for gaining rulership of land. In other words, Śri Krishna wants to tell Arjuna that he should not fight the war because he will be one of the beneficiaries. In that case, he can also try to avoid the war if the real benefit lies in avoiding the same. So far as this type of thinking is involved in waging the war, he will remain confused over the issue of whether the actual benefit lies in waging the war or avoiding it.

Nevertheless, when he comes out of the selfish interest behind waging war and thinks from the point of entire humanity involving the national/global interest, then the position will be clear that the rule of the nation in the hands of a person like Duryodhana, who does not leg behind even outraging the modesty of his own sister in law and is inspired by his selfish interest and guided by the persons who want to earn a profit for themselves out of his rule, is not suitable for nation and people.

Duryodhana and his party's motive for gaining power of kingship was to enjoy/exploit it for their selfish motives and not to serve the nation and people at large. Today, we have seen that people have made politics a business. Everyone wants to join politics to reap benefits for himself and his family and not to serve the nation or society selflessly. Today's politicians can also learn much from Śri Krishna's message of karma-yoga and change their attitude towards politics.

अर्जुन उवाच

Arjuna said

संन्यासं कर्मणां कृष्ण पुनर्योगं च शंससि।
यच्छ्रेय एतयोरेकं तन्मे ब्रूहि सुनिश्चितम्॥ ५.१॥

*Saṁnyāsaḥ karmaṇāṁ kṛṣṇa punaryogaṁ ca śansasi,*
*yacchreya etayor ekaṁ tanme brūhi suniścitam. (5.1)*

Arjuna said— O Krishna, on one side, you praise renunciation of kāmya actions; on the other hand, you advocate Karma-Yoga [performance of nitya karmas without motive and attachment]. Tell me, definitely, which one is better of the two. (See also 5.05).

Note: Defending the country from anti-national forces in war is nitya karma (obligatory duty) of a kṣatriya.

श्री कृष्ण उवाच

Śri Krishna said

संन्यासः कर्मयोगश्च निःश्रेयसकरावुभौ।
तयोस्तु कर्मसंन्यासात्कर्मयोगो विशिष्यते॥ ५.२॥

*Saṁnyāsaḥ karmayogaśca niḥśreyasa-karāvubhau,*
*tayos tu karmasannyāsāt karmayogo viśiṣyate. (5.2)*

Śri Krishna said— Karma-saṁnyāsa [renunciation of kāmya karmas], and Karma-yoga [renunciation of the fruits of nitya karmas] both lead to emancipation.

However, of the two, karma-yoga [doing nitya-karmas without any motive and attachment] is superior to Karma-saṁnyāsa [renunciation of kāmya karmas].

ज्ञेय: स नित्यसंन्यासी यो न द्वेष्टि न काङ्क्षति ।
निर्द्वन्द्वो हि महाबाहो सुखं बन्धात्प्रमुच्यते ॥ ५.३ ॥
*jñeyaḥ sa nitya-sannyāsi yo na dveṣṭi na kāṅkṣati,*
*nirdvandvo hi mahā-bāho sukhaṁ bandhāt pramucyate.*

Only a person who neither hates nor desires [hates or desires are associated with acts of kāmya karmas—actions done for the fulfilment of some desire] should be considered a true/eternal saṁnyāsī or renunciat. Thus, free from the dualities of hate and desire, O Arjuna, one is easily liberated from bondage.

साङ्ख्ययोगौ पृथग्बाला: प्रवदन्ति न पण्डिता: ।
एकमप्यास्थित: सम्यगुभयोर्विन्दते फलम् ॥ ५.४ ॥
*Saṅkhya-yogau pṛthag bālāḥ pravadanti na paṇḍitāḥ,*
*ekam apyāsthitaḥ samyag ubhayor vindate phalam. (5.04)*

The ignorant speak of Sāṅkhya (knowledge of embodiment) as different from Yoga (action for disembodiment), but not the wise. The person who has mastered himself/herself gets the benefits of both. [One {Sāṅkhya} gives the knowledge how a soul gets disembodied, and another {Yoga} tells us the method for disembodiment of soul or mokṣa). Having known one, the fruit of both is achieved. For instance, if a seeker knows how he got embodied, he can get himself disembodied. If he excels in the method of disembodiment, he will be able to understand how he got embodied.

Note: Sāṅkhya gives the knowledge as to how Puruṣa (soul), due to its sanskāras of the material world, comes in union with prakṛti and takes birth. Taking birth of the soul as a physical body is called its embodiment or bondage. Yoga is an applied aspect; it tells how to get itself disembodied or attain emancipation. As such, Sāṅkhya and Yoga are two sides of the same coin.

यत्साङ्ख्यैः प्राप्यते स्थानं तद्योगैरपि गम्यते ।
एकं साङ्ख्यं च योगं च यः पश्यति स पश्यति ॥ ५.५ ॥
*yat sāṅkhyaiḥ prāpyate sthānaṁ tad yogair api gamyate,*
*ekaṁ sāṅkhyaṁ ca yogaṁ ca yaḥ paśyati sa paśyati. (5.5)*

Whatever is achieved by the experts of Sāṅkhya (the knowledge of embodiment), the same is achieved by yoga experts (method of disembodiment). The true seeker finds no difference between the Sāṅkhya (knowledge of embodiment) and Yoga (method of disembodiment). (See also 6.1 and 6.2)

Note: If one can know how one gets embodied, he will also find the way of disembodiment. Similarly, one who is acquainted with the method of disembodiment, also knows the process of embodiment. This is like if one can go stairs up, then he knows how to go down and vice versa. If one knows how to lift one foot, other foot will follow. If one knows how to breath in, he knows how to breath out.

संन्यासस्तु महाबाहो दुःखमाप्तुमयोगतः ।
योगयुक्तो मुनिर्ब्रह्म नचिरेणाधिगच्छति ॥ ५.६ ॥
*Saṁnyāsas tu mahābāho duḥkham āptum ayogataḥ,*
*yoga-yukto munir brahma nacireṇādhigacchati. (5.06)*

But Saṁnyāsa [renunciation from kāmya karmas], O Arjuna, is difficult to attain without the practice of yoga. A saṁnyāsī [renunciate of kāmya karmas] who does the practice of yoga quickly attains Brahman. (See also 4.31, and 4.38) (5.6)

योगयुक्तो विशुद्धात्मा विजितात्मा जितेन्द्रियः ।
सर्वभूतात्मभूतात्मा कुर्वन्नपि न लिप्यते ॥ ५.७ ॥
*yoga-yukto viśuddh-ātmā vijit-ātmā jitendriyaḥ,*
*sarva-bhūtātma bhūtātmā kurvann api na lipyate. (5.7)*

A person who has established in yoga; whose mind is pure; who has control over his mind, senses and is not led by sensory pleasures; who sees oneness in all beings; remains unattached to material world in spite of his engagements into worldly affairs.

नैव किंचित्करोमीति युक्तो मन्येत तत्त्ववित् ।
पश्यञ्श्रुण्वन्स्पृशञ्जिघ्रन्नश्नंगच्छन्स्वपन्श्वसन् ॥ ५.८ ॥
*naiva kiñcit karomīti yukto manyeta tattavavit,*
*paśyañ-śṛṇvan-spṛśañ-jighran-naśnan-gacchan-svapañ-śvasan. (5.8)*

A person who has attained perfection in yoga, who knows the truth and thinks: 'I do nothing at all' while seeing, hearing, touching, smelling, eating, walking, sleeping, and breathing. Since these are the routine activities of sense organs and not inspired by any motive.

प्रलपन्विसृजन्गृह्णन्नुन्मिषन्निमिषन्नपि ।
इन्द्रियाणीन्द्रियार्थेषु वर्तन्त इति धारयन् ॥ ५.९ ॥
*pralapan-visarjan-gṛhṇann-unmiṣnn-api,*
*indriyāṇ-indriyārtheṣu vartanta iti dhārayan (5.9)*

While speaking, giving, taking, opening, and closing the eyes, a yogī believes that only the senses operate upon their stimuli. He is not involved with them, these are taking place as essential reflexes. Śri Krishna wants to say that when reflexes or sensory activities take place automatically, they do not come within the ambit of the definition of work. Only those activities that are carried out intentionally are called karmas or actions. If the intention involves selfish interest, that work is called as sakāma; if the intention involves altruistic interest, that is known as niṣkāma karma yoga. (See also 3.27, 13.29, and 14.19)

ब्रह्मण्याधाय कर्माणि सङ्गं त्यक्त्वा करोति यः ।
लिप्यते न स पापेन पद्मपत्रमिवाम्भसा ॥ ५.१० ॥
*brahmaṇyādhāya karmāṇi saṅgaṁ tyaktvā karoti yaḥ,*
*lipyate na sa pāpena padma-patram-ivāmbhasā. (5.10)*

One who works for Brahman like a servant for his master without any desire for selfish gain or profit, even for mokṣa, remains untouched by pāpa as a lotus leaf is untouched by water.

कायेन मनसा बुद्ध्या केवलैरिन्द्रियैरपि ।
योगिनः कर्म कुर्वन्ति सङ्गं त्यक्त्वात्मशुद्धये ॥ ५.११ ॥
*kāyena manasā buddhyā kevalair indriyair api,*
*yoginaḥ karma kurvanti saṅgaṁ tyaktvātmaśuddhaye. (5.11)*

Karma-yogīs perform actions by body, mind, intellect, and senses only for Brahman (*saṅgaṁ tyaktvā*) without any selfish motive, and for self-purification.

युक्तः कर्मफलं त्यक्त्वा शान्तिमाप्नोति नैष्ठिकीम् ।
अयुक्तः कामकारेण फले सक्तो निबध्यते ॥ ५.१२ ॥
*yuktaḥ karma-phalaṁ tyaktvā śāntim āpnoti naiṣṭhikīm,*
*ayuktaḥ kāmakāreṇa phale sakto nibadhyate. (5.12)*

(*yuktaḥ*) 'All actions are for God and not for my selfish gain', a yogī who has made up his/her mind like this and who has abandoned kāmya karmas and the desire for fruits of nitya karmas, he attains supreme peace in the form of mokṣa (*naiṣṭhikiṁ śāntiṁ*) by establishing himself/herself in his/her true nature called jñāna. The sequence is like this:

Self-purification, attainment of knowledge, renunciation of all kāmya karmas, renunciation of selfish motives behind nitya karmas, and finally establishing in one's true nature. While others (*ayuktaḥ*) who are doing all actions for themselves (*kāmakāreṇa*) inspired by kāmya karmas (*phale saktaḥ*) for gaining some fruit (*nibadhyate*) get trapped in bondage.

सर्वकर्माणि मनसा संन्यस्यास्ते सुखं वशी ।
नवद्वारे पुरे देही नैव कुर्वन्न कारयन् ॥ ५.१३ ॥
*sarvakarmāṇi manasā sannyasyāste sukhaṁ vaśi,*
*nava-dvāre pure dehi naiva kurvanna kārayan. (5.13)*

A person (*vaśī*) having subdued senses (*saṁnyasya*) and having renounced (*sarva karmāṇi*) all kāmya karmas (*manaśa*) applying his rational mind (*āste*) dwells (*sukhaṁ*) happily (*pure*) in the city of (*navadvāre*) the nine gates [physical body consisting of two eyes, two ears, two nostrils, one mouth, urinary tract and excretory organ]. He (*naiva*) neither performs kāmya actions nor nitya actions in his self-interest (*na*) nor (*kārayan*) makes his body and sense organs do action.

न कर्तृत्वं न कर्माणि लोकस्य सृजति प्रभुः ।
न कर्मफलसंयोगं स्वभावस्तु प्रवर्तते ॥ ५.१४ ॥
*na kartṛtvaṁ na karmāṇi lokasya saṛjati prabhuḥ,,*
*na karma-phala-sañyogaṁ svabhāvas tu pravartate. (5.14)*

Īśvara neither creates doership of souls nor creates essential actions like constructions of homes, pots, and vehicles to be performed by souls nor does He associate actions with their fruits. It is all taking place naturally. That is, it is all within the nature of human beings to consider themselves as doers and do some action and associate actions with fruits.

नादत्ते कस्यचित्पापं न चैव सुकृतं विभुः ।
अज्ञानेनावृतं ज्ञानं तेन मुह्यन्ति जन्तवः ॥ ५.१५ ॥
*nādatte kasyacitpāpaṁ na caiva sukṛtaṁ vibhuḥ,*

*ajñānen āvaṛtaṁ jñānaṁ tena muhyanti jantavaḥ. (5.15)*

Īśvara neither accepts pāpa [actions responsible for the downfall of a human-being] nor the good deeds gifted by any devotee. The knowledge of truth [that they are pure spiritual element and not the body] is covered by [the veil of] ignorance, thereby people are deluded that they do it, they make others do it, they eat, they feed, etc.

ज्ञानेन तु तदज्ञानं येषां नाशितमात्मनः ।
तेषामादित्यवज्ज्ञानं प्रकाशयति तत्परम् ॥ ५.१६ ॥
*jñānena tu tad ajñānaṁ yeṣāṁ nāśitam ātmanaḥ,*
*teṣām āditya-vaj-jñānaṁ prakāśayati tatparam. (5.16)*

But who have destroyed their ignorance with the help of the knowledge of truth, their knowledge reveals the Supreme power like the sun [reveals the physical world].

तद्बुद्धयस्तदात्मानस्तन्निष्ठास्तत्परायणाः ।
गच्छन्त्यपुनरावृत्तिं ज्ञाननिर्धूतकल्मषाः ॥ ५.१७ ॥
*tad buddhayas tad ātmānas tanniṣṭhās tat parāyaṇāḥ,*
*gacchantya punarāvṛttiṁ jñāna-nirdhūta-kalmaṣāḥ. (5.17)*

Whose mind [intellect] and soul have become one with the Supreme power, who are firmly established in Him and completely attached to Him, they do not take birth again and again by destroying their ignorance by the knowledge [realisation] of Supreme Being.

विद्याविनयसंपन्ने ब्राह्मणे गवि हस्तिनि ।
शुनि चैव श्वपाके च पण्डिताः समदर्शिनः ॥ ५.१८ ॥
*vidyā-vinaya-sampanne brāhmaṇe gavi hastini,*
*śuni caiva śvapāke ca paṇḍitāḥ samadarśinaḥ. (5.18)*

Enlightened persons endowed with vinaya [tranquility] look upon a learned, a cow, an elephant, or a dog or the chanḍāla [a person working in crematorium place for cremation of dead bodies] with an equal eye.

इहैव तैर्जितः सर्गो येषां साम्ये स्थितं मनः ।
निर्दोषं हि समं ब्रह्म तस्माद् ब्रह्मणि ते स्थिताः ॥ ५.१९ ॥
*ihaiva tair jitaḥ sargo yeṣāṁ sāmye sthitaṁ manaḥ,*
*nirdoṣaṁ hi samaṁ brahma tasmād brahmaṇi te sthitāḥ. (5.19)*

Here on the earth itself, (*sargaḥ*) life is conquered by those whose mind is set in equality or impartiality. Since the Almighty Brahman is free from all blamishes and He is impartial to all, so a person whose mind is set in impartiality is established in Brahman. (See also 18.55)

न प्रहृष्येत्प्रियं प्राप्य नोद्विजेत्प्राप्य चाप्रियम् ।
स्थिरबुद्धिरसंमूढो ब्रह्मविद् ब्रह्मणि स्थितः ॥ ५.२० ॥
*na prahṛṣyet priyaṁ prāpya nodvijet prāpya cāpriyam,*
*Sthira-buddhira-sammūḍho brahmavid brahmaṇi sthitaḥ. (5.20)*

The notion of impartiality, as described in the above stanza, is elaborated here. One who neither rejoices on obtaining the pleasant things nor grieves on obtaining the unpleasant things, who does not have a wavering mind, who is undeluded, and who knows [realises] Brahman; such a person is established in Brahman.

बाह्यस्पर्शेष्वसक्तात्मा विन्दत्यात्मनि यत्सुखम् ।
स ब्रह्मयोगयुक्तात्मा सुखमक्षयमश्नुते ॥ ५.२१ ॥
*bāhya-sparśeṣvasaktātmā vindatyāmani yat-sukham,*
*sa brahma-yoga-yuktātmā sukham akṣayam aśnute. (5.21)*

A person whose mind is unattached to external stimuli, who discovers the joy within himself/herself, is said to be united with Brahman in samādhi and enjoys eternal bliss.

ये हि संस्पर्शजा भोगा दुःखयोनय एव ते ।
आद्यन्तवन्तः कौन्तेय न तेषु रमते बुधः ॥ ५.२२ ॥
*ye hi sansparśajā bhogā duḥkha-yonaya eva te,*

*ādyantavantaḥ kaunteya na teṣu ramate budhaḥ. (5.22)*

Pleasure derived from the contact of senses with their external stimuli is verily the source of misery. Such pleasure cannot be eternal since it has a beginning and an end. The wise, O Arjuna, does not rejoice in the external stimuli of their senses. (See also 18.38)

शक्नोतीहैव यः सोढुं प्राक्शरीरविमोक्षणात् ।
कामक्रोधोद्भवं वेगं स युक्तः स सुखी नरः ॥ ५.२३ ॥
*śaknotīhaiva yaḥ soḍhuṁ prāk śarīra-vimokṣaṇāt,*
*kāmakrodhodbhavaṁ vegaṁ sa yuktaḥ sa sukhī naraḥ. (5.23)*

One who can withstand the impulse of lust and anger before leaving his body [death] is a yogī and a happy person.

योऽन्तःसुखोऽन्तरारामस्तथान्तर्ज्योतिरेव यः ।
स योगी ब्रह्मनिर्वाणं ब्रह्मभूतोऽधिगच्छति ॥ ५.२४ ॥
*yo'ntaḥsukho'ntarārāmas tathāntar-jyotireva yaḥ,*
*sa yogī brahma-nirvāṇaṁ brahmabhūto'dhigacchati. (5.24)*

One who finds happiness within himself, who rejoices within himself, and who is illuminated by the inner enlightenment; such a yogī becomes one with Brahman and attains supreme Nirvāṇa [emancipation].

लभन्ते ब्रह्मनिर्वाणमृषयः क्षीणकल्मषाः ।
छिन्नद्वैधा यतात्मानः सर्वभूतहिते रताः ॥ ५.२५ ॥
*labhante brahma-nirvāṇam-ṛṣyaḥ kṣīṇa-kalmaṣāḥ,*
*chinna-dvaidhā yatātmānaḥ sarvabhūta-hite ratāḥ. (5.25)*

Seers, whose fruits of pāpa karmas [actions responsible for the downfall of a human being] have ended, whose doubts have been dispelled by knowledge, whose minds are controlled, and who are engaged in activities suitable to all beings [non-violence], attain the Supreme Brahman.

कामक्रोधवियुक्तानां यतीनां यतचेतसाम् ।
अभितो ब्रह्मनिर्वाणं वर्तते विदितात्मनाम् ॥ ५.२६ ॥
*kāma-krodh-aviyuktānāṁ yatīnaṁ yatacetasām,*
*abhito brahma-nirvāṇaṁ vartate vidit-ātmanām. (5.26)*

A Self-realised person who is free from lust and anger, and who has subdued the mind and senses easily attains Nirvāṇa [emancipation].

स्पर्शान्कृत्वा बहिर्बाह्यांश्चक्षुश्चैवान्तरे भ्रुवोः ।
प्राणापानौ समौ कृत्वा नासाभ्यन्तरचारिणौ ॥ ५.२७ ॥
*sparśān kṛtvā bahir bāhyāñś cakṣuścaivāntare bhruvoḥ,*
*prāṇāpānau smau kṛtvā nāsābhyantaracāriṇau. (5.27)*

Shutting out [ignoring] all external stimuli; focussing the eyes between eyebrows; harmonising the inhalations and exhalations moving through the nostrils; (See also 4.29, 6.13)

यतेन्द्रियमनोबुद्धिर्मुनिर्मोक्षपरायणः ।
विगतेच्छाभयक्रोधो यः सदा मुक्त एव सः ॥ ५.२८ ॥
*yatendriya-mano-buddhir-munir-mokṣaparāyaṇaḥ,*
*vigatecchā-bhaya-krodho yaḥ sadā mukta eva saḥ. (5.28)*

With senses, mind, and intellect under control, who has become a muni or saṁnyāsi by meditating upon Iśvara, having liberation as the prime goal, free from lust, anger, and fear, such a sage is verily liberated.

भोक्तारं यज्ञतपसां सर्वलोकमहेश्वरम् ।
सुहृदं सर्वभूतानां ज्ञात्वा मां शान्तिमृच्छति ॥ ५.२९ ॥
*bhoktāraṁ yajña-tapasāṁ sarvaloka-maheśrvaram,*
*suhṛdaṁ sarva-bhūtānāṁ jñātvā māṁ śāntim ṛcchati. (5.29)*

Such a sage (*jñātvā*) perceiving or knowing (*māṁ*) the Almighty Brahman, who is the great Lord of all the worlds, a friend of all beings and who is pleased by yajñas and austerities, attains peace.

ॐ तत्सदिति श्रीमद् भगवद्गीतासूपनिषत्सु ब्रह्मविद्यायां योगशास्त्रे श्रीकृष्णार्जुनसंवादे संन्यासयोगो नाम पंचमोऽध्याय: ॥ ५ ।

Here ends the fifth chapter, named Saṁnyāsa yoga in the *Bhagvadgitā*, dealing with the Brahmavidyā as propounded in the Upaniṣad and Yogaśāstra in the form of a dialogue between Śri Krishna and Arjuna.

# अथ षष्ठोऽध्यायः

## ध्यानयोगः

# Chapter 6

[Yoga of Meditation]

This chapter is known as a chapter dealing with Dhyāna Yoga (or Yoga of Meditation). Śri Krishna wants to tell confused Arjuna that yoga for altruistic welfare is the best among all other forms of yoga. Krishna is a supporter of this form of yoga. Since the purpose of life is shared prosperity and not an individual prosperity. Rishi Dayananda followed a similar principle when formulating the 9th Principal of Arya Samaj. Accordingly, the welfare of an Individual lies in the welfare of the entire society or shared or altruistic welfare. Śri Krishna gives here two concepts of the self—one Individual self, characterised by the life of an Individual being. The individuated self is attributed to the first person, such as Aham/Māma, etc.; conversely, it is the Universal Self characterised by the life of the entire Universe. The Individuated Self remains confined within the periphery of ahaṁ and mama (I and my), but the universal self encompasses the entire Universe. Śri Krishna tells Arjuna to universalise this ahaṁ, mām and mama (I, me, and my). Rise above all aham and see it pervading the entire Universe. Then only he will be a real yogī defined by Śri Krishna. Universalisation of aham (I) is the actual goal of life. So Arjuna is to fight the war not keeping his individuated self-interest in mind but in mind the interest of entire humankind. In this chapter, Śri Krishna sheds a little light on the life hereafter. He conveys that the sanskāras of previous lives do not leave us so easily. Our present life is moulded based upon the sanskāras of previous lives. If an individual has earned good sanskāras but has fallen from the actual path, his good sanskāras help him tread upon the same good path next time. Sanskāras are the psychological genes formed from our reaction to the outside world and the karmas we perform. According to the Vedic philosophy, it is not the biological genes that act as the seed of our life. However, the psychological genes or sanskāras of an individual transform into biological genes and act as the seed for his/her next life. Vedānta philosopher also support it, *sanskāra bijāt sṛṣṭi.*

श्री कृष्ण उवाच

Śri Krishna Said

अनाश्रित: कर्मफलं कार्यं कर्म करोति य: ।
स संन्यासी च योगी च न निरग्निर्न चाक्रिय: ॥ ६.१ ॥
*anāśritaḥ karma-phalaṁ kāryaṁ karma karoti yaḥ,*
*sa sannyāsi ca yogī ca na niragnir na cākriyaḥ. (6.01)*

Śri Krishna Said— One who performs the nitya karmas without seeking benefit for oneself is a saṁnyāsī and a yogī in real sense and not the one who does not enkindle fire in various yajñas and who doesn't perform any action of tapa (austerity) and dāna (charity), etc.

**Saṁnyāsa**: Abandonment of kāmya-karmas and lack of desire for fruits of nitya karmas is Saṁnyāsa

Lack of desire for fruits of nitya-karmas causing chittavikṣepa [distraction of mind from its objects] is yoga.

यं संन्यासमिति प्राहुर्योगं तं विद्धि पाण्डव ।
न ह्यसंन्यस्तसङ्कल्पो योगी भवति कश्चन ॥ ६.२ ॥
*yaṁ Saṁnyāsam iti prāhur yogaṁ taṁ viddhi pāṇḍava,*
*na hyasannyasta-saṅkalpo yogī bhavati kaścana. (6.02)*

O son of Pāṇḍu, know that yoga which is called as saṁnyāsa. No one can become a Karma-yogī without renouncing the saṅkalpas leading to the desire for fruits of actions. (See also 5.1, 5.5, 6.1, and 18.2).

Note: Saṅkalpa here is sanskāra.

आरुरुक्षोर्मुनेर्योगं कर्म कारणमुच्यते ।
योगारूढस्य तस्यैव शमः कारणमुच्यते ॥ ६.३ ॥
*āruruk ṣormuneryogaṁ karma kāraṇamucyaate,*
*yogāruḍhasya tasyaiva śmaḥ kāraṇamucyate. (6.03)*

Nitya karmas (without desire for fruits) are said to be the secret behind the success in (*ārurukṣu*) climbing the ladder of yoga. Śama or upaśama (withdrawal even from nitya karma) is the means for (*yogarūḍhatā*) establishing in dhyāna yoga.

यदा हि नेन्द्रियार्थेषु न कर्मस्वनुषज्जते ।
सर्वसङ्कल्पसंन्यासी योगारूढस्तदोच्यते ॥ ६.४ ॥
*yadā hi nendriyārtheṣu na karmasvanuṣajjate,*
*Sarvasaṅkalpa-sannyāsī yogārūḍhas tadocyate. (6.04)*

A seeker is said to have (*yogārūḍha*) established in dhyāna yoga and (*sarvasaṅkalpa-saṁnyāsī*) renunciator of all saṅkalpas [sanskāra based desires] leading to the bhoga [sensory and sensual enjoyments] here and hereafter, when he is not attracted to the outside stimuli of sense organs as well as nitya [daily duties], naimittika (actions to be done to celebrate some occasion), kāmya (actions to be performed with some desire in mind) and niṣiddha [prohibited] karmas [actions] finding them to be serving none of his purposes.

Note: There are two types of bhogas: One the reward of fruits done by us, second the consuming natural resources and sensory enjoyment. Saṅkalpa is the cause of all desires. संकल्प मूला हि सर्वे कामाः *saṁkalpa mūlā hi sarve kāmāḥ.*

उद्धरेदात्मनात्मानं नात्मानमवसादयेत्।
आत्मैव ह्यात्मनो बन्धुरात्मैव रिपुरात्मनः॥ ६.५॥
*uddhared ātmanātmānaṁ nātmānam avasādayet,*
*ātmaiva hyātmano bandhur ātmaiva ripur ātmanaḥ. (6.05)*

Thus in view of the above facts, a seeker must elevate himself, and not degrade. Since a seeker is himself his friend [if he elevates himself], and himself his enemy [if he degrades himself].

बन्धुरात्मात्मनस्तस्य येनात्मैवात्मना जितः।
अनात्मनस्तु शत्रुत्वे वर्तेतात्मैव शत्रुवत्॥ ६.६॥
*bandhur ātmātmanas tasya yenātmaivātmanā jitaḥ,*
*anātmanas tu śatrutve vartet ātmaiva śatruvat. (6.06)*

A seeker who (*ātmanā*) himself has taken (*ātmā*) his body (*jitaḥ*) in his control is called (*ātmanaḥ*) one's own (*bandhu*) friend. On the other hand, a seeker is called (*ātmaiva*) his own (*śatrutve śatruvat*) enemy, (*anātmanaḥ*) if he has failed to control his body.

जितात्मनः प्रशान्तस्य परमात्मा समाहितः।
शीतोष्णसुखदुःखेषु तथा मानापमानयोः॥ ६.७॥
*jitātmanaḥ praśāntasya paramātmā samāhitaḥ,*
*śitoṣṇa-sukha-duḥkheṣu tathā mānāpamānayoḥ. (6.07)*

(*jitātmanaḥ*) One who has conquered oneself, (*praśāntasy*); who is always happy, he/she is ever steadfast with the Supreme Self. He/she is indifferent to heat, cold, pleasure, pain, honour or dishonour.

ज्ञानविज्ञानतृप्तात्मा कूटस्थो विजितेन्द्रियः।
युक्त इत्युच्यते योगी समलोष्टाश्मकांचनः॥ ६.८॥
*jñāna-vijñāna-tṛptātmā kūṭastho vijitendriyaḥ,*
*yukta ityucyate yogī sama-loṣṭāśma-kāñcanaḥ. (6.08)*

A yogī is called (*yukta*) established in samādhi who has (*jñāna*) understood the Śāstras properly and realized or experienced whatever described in the Śāstras; who is satisfied that nothing is to be known more or further; who is equanimous, who has control over one's [mind and] senses; for whom a lump of clay, a stone, and gold (*sama*) are of equal importance.

सुहृन्मित्रार्युदासीनमध्यस्थद्वेष्यबन्धुषु ।
साधुष्वपि च पापेषु समबुद्धिर्विशिष्यते ॥ ६.९ ॥
*suhṛnmitrāryudāsina-madhyastha-dveaṣya-bandhuṣu,*
*sādhuṣvapi ca pāpeṣu sama-buddhir viśiṣyate. (6.09)*

A person is considered superior who equally treats a (*suhṛt*) person who helps us without expecting anything in return; (*mitra*) who is affectionate; (*ari*) who is enemy; (*udāsīna*) who is impartial (*madhyastha*) well-wisher of both the opposing parties; (*dveṣya*) who is not our well-wisher; (*bandhu*) who is close relative; (*sādhuṣu*) who is good person acting according to Śāstras; and (*pāpeṣu*) who commit prohibited acts or creates troubles for others.

योगी युञ्जीत सततमात्मानं रहसि स्थितः ।
एकाकी यतचित्तात्मा निराशीरपरिग्रहः ॥ ६.१० ॥
*yogī yuñjīta satatam ātmānaṁ rahasi sthitaḥ,*
*ekākī yata-cittātmā nirāśīra parigrahaḥ. (6.10)*

(*Yogī*) Let a Yogi — (*sthitaḥ*) sit (*rahasi*) in solitude (*ekākī*) alone [after taking Saṁnyāsa]-- (*yat chitta-ātmā*) having mind, body and senses under his/her control, free from (*āśīḥ*) desires and (*aparigraha*) possessiveness, (*satataṁ*) and try constantly to stabilize (*ātmānaṁ*) his mind.

शुचौ देशे प्रतिष्ठाप्य स्थिरमासनमात्मनः ।
नात्युच्छ्रितं नातिनीचं चैलाजिनकुशोत्तरम् ॥ ६.११ ॥

*śucau deśe pratiṣṭhāpya sthiram āsanam ātmanaḥ,*
*nātyucchritaṁ nātinīcaṁ cailājinakuśottaram. (6.11)*

The yogī should sit on a firm seat that is neither too high nor too low, covered with Kuśa grass, or a skin of trees, both covered with a cloth in a clean spot.

तत्रैकाग्रं मनः कृत्वा यतचित्तेन्द्रियक्रियः ।
उपविश्यासने युञ्ज्याद्योगमात्मविशुद्धये ॥ ६.१२ ॥
*tatraikāgraṁ manaḥ kṛtvā yata-chittendriya-kriayaḥ,*
*uapaviśyāsane yuñjyād-yogam-ātma-viśuddhaye. (6.12)*

Sitting [in a comfortable position] and concentrating the mind on a single object, controlling the activities of the senses and mind, let the yogī practice yoga for self-purification.

समं कायशिरोग्रीवं धारयन्नचलं स्थिरः ।
संप्रेक्ष्य नासिकाग्रं स्वं दिशश्चानवलोकयन् ॥ ६.१३ ॥
*samaṁ kāya-śirogrivaṁ dhārayann acalaṁ sthiraḥ,*
*saṁprekṣya nāsikāgaraṁ svaṁ diśaś cānavalokayan. (6.13)*

While practising yoga, one should ensure that the (*kāyaṁ*) waist, spine, chest, (*grīvaṁ*) neck, and (*śiraḥ*) head are erect, motionless and steady; eyes are fixed steadily, and one does not look around. (See also 4.29, 5.27 and 8.10)

प्रशान्तात्मा विगतभीर्ब्रह्मचारिव्रते स्थितः ।
मनः संयम्य मच्चित्तो युक्त आसीत मत्परः ॥ ६.१४ ॥
*praśāntāntātmā vigatabhīr brahmacārivrate sthitaḥ,*
*manaḥ sañyamya maccitto yukta āsita matparaḥ. (6.14)*

[Krishna gives here a simple technique to Arjuna to come out of war stress]. With a peaceful mind, without any fear, observing the vow of Brahmachārī [having one's mind concentrated upon Brahman, service of guru, and depending upon alms for food], having withdrawn the mind from the outside world, (*macchittaḥ*) concentrate on Paramātmā (*matparaḥ*) considering Him the supreme and best.

युञ्जन्नेवं सदात्मानं योगी नियतमानसः ।
शान्तिं निर्वाणपरमां मत्संस्थामधिगच्छति ॥ ६.१५ ॥
*yuñjannevaṁ sadātmānaṁ yogī niyata-mānasaḥ,*
*śāntiṁ nirvāṇa-paramāṁ matsansthām adhigacchati. (6.15)*

Thus, (*yuñjannevaṁ*) having meditated upon Brahman, (*niyatmānamaḥ*) with controlled mind, (*sadā*) always (*ātmānaṁ*) establishing himself in Brahman, a yogī attains peace culminating into nirvāṇa or mokṣa (*matsaṁsthām*) located in Brahman.

नात्यश्नतस्तु योगोऽस्ति न चैकान्तमनश्नतः ।
न चातिस्वप्नशीलस्य जाग्रतो नैव चार्जुन ॥ ६.१६ ॥
*nātyaśnatastu yogo'sti na caikāntam anaśnataḥ,*
*na cātisvapnaśilasya jāgrato naiva cārjuna. (6.16)*

The success in yoga is not possible, O Arjuna, for the one who eats too much, or who does not eat at all; who sleeps too much, or who keeps awake all the time.

युक्ताहारविहारस्य युक्तचेष्टस्य कर्मसु ।
युक्तस्वप्नावबोधस्य योगो भवति दुःखहा ॥ ६.१७ ॥
*yukt-āhāra-vihārasya yuktaceṣṭasya karmasu,*
*yukta-svapnāvabodhasya yogo bhavati duḥkhahā. (6.17)*

But, for the one who observes restraint in eating and sensory pleasures, who involves into actions in a restrained manner, who has regulated his sleep, and waking habits, this dhyāna yoga removes (all) sorrows.

यदा विनियतं चित्तमात्मन्येवावतिष्ठते ।
निःस्पृहः सर्वकामेभ्यो युक्त इत्युच्यते तदा ॥ ६.१८ ॥
*yadā viniyataṁ cittam ātmanyevāvatiṣthate,*
*niḥspṛhaḥ sarvakāmebhyo yukta ityucyate tadā. (6.18)*

When the mind is restrained and become stable in itself [without being attracted by outside stimuli], then a person gets freedom from desires of sensory objects and is said to be yukta [established in samādhi].

यथा दीपो निवातस्थो नेङ्गते सोपमा स्मृता ।
योगिनो यतचित्तस्य युञ्जतो योगमात्मनः ॥ ६.१९ ॥
*yathā dīpo nivātastho neṅgate sopamā smṛtā,*
*yogino yatacittasya yuñjato yogamātmanaḥ. (6.19)*

As a lamp doesn't flicker in a windless place, (*sā upamā*) similar is (*smṛtā*) said to be the condition (*yoginaḥ*) of a yogī (*yat chittasyā*) whose mind is restrained and (*yuñjataḥ*) who has established in Samādhi (*yogamātmanaḥ*) during the course of doing dhyāna yoga.

यत्रोपरमते चित्तं निरुद्धं योगसेवया ।
यत्र चैवात्मनात्मानं पश्यन्नात्मनि तुष्यति ॥ ६.२० ॥
*yatroparamate cittaṁ niruddhaṁ yogasevayā,*
*yatra caivātmanātmānaṁ paśyannātmani tuṣyati. (6.20)*

When the mind is restrained by the practice of yoga and is withdrawn from worldly allurements, one becomes content beholding the Self through the mind purified by samādhi.

सुखमात्यन्तिकं यत्तद् बुद्धिग्राह्यमतीन्द्रियम् ।
वेत्ति यत्र न चैवायं स्थितश्चलति तत्त्वतः ॥ ६.२१ ॥
*sukhamātyantikaṁ yattadbuddhigrāhmatīndirayam,*
*vetti yatra na caivāyaṁ sthitaśchalati tattvataḥ. (6.21)*

One experiences (*ātyantikam*) infinite (*sukham*) bliss resulting from a purified mind, which is beyond the reach of the senses. The time when such bliss is experienced by a yogī, he is never separated from the absolute reality.

यं लब्ध्वा चापरं लाभं मन्यते नाधिकं ततः ।
यस्मिन्स्थितो न दुःखेन गुरुणापि विचाल्यते ॥ ६.२२ ॥
*yaṁ labdhvā cāparaṁ lābhaṁ manyate nādhikaṁ tataḥ,*
*yasmin sthito na duḥkhena guruṇāpi vicālyate. (6.22)*

After realizing the absolute reality, one does not regard any other gain superior to it. Having established in absolute reality, one is not moved even by the greatest calamity.

तं विद्याद् दुःखसंयोगवियोगं योगसंज्ञितम् ।
स निश्चयेन योक्तव्यो योगोऽनिर्विण्णचेतसा ॥ ६.२३ ॥
*taṁ vidyād duḥkh-sañyoga-viyogaṁ yoga-sañjñitam,*
*sa niścayena yoktavyo yogo'nirviṇṇacetasā. (6.23)*

The [state of] yoga should be known as a severance of union with sorrow. This yoga should be practised with firm determination and perseverance (*anirviṇṇachetasā*) without any mental fatigue.

सङ्कल्पप्रभवान्कामांस्त्यक्त्वा सर्वानशेषतः ।
मनसैवेन्द्रियग्रामं विनियम्य समन्ततः ॥ ६.२४ ॥
*saṅkalpaprabhavān kāmāṁstyaktvā sarvān aśeṣataḥ,*
*manasaivendriyagrāmaṁ viniyamya samantataḥ. (6.24)*

How to practice yoga? Abandon all desires born of sanskāras, and completely restrain the senses from their stimuli with the help of a rational mind.

शनैः शनैरुपरमेद् बुद्ध्या धृतिगृहीतया ।
आत्मसंस्थं मनः कृत्वा न किंचिदपि चिन्तयेत् ॥ ६.२५ ॥
*śanaiḥ śanairuparamedbuddhyā dhṛtigaṛhītayā,*
*ātmasaṁsthaṁ manaḥ kṛtvā na kiñcidapi cintayet. (6.25)*

One should gradually restrain one's mind (*buddhyā*) wisely and (*dhṛtigṛhītayā*) patiently, and try (*ātma-sanstha*) to absorb one's mind in one's own self without involving any thought.

यतो यतो निश्चरति मनश्चंचलमस्थिरम्।
ततस्ततो नियम्यैतदात्मन्येव वशं नयेत्॥ ६.२६॥
*yato yato niścarati manaś cañcalam asthiram,*
*tatastato niyamyaitadātmanyeva vaśaṁ nayet. (6.26)*

Wheresoever this restless and unsteady mind wanders away, one should withdraw his mind from that stimuli, bring it back to one's own control.

प्रशान्तमनसं ह्येनं योगिनं सुखमुत्तमम्।
उपैति शान्तरजसं ब्रह्मभूतमकल्मषम्॥ ६.२७॥
*praśāntamanasaṁ hyenaṁ yoginaṁ sukham uttamam,*
*upaiti śāntarajasaṁ brahmabhūtam akalmaṣam. (6.27)*

Supreme bliss comes to a yogī who realises the Brahman (*universal self*) and whose mind is tranquil, whose desires are under control, and (*akalmaṣaṁ*) who is free from adharma.

युञ्जन्नेवं सदात्मानं योगी विगतकल्मषः।
सुखेन ब्रह्मसंस्पर्शमत्यन्तं सुखमश्नुते॥ ६.२८॥
*yuñjannevaṁ sadātmānaṁ yogi vigatakalmaṣaḥ,*
*sukhena brahmasaṁsparśamatyantaṁ sukhamaśnute. (6.28)*

Such a yogī, who is free from distractions of yoga, (*yuñjanneva*) who constantly engages the mind in samādhi, (*aśnute*) enjoys (*atyantaṁ*) the infinite (*sukham*) bliss by (*brahma-sansarpa*) contact with Brahman.

सर्वभूतस्थमात्मानं सर्वभूतानि चात्मनि।
ईक्षते योगयुक्तात्मा सर्वत्र समदर्शनः॥ ६.२९॥
*sarvabhūtastham ātmānaṁ sarvabhūtāni cātmani,*
*īkṣate yoga-yuktātmā sarvatra sama-darśanaḥ. (6.29)*

Because of establishing his mind in samādhi, a yogī perceives the Brahman in all beings and all beings in Brahman. He also treats every being equally. (See also

4.35)

योो मां पश्यति सर्वत्र सर्वं च मयि पश्यति।
तस्याहं न प्रणश्यामि स च मे न प्रणश्यति ॥ ६.३० ॥
*yo māṁ paśyati sarvatra sarvaṁ ca mayi paśyati,*
*tasyāhaṁ na praṇaśyāmi sa ca me na praṇaśyati. (6.30)*

For example, a seeker who perceives Brahman pervading everything and everything in Brahman, he becomes inseparable from the Brahman and the Brahman becomes inseparable from him.

सर्वभूतस्थितं यो मां भजत्येकत्वमास्थितः।
सर्वथा वर्तमानोऽपि स योगी मयि वर्तते ॥ ६.३१ ॥
*sarvabhūta-sthitaṁ yo māṁ bhajatyekatvamāsthitaḥ,*
*sarvathā vartamāno'pi sa yogī mayi vartate. (6.31)*

Thus a yogī who meditates upon Brahman abiding in all beings equally and (*sarvathā vartamānaḥ api*) sees all beings with an equal eye, merges with Brahman.

आत्मौपम्येन सर्वत्र समं पश्यति योऽर्जुन।
सुखं वा यदि वा दुःखं स योगी परमो मतः ॥ ६.३२ ॥
*ātmaupamyena sarvatra samaṁ paśyati yo'rjuna,*
*sukhaṁ vā yadi duḥkhaṁ sa yogi paramo mataḥ. (6.32)*

One is considered as the best yogī, who considers every being like oneself, and who can feel the pain and pleasures of others as one's own, O Arjuna.

अर्जुन उवाच
Arjuna said
योऽयं योगस्त्वया प्रोक्तः साम्येन मधुसूदन।
एतस्याहं न पश्यामि चंचलत्वात्स्थितिं स्थिराम् ॥ ६.३३ ॥
*yo'yaṁ yogastvayā proktaḥ sāmyena madhusūdana,*
*eatasyāhaṁ na paśyāmi cañcalatvātsthitiṁ sthirām. (6.33)*

Arjuna Said— O Madhusūdana [destroyer of foes], I don't see the yoga of equanimity stated by you can be done, because of fickleness of mind.

चंचलं हि मनः कृष्ण प्रमाथि बलवद् दृढम्।
तस्याहं निग्रहं मन्ये वायोरिव सुदुष्करम्॥ ६.३४॥
*cañcalaṁ hi manaḥ kṛṣṇa pramāthi balavaddṛḍham,*
*tasyāhaṁ nigrahaṁ manye vāyor iva suduṣkaram. (6.34)*

As the mind, indeed, is very unsteady, (*pramāthi*) subduer of body and sense organs, powerful, and firm, O Krishna. I think restraining the mind is as difficult as restraining the wind.

श्री कृष्ण उवाच
Krishna Said

असंशयं महाबाहो मनो दुर्निग्रहं चलम्।
अभ्यासेन तु कौन्तेय वैराग्येण च गृह्यते॥ ६.३५॥
*asañśayaṁ mahābāho mano dur-nigrahaṁ calam,*
*abhyāsena tu kaunteya vairāgyeṇa ca gṛhyate. (6.35)*

Śri Krishna said— Undoubtedly, O Arjuna, the mind is restless and difficult to restrain, but it can be subdued by abhyāsa [practice of repeting one and same vṛtti of chitta], and vairāgya [detachment], O son of Kunti. Yoga Darśana also says: *abhyāsa vairāgyābhyām tannirodhaḥ*, that is, the mind can be restrained through constant practice and detachment.

Note: Abhyāsa is the repetition of the same vṛtti of chitta.

Vairāgya is unwillingness developed towards bhogas [sensory and sensual pleasures] desired by us by finding fault with the visible and invisible bhogas by us.

असंयतात्मना योगो दुष्प्राप इति मे मतिः।
वश्यात्मना तु यतता शक्योऽवाप्तुमुपायतः॥ ६.३६॥
*asañyatātmanā yogo duṣprāpa iti me matih,*
*vaśyātmanā tu yatatā śakyo'vāptum upāyataḥ. (6.36)*

In my opinion, yoga is difficult for those who have (*asañyatātmā*) failed to control their mind through abhyāsa and vairāgya. However, yoga is attainable by those who can control their minds through abhyāsa and vairāgya.

**Question:** Inquistive about the fate of a yogī, who is able to withdraw himself/herself from the kāmya karmas that are instrumental in bondage of life [embodiment of soul], but who has not been successful in attaining mokṣa as the fruit of yoga, Arjuna asked:

अर्जुन उवाच

Arjuna said

अयतिः श्रद्धयोपेतो योगाच्चलितमानसः ।
अप्राप्य योगसंसिद्धिं कां गतिं कृष्ण गच्छति ॥ ६.३७ ॥
*ayatiḥ śraddhayopeto yogāccalitamānasaḥ,*
*aprāpya yogasansiddhiṁ kāṁ gatiṁ kṛṣṇa gacchati. (6.37)*

Arjuna said— O Krishna, what happens to a yogī who is (*ayatiḥ*) not putting efforts in yoga, (*śraddhayā upetaḥ*) in spite of his/her positive attitude towards yoga, who (*chalita*) has deviated (*yogāt*) from (the path of) yoga. (*kā gatiṁ gacchati*) What will be the fate of a yogī who has failed (*yoga-sansiddhiṁ*) in attaining mokṣa as the fruit of yoga?

कच्चिन्नोभयविभ्रष्टश्छिन्नाभ्रमिव नश्यति ।
अप्रतिष्ठो महाबाहो विमूढो ब्रह्मणः पथि ॥ ६.३८ ॥
*Kaccinnobhaya-vibhraṣtaś-chinnābhram-iva naśyati,*
*apratiṣtho mahābāho vimūḍho brahmaṇaḥ pathi. (6.38)*

Does he (*na*) not (*naśyati*) downgraded to the lower species (*iva*) like a (*chhinna*) dispersing (*abhraṁ*) cloud, O Krishna (*ubhaya-bhraṣṭa*) having lost both path of yoga and path of karma, (*apratiṣṭhaḥ*) supportless, (vimūḍhaḥ) and getting astray (*pathi*) on the path (*brahmaṇaḥ*) of realisation of the Universal Self or Brahman?

Note: Here nāśa means to be downgraded to the lower species. Āchārya Śaṅkara says: नाशो नाम पूर्वस्माद् हीनजन्मनः प्राप्तिः। Nāśa here means to be downgraded to the lower species as compared to the previous life.

एतन्मे संशयं कृष्ण छेत्तुमर्हस्यशेषतः।
त्वदन्यः संशयस्यास्य छेत्ता न ह्युपपद्यते॥ ६.३९॥
*etanme sañśayaṁ kṛṣṇa chettum arhasyaśeṣataḥ,*
*tvadanyaḥ sañśayasyāsya chettā na hyupapadyate. (6.39)*

O Krishna, only you are able to completely dispel this doubt of mine. Because there is none, other than you, who can dispel this doubt. (See also 15.15)

श्री कृष्ण उवाच
Śri Krishna Said

पार्थ नैवेह नामुत्र विनाशस्तस्य विद्यते।
न हि कल्याणकृत्कश्चिद् दुर्गतिं तात गच्छति॥ ६.४०॥
*pārtha naiveha nāmutra vināśastasya vidyate,*
*nahi kalyāṇakṛtkaścid durgatiṁ tāta gacchati. (6.40)*

Śri Krishna said— O son of Pṛthā, a yogī who has falled from the path of yoga is not downgraded in this life or life hereafter. My dear friend, whoever is engaged in noble acts, is never faces (*durgatiṁ*) downgradation [to lower species].

प्राप्य पुण्यकृतां लोकानुषित्वा शाश्वतीः समाः।
शुचीनां श्रीमतां गेहे योगभ्रष्टोऽभिजायते॥ ६.४१॥
*prāpya puṇyakṛtāṁ lokānuṣitvā śāśvatīḥ samāḥ,*
*śucīnāṁ śrimatāṁ gehe yogabhraṣto'bhijāyate. (6.41)*

A fallen yogī [unsuccessful on the path of yoga] lives for many years in those species that are generally attained by (*puṇyakṛtāṁ*) those who do not observe violence against anybody through mind, speech and acts and do welfare acts. Consequent upon which, he is reborn in the house of the persons (*śuchīnāṁ*) who act according to the Śāstra and (*śrīmatāṁ*) and are endowed with material and spiritual prosperity.

अथवा योगिनामेव कुले भवति धीमताम् ।
एतद्धि दुर्लभतरं लोके जन्म यदीदृशम् ॥ ६.४२ ॥
*athavā yogināmeva kule bhavati dhīmatām,*
*etaddhi durlabhataraṁ loke janma yadidṛśam. (6.42)*

Or such a yogī is born in a family of wise and poor yogīs [who are not materially prosperous]. A birth in the family of yogīs is, indeed, very difficult to attain in this world.

तत्र तं बुद्धिसंयोगं लभते पौर्वदेहिकम् ।
यतते च ततो भूयः संसिद्धौ कुरुनन्दन ॥ ६.४३ ॥
*tatra taṁ buddhisaṁyogaṁ labhate paurvadehikam,*
*yatate ca tato bhūyaḥ saṁsiddhau kurunandana. (6.43)*

When a fallen yogī is reborn in the family of a yogī, O Son of Kurus, he/she is exposed to the sanskāras of yoga attained by him/her in previous births of a fallen yogī. So, he/she puts more efforts [strives more intensely] to attain the fruit of yoga [mokṣa].

पूर्वाभ्यासेन तेनैव ह्रियते ह्यवशोऽपि सः ।
जिज्ञासुरपि योगस्य शब्दब्रह्मातिवर्तते ॥ ६.४४ ॥
*pūrvābhyāsena tenaiva hriyate hyavaśo'pi saḥ,*
*jijñāsurapi yogasya śabdabrahmātivartate. (6.44)*

Furthermore, (*tena eva*) due to the practice of yoga done by him/her (*pūrvābhyāsena*) in the previous life, he/she is (*avaśaḥ*) forcefully (*hriyate*) attracted to yoga due to the dominance of sanskāras of yoga.

Note: If other evil sanskāras are dominant, he/she cannot tread the path of yoga, even if he/she takes birth in the house of a yogī. Even a saṁnyāsī [who has abandoned all kāmya karmas leading to his/her embodiment; who is unsuccessfully following the path of yoga surpasses a learned Vedic scholar so far as the spiritual elevation is concerned.

प्रयत्नाद्यतमानस्तु योगी संशुद्धकिल्बिषः ।
अनेकजन्मसंसिद्धस्ततो याति परां गतिम् ॥ ६.४५ ॥
*prayatnād yatamānas tu yogī sanśuddha-kilbiṣaḥ,*
*aneka-janma-sansiddhas-tato yāti parāṁ gatim. (6.45)*

The learned yogī who diligently strives for yoga, (*sanśuddh-kilbiṣaḥ*) having purged his/her sanskāras of karmas leading to his/her birth and death in many lives, (*sansiddhaḥ*) becomes siddha [successful in yoga] and attains supreme goal (*mokṣa*).

तपस्विभ्योऽधिको योगी ज्ञानिभ्योऽपि मतोऽधिकः ।
कर्मिभ्यश्चाधिको योगी तस्माद्योगी भवार्जुन ॥ ६.४६ ॥
*tapasvibhyo'dhiko yogī jñānibhyo'pi mato'dhikaḥ,*
*karmibhyaścādhiko yogī tasmād yogī bhavārjuna. (6.46)*

A yogī is superior to an ascetic. A yogī is considered superior to a scholar of Veda and Śāstras. A yogī is superior to those who perform Agnihotra, etc. yajñas. Therefore, O Arjuna, you should become a yogī.

योगिनामपि सर्वेषां मद्गतेनान्तरात्मना ।
श्रद्धावान्भजते यो मां स मे युक्ततमो मतः ॥ ६.४७ ॥
*yogināmapi sarveṣāṁ madgatenāntarātmanā,*
*śraddhāvān bhajate yo māṁ sa me yuktatamo mataḥ.*

A yogī who (*bhajate*) meditates (*madgatena*) upon Brahman (*śraddhāvān*) with a positive mind and attitude (*antarātmanā*) from the core of his heart, (*saḥ*) he is (*mataḥ*) considered to be (*yukta-tamaḥ*) very near to (*me*) Brahman (*sarveṣaṁ yogināṁ*) as compared to those whose subject matter of meditation is other than Brahman. (See also 12.02 and 18.66).

ॐ तत्सदिति श्रीमद् भगवद्गीतासूपनिषत्सु ब्रह्मविद्यायां योगशास्त्रे श्रीकृष्णार्जुनसंवादे ध्यानयोगो नाम षष्ठोऽध्याय: ॥

Here ends the sixth chapter, named Dhyāna yoga in the *Bhagvadgitā*, dealing with the Brahmavidyā as propounded in the Upaniṣad and Yogaśāstra in the form of dialogue between Śri Krishna and Arjuna.

# अथ सप्तमोऽध्याय:

## ज्ञानविज्ञानयोग:

# Chapter 7

[Knowledge or Correct Information and its Realisation]

This chapter is known as Jñāna and Vijñāna Yoga. Ādi Śaṅkara defines Jñāna and Vijñāna as follows: *jñānam viṣaya viṣayānubhūtir vijñānam.* That is Jñāna is correct information, and the realisation or experience of information is Vijñāna. Many things in this world are to be known, like Brahman, soul, and matter. The information of Brahman and soul is available easily, but their realisation is difficult. Information of Brahman is Jñāna, but when Brahman is subjected to experience realisation, it becomes Vijñāna. This chapter deals with many aspects of Jñana and Vijñana. Here, terms like Prakṛti, Ātmā, and Brahman have been elucidated by Śri Krishna. Śri Krishna also shares his information and realisation about Ātman and Brahman with Arjuna.

श्री कृष्ण उवाच
Śri Krishna said

मय्यासक्तमना: पार्थ योगं युञ्जन्मदाश्रय: ।
असंशयं समग्रं मां यथा ज्ञास्यसि तच्छृणु ॥ ७.१ ॥
*mayyāsaktamanāḥ pārtha yogaṁ yuñjanmadāśrayaḥ,*
*asaṁśayaṁ samagraṁ māṁ yathā jñāsyasi tacchṛṇu. (7.01)*

Śri Krishna said— O Arjuna, after getting established in Brahman, if one observes samadhi upon Brahman, listen in detail how can he/she do so?

ज्ञानं तेऽहं सविज्ञानमिदं वक्षयाम्यशेषत: ।

यज्ज्ञात्वा नेह भूयोऽन्यज्ज्ञातव्यमवशिष्यते ॥ ७.२ ॥
*jñānaṁ te'haṁsavijñānamidaṁ vakṣyāmyaśeṣataḥ,*
*yajjñātvā neha bhūyo'nyajjñātavyamavaśiṣyate. (7.02)*

I shall fully share information with you along with my experience about it. After knowing that nothing more remains to be known in this world.

मनुष्याणां सहस्रेषु कश्चिद्यतति सिद्धये ।
यततामपि सिद्धानां कश्चिन्मां वेत्ति तत्त्वत: ॥ ७.३ ॥
*manuṣyāṇāṁ sahasreṣu kaścid yatati siddhaye,*
*yatatām api siddhānāṁ kaścinmāṁ vetti tattvataḥ. (7.03)*

Scarcely one out of thousands of seekers strive for yoga-siddhi (self-realisation). Scarcely any one of the striving seekers truly realises self and Brahman.

भूमिरापोऽनलो वायु: खं मनो बुद्धिरेव च ।
अहंकार इतीयं मे भिन्ना प्रकृतिरष्टधा ॥ ७.४ ॥
*bhūmir āpo'nalo vāyuḥ khaṁ mano buddhireva ca,*
*ahaṅkāra itīyaṁ bhinnā prakṛtir aṣṭadhā. (7.04)*

The mind, intellect, ahaṁkāra, bhūtākāśa (space), air, fire, water, and earth are the eightfold transformation of the Prakṛti. (See also 13. 5)

[That which creates diversity, and all that can be seen or known is called Prakṛti. Prakṛiti is also the material cause of creation, according to the Sāṅkhya doctrine. Prakṛti is also referred to as asat, perishable, body, matter, nature, material nature, māyā, mahat, and manifest state].

अपरेयमितस्त्वन्यां प्रकृतिं विद्धि मे पराम् ।
जीवभूतां महाबाहो ययेदं धार्यते जगत् ॥ ७.५ ॥
*apreyamitas tvanyāṁ prakṛtiṁ viddhi me parām,*
*jivabhūtāṁ mahābāho yayedaṁ dhāryate jagat. (7.05)*

This Prakṛti [consisting of the eight parts mentioned

above] is known as aparā; different from this is the parā prakṛti. Both Parā and Aparā prakṛtis [are consisted in Brahman] and are the source of the entire living and non-living world, O mighty armed Arjuna.

Note: Puruṣa is the individuated soul. It is also referred to as sat, imperishable, ātmā, spirit, self, and soul. Prakṛti is the matter. Both are consisted in Brahman.

एतद्योनीनि भूतानि सर्वाणीत्युपधारय।
अहं कृत्स्नस्य जगत: प्रभव: प्रलयस्तथा॥ ७.६॥
*eatadyoninī bhūtāni sarvāṇītyupadhāraya,*
*ahaṁ kṛtsnasya jagataḥ prabhavaḥ pralayas tathā. (7.06)*

You should know that Parā and Aparā prakṛtis consisted in Brahman are the source of the origin of entire material and immaterial world. As such Brahman is the root cause [efficient cause] of the origin and dissolution of living and non-living worlds.

मत्त: परतरं नान्यत्किंचिदस्ति धनंजय।
मयि सर्वमिदं प्रोतं सूत्रे मणिगणा इव॥ ७.७॥
*mattaḥ parataraṁ nānyat kiñcid asti Dhanañjaya,*
*mayi sarvam idaṁ protaṁ sūtre maṇigaṇā iva. (7.07)*

O Conqueror of wealth, there is nothing greater than Brahman. This entire living world is woven around Brahman like jewels around the thread of a necklace.

रसोऽहमप्सु कौन्तेय प्रभास्मि शशिसूर्ययो:।
प्रणव: सर्ववेदेषु शब्द: खे पौरुषं नृषु॥ ७.८॥
*raso'ham apsu kaunteya prabhāsmi śaśisūryayoḥ,*
*praṇavaḥ sarvavedeṣu śabadaḥ khe pauruṣaṁ nṛṣu. (7.08)*

O Son of Kunti, this Brahman is the very essence of existence in the objects. For example, Brahman is present as taste in the waters, as the lustre in the Moon and Sun, as Om in all the Vedas, as the sound in the space, and the manhood in men. If this essential element Brahman is removed from the concerned objects, their existence is at stake.

पुण्यो गन्धः पृथिव्यां च तेजश्चास्मि विभावसौ।
जीवनं सर्वभूतेषु तपश्चास्मि तपस्विषु॥ ७.९॥
*puṇyo gandhaḥ pṛthivyāṁ ca tejaścāsmi vibhāvasau,*
*jivanaṁ sarvabhūteṣu tapaś cāsmi tapasviṣu. (7.09)*

This Brahman is marked by sweet fragrance in the earth, heat in the fire, life in all living beings, and the austerity in the ascetics.

बीजं मां सर्वभूतानां विद्धि पार्थ सनातनम्।
बुद्धिर्बुद्धिमतामस्मि तेजस्तेजस्विनामहम्॥ ७.१०॥
*bījaṁ māṁ sarvabūtānāṁ viddhi pārtha sanātanam,*
*buddhir buddhimatām asmi tejas tejasvinām aham. (7.10)*

O Son of Pṛthā, Brahman should be known as the (*sanātana*) perennial source [efficient cause] of all creatures. This Brahman is the intelligence of the intelligent, and the brilliance of the brilliant. (See also 9.18 and 10.39)

बलं बलवतां चाहं कामरागविवर्जितम्।
धर्माविरुद्धो भूतेषु कामोऽस्मि भरतर्षभ॥ ७.११।
*balaṁ balavatāṁ cāhaṁ kāma-rāga-vivarjitam,*
*dharmāviruddho būteṣu kāmo'smi bharatarṣabha. (7.11)*

The strength of the strong uncorrupted by desire and attachment, exists due to Brahman. Desire in human beings in consonance with Dharma is due to Brahman, O Best of the line of Bharatas.

ये चैव सात्त्विका भावा राजसास्तामसाश्च ये।
मत्त एवेति तान्विद्धि न त्वहं तेषु ते मयि॥ ७.१२॥
*ye caiva sāttvikā bhāvā rājasās tāmasāśca ye,*

*matta eveti tān viddhi na tvahaṁ teṣu te mayi. (7.12)*

All the three states, Sāttvika, Rājasika, and Tāmasika, in the living beings caused by their sanskāras are regulated by Brahman. Brahman is not dependent on the guṇas, but the guṇas are dependant upon Brahman for their manifestation. (See also 9.4 and 9.5).

त्रिभिर्गुणमयैर्भावैरेभिः सर्वमिदं जगत्।
मोहितं नाभिजानाति मामेभ्यः परमव्ययम्॥ ७.१३॥
*tribhir guṇamayair bhāvair ebhiḥ sarvam idaṁ jagat,*
*mohitaṁ nābhijānāti mām ebhyaḥ param avyayam. (7.13)*

The deluded one thinks that the whole world is formed of these three guṇas and do not know the Brahman Who exists transcending these guṇas, and Who is imperishable.

दैवी ह्येषा गुणमयी मम माया दुरत्यया।
मामेव ये प्रपद्यन्ते मायामेतां तरन्ति ते॥ ७.१४॥
*daivi hyeṣā guṇamayī mama māyā duratyayā,*
*māmeva ye prapadyante māyām etāṁ taranti te. (7.14)*

(*māyā*) This network (*guṇmayī)* of three guṇas is made up of (*daivī*) prakṛti (*mama*) consisted in Brahman which (*duratyayā*) difficult to transcend. Only those who are able to realise (*māma*) Brahman, are able to transcend this network of the three guṇas, i.e. attain mokṣa (See also 14.26, 15.19, and 18.66)

न मां दुष्कृतिनो मूढाः प्रपद्यन्ते नराधमाः।
माययापहृतज्ञाना आसुरं भावमाश्रिताः॥ ७.१५॥
*na māṁ duṣkṛtino mūḍhāḥ prapadyante narādhamāḥ,*
*māyayā-pahṛta-jñānā āsuraṁ bhāvam āśritāḥ. (7.15)*

The evildoers, the deluded ones, the wretched persons whose wisdom has been taken over by worldly allurements and who are involved in the material world, cannot realise Brahman.

चतुर्विधा भजन्ते मां जनाः सुकृतिनोऽर्जुन।
आर्तो जिज्ञासुरर्थार्थी ज्ञानी च भरतर्षभ॥ ७.१६॥
*caturvidhā bhajante māṁ janāḥ sukṛtino'rjuna,*
*ārto jijñāsur arthārthī jñāni ca bharatarṣabha. (7.16)*

O Arjuna, (*mām*) Brahman is realised by four types of persons turned to be virtuous. Those who are either distressed, or seekers of Self and Brahman, or seekers of material prosperity, or the enlightened ones who have realised the truth.

तेषां ज्ञानी नित्ययुक्त एकभक्तिर्विशिष्यते।
प्रियो हि ज्ञानिनोऽत्यर्थमहं स च मम प्रियः॥ ७.१७॥
*teṣāṁ jñānī nityayukta ekabhaktir viśiṣyate,*
*priyo hi jñānino'tyartham ahaṁ sa ca mama priyaḥ. (7.17)*

Of the four mentioned above, the enlightened one always remains merged with Brahman, and he does not consider other gods and goddesses worth meditating on, so he is devoted to Brahman alone by all means. He is regarded as the best of the other three since he is close to Brahman.

उदाराः सर्व एवैते ज्ञानी त्वात्मैव मे मतम्।
आस्थितः स हि युक्तात्मा मामेवानुत्तमां गतिम्॥ ७.१८॥
*udārāḥ sarva evaite jñānī tvātmaiva me matam,*
*āsthitaḥ sa hi yuktātmā māma evānuttamāṁ gatim. (7.18)*

The other three virtuous ones [the distressed one, seekers of Brahman and material prosperity] are indeed good, but the enlightened one becomes one with Brahman. Having established in Brahman in samādhi, he attains the supreme goal (*mokṣa*).

बहूनां जन्मनामन्ते ज्ञानवान्मां प्रपद्यते।
वासुदेवः सर्वमिति स महात्मा सुदुर्लभः॥ ७.१९॥

*bahūnāṁ janmanāmante jñānavān māṁ prapadyate,*
*vāsudevaḥ sarvam iti sa mahātmā sudurlabhaḥ. (7.19)*

After many births, the enlightened one, having attained perfection in the sanskāras of self-realisation, realises Brahman (*mokṣa*), as Vāsudeva Brahman is the final destination for all. Such an enlightened one is called Mahātmā [universalized soul] and is rarely traced in the world.

कामैस्तैस्तैर्हृतज्ञाना: प्रपद्यन्तेऽन्यदेवता: ।
तं तं नियममास्थाय प्रकृत्या नियता: स्वया ॥ ७.२० ॥
*kāmais tais tair hṛta-jñānāḥ prapadyante'nyadevatāḥ,*
*taṁ taṁ niyamam āsthāya prakṛtyā niyatāḥ svayā. (7.20)*

They, whose wisdom has been carried away by various (*taiḥ taiḥ kāmaiḥ*) mundane desires like progeny, prosperity, material comforts, etc., (*āsthāya*) impelled by (*svayā*) their own (*prakṛtyā*) sanskāras accumulated in the past lives, (*prapadyante*) meditate upon (*devatāḥ*) deities (*anyāḥ*) other than Brahman.

यो यो यां यां तनुं भक्त: श्रद्धयार्चितुमिच्छति ।
तस्य तस्याचलां श्रद्धां तामेव विदधाम्यहम् ॥ ७.२१ ॥
*yo yo yāṁ yāṁ tanuṁ bhaktaḥ śraddhayā-rcitum icchati,*
*tasya tasyācalāṁ śraddhāṁ tāmeva vidadhāmyaham. (7.21)*

[There are many species in this world. Every species has its own body and temperament]. In this śloka, it is said that whatever species' temperament or mannerism a person wants to follow with a positive bend of mind, the sanskāras of the same species are firmly impressed in his mind.

Note: Those sanskāras lead him to take birth in the same species in the future. [So, it is necessary to follow the temperament and mannerism of the species you want to take birth in the next life].

स तया श्रद्धया युक्तस्तस्याराधनमीहते ।
लभते च ततः कामान्मयैवः विहितान्हितान् ॥ ७.२२ ॥
*sa tayā śraddhayā yuktas tasy-ārādhanam īhate,*
*labhate ca tataḥ kāmān mayaiva vihitān hi tān. (7.22)*

Having accumulated those Sanskāras of a particular species, he wants to act according to them. So, he is rewarded according to his actions as per the rule of Almighty.

Note: Here it is said that the rewards of various actions have been fixed by Brahman.

अन्तवत्तु फलं तेषां तद्भवत्यल्पमेधसाम् ।
देवान्देवयजो यान्ति मद्भक्ता यान्ति मामपि ॥ ७.२३ ॥
*antavattu phalaṁ teṣāṁ tad bhavatyalpamedhasām,*
*devān devayajo yānti madbhaktā yānti māmapi. (7.23)*

The shortsighted people do such acts as are rewarded termporarily for a shortwhile [and far sighted persons do such acts are rewarded for infinite period]. The worshippers of material things cycles back to material world in one form or another and worshippers of Brahman, attains Him.

अव्यक्तं व्यक्तिमापन्नं मन्यन्ते मामबुद्धयः ।
परं भावमजानन्तो ममाव्ययमनुत्तमम् ॥ ७.२४ ॥
*avyaktaṁ vyaktim āpannaṁ manyante māma-buddhayaḥ,*
*paraṁ bhāvam ajānanto mamāvyayam anuttamam. (7.24)*

(*abuddhyaḥ*) The ignorants think unmanifest ātman as manifest one. They do so because they do not know the actual nature of imperishable ātman.

नाहं प्रकाशः सर्वस्य योगमायासमावृतः ।
मूढोऽयं नाभिजानाति लोको मामजमव्ययम् ॥ ७.२५ ॥
*nāhaṁ prakāśaḥ sarvasya yoga-māyā-samāvṛtaḥ,*

*mūḍho'yaṁ nābhijānāti loko mām ajam avyayam. (7.25)*

Veiled by (*māyā*) the material body made of yoga [mixure of three guṇas], ātman is not visible to all persons. The people deluded by worldy allurements are not able to know the real eternal and imperishable nature of ātman.

Note: The ignorant people do not know that this ātman neither dies nor takes birth.

वेदाहं समतीतानि वर्तमानानि चार्जुन।
भविष्याणि च भूतानि मां तु वेद न कश्चन॥ ७.२६॥
*vedāhaṁ samatītāni vartamānāni cārjuna,*
*bhaviṣyāṇī ca bhūtāni māṁ tu veda na kaścana. (7.26)*

Brahman knows, O Arjuna, all beings that have born in the past, that exist in the present, and that will be born in the future. But nobody really knows about Brahman, except those who have realised Him.

इच्छाद्वेषसमुत्थेन द्वन्द्वमोहेन भारत।
सर्वभूतानि संमोहं सर्गे यान्ति परंतप॥ ७.२७॥
*icchā-dveṣa-samutthena dvandva-mohena bhārata,*
*Sarva-bhūtāni sammohaṁ sarge yānti parantapa. (7.27)*

(*sarva-bhūtānī*) All beings are (*saṁmohaṁ*) wrapped in utter delusion (*dvandva-mohena*) of pleasure and pain (*sarge*) after taking birth (*samutthena*) due to the (*icchā*) likes and (*dveṣa*) dislikes, (*Bhārata*) O son of Bharatas. So long as they remain deluded, they continue to worship material things.

येषां त्वन्तगतं पापं जनानां पुण्यकर्मणाम्।
ते द्वन्द्वमोहनिर्मुक्ता भजन्ते मां दृढव्रताः॥ ७.२८॥
*yeśāṁ tvantagataṁ pāpaṁ janānāṁ puṇya-karmaṇām,*
*te dvandva-moha-nirmuktā bhajante māṁ dṛḍhavratāḥ. (7.28)*

(*puṇya-karmaṇāṁ janānām*) The virtuous persons,

whose (*pāpaṁ*) negative sanskāras (*antagataṁ*) have come to an end, (*vinirmuktaḥ*) become free from the (*moha*) delusion of (*dvandva*) pleasure and pain and (*māṁ bhajante*) attain self-realisation (*dṛḍhavratā*) due to their firm resolve.

जरामरणमोक्षाय मामाश्रित्य यतन्ति ये।
ते ब्रह्म तद्विदुः कृत्स्नमध्यात्मं कर्म चाखिलम्॥ ७.२९॥
*jarā-maraṇa-mokṣāya mām āśritya yatanti ye,*
*te brahma tad viduḥ kṛtsnam adhyātmaṁ karma cākhilam. (7.29)*

Those who strive for emancipation and freedom from old age and death following the path of self-realisation, they will be able to realise Brahman, the true nature of ātman, karma-system and His creative power.

साधिभूताधिदैवं मां साधियज्ञं च ये विदुः।
प्रयाणकालेऽपि च मां ते विदुर्युक्तचेतसः॥ ७.३०॥
*sādhibhūtādhidaivaṁ māṁ sādhiyajñaṁ ca ye viduḥ,*
*prayāṇakāle'pi ca māṁ te vidur yukta cetasaḥ. (7.30)*

The person, who knows Brahman alongwith Adhibhūta [perishable physical world], the Adhidaiva [the cosmic world]; also the Adhiyajña [process of creation, life and death of living beings], they do realise Brahman or merge with Brahman after leaving their material bodies.

ॐ तत्सदिति श्रीमद् भगवद्गीतासूपनिषत्सु ब्रह्मविद्यायां योगशास्त्रे श्रीकृष्णार्जुनसंवादे ज्ञानविज्ञानयोगो नाम सप्तमोऽध्याय:॥ ७॥

Here ends the seventh chapter named Jñāna-vijñāna yoga in the *Bhagvadgitā* dealing with the Brahmavidyā as propounded in the Upaniṣad and Yogaśāstra in the form of dialogue between Śri Krishna and Arjuna.

# अथ अष्टमोऽध्यायः

## अक्षरब्रह्मयोगः

# Chapter 8

[Merging with Imperishable Brahman]

In this chapter, Śri Krishna defines terms like adhyātama, adhidaivata, adhibhūta and adhiyajña, etc., at the request of Arjuna. He tells Arjuna the importance of sanskāras and karmas for attaining the next life. He tells the importance of Brahman and Om in attaining mokṣa. This chapter is significant for understanding the meaning of technical terms used in Indian philosophy because most of the terms are used by us without knowing their intended meaning.

अर्जुन उवाच

Arjuna said

किं तद् ब्रह्म किमध्यात्मं किं कर्म पुरुषोत्तम।
अधिभूतं च किं प्रोक्तमधिदैवं किमुच्यते॥ ८.१॥
*kiṁ tad brahma kimadhyātmaṁ kiṁ puruṣottama,*
*adhibhūtaṁ ca kiṁ proktam adhidaivaṁ kimucyate. (8.01)*

Arjuna said— O Krishna, what is Brahman? What is Adhyātma? What is Karma? What is called Adhibhūta? Moreover, what is known as Adhidaivata?

अधियज्ञः कथं कोऽत्र देहेऽस्मिन्मधुसूदन।
प्रयाणकाले च कथं ज्ञेयोऽसि नियतात्मभिः॥ ८.२॥
*adhiyajñaḥ kathaṁ ko'tra dehe'smin madhusūdana,*
*prayāṇakāle ca kathaṁ jñeyo'si niyatātmabhiḥ. (8.02)*

O Slayer of enemies, how would you define Adhiyajña, and who dwells in the body? How can He be realised at the time of death by (*niyatātmabhiḥ*) yogīs?

श्री कृष्ण उवाच

Śri Krishna said

अक्षरं ब्रह्म परमं स्वभावोऽध्यात्ममुच्यते।
भूतभावोद्भवकरो विसर्गः कर्मसंज्ञितः॥ ८.३॥
*akṣaraṁ brahma paramaṁ svabhāvo'dhyātmamucyate,*
*Bhūtabhāv-odbhavakaro visargaḥ karmasañjñitaḥ. (8.03)*

Śri Krishna said— Brahman is supreme and imperishable. One's own soul is called Adhyātma. Act of creation that causes the origin of all beings is called Karma.

अधिभूतं क्षरो भावः पुरुषश्चाधिदैवतम्।
अधियज्ञोऽहमेवात्र देहे देहभृतां वर॥ ८.४॥
*adhibhūtaṁ kṣaro bhāvaḥ puruṣaścādhidaivatam,*
*adhiyajño'hamevātra dehe dehabhṛtāṁ vara. (8.04)*

Adhibhūta has the nature of perishability. As such animate beings and inanimate objects are called Adhibhūta, and the Puruṣa [Brahmāṇḍa Puruṣa/universe] is called Adhidaivata. The Brahman who has pervaded the bodies of jīvas is called Adhiyajña.

अन्तकाले च मामेव स्मरन्मुक्त्वा कलेवरम्।
यः प्रयाति स मद्भावं याति नास्त्यत्र संशयः॥ ८.५॥
*antakāle ca māmeva smaran muktvā kalevaram,*
*yaḥ prayāti sa madbhāvaṁ yāti nāstyatra sañśayaḥ. (8.05)*

The next life of an Individual is determined by the sanskāras or bhāva he/she enjoys at the time of death. If an individual has the sanskāra of self-realisation or Brahma-realisation, he/she will certainly attain Brahman after death, there is no doubt about it.

यं यं वाऽपि स्मरन्भावं त्यजत्यन्ते कलेवरम्।
तं तमेवैति कौन्तेय सदा तद्भावभावितः॥ ८.६॥
*yaṁ yaṁ vāpi smaran bhāvaṁ tyajatyante kalevaram,*

*taṁ tamevaiti Kaunteya sadā tadbhāvabhāvitaḥ. (8.06)*

Whatever bhāva or sanskāra is dominant [due to abhyāśa of meditation] at the time of leaving the body, (*eti*) one attains the body of (*tadbhāva-bhāvitaḥ*) the same sanskāras in the next life, [Kaunteya] O Arjuna. For example, if the tāmasika Sanskāras are dominant, an individual attains the body dominant with tāmasika sanskāras.

तस्मात्सर्वेषु कालेषु मामनुस्मर युध्य च।
मय्यर्पितमनोबुद्धिर्मामेवैष्यस्यसंशयः ॥ ८.७ ॥
*tasmātsarveṣu kāleṣu mām anusmara yudhya ca,*
*mayyarpita mano-buddhir mām eva iṣyasy-asañśayam.(8.07)*

Therefore, always meditate upon Brahman and do your duty. If you are able to surrender your mind to Brahman, you shall certainly attain Him, there is no doubt about it.

अभ्यासयोगयुक्तेन चेतसा नान्यगामिना।
परमं पुरुषं दिव्यं याति पार्थानुचिन्तयन् ॥ ८.८ ॥
*abhyāsa-yoga-yuktena cetasā nānya-gāminā,*
*paramaṁ puruṣaṁ divyaṁ yāti pārthānucintayan. (8.08)*

An individual who has disciplined his mind through the practice of Yoga does not attend any other issue save Brahman, attains the Supreme power, O Son of Pṛthā.

कविं पुराणमनुशासितारमणोरणीयांसमनुस्मरेद्यः।
सर्वस्य धातारमचिन्त्यरूपं आदित्यवर्णं तमसः परस्तात् ॥ ८.९ ॥
*kaviṁ purāṇam anuśāsitāram,*
*aṇor aṇiyānsam anusmared yaḥ.*
*sarvasya dhātāram acintya-rūpam,*
*āditya-varṇaṁ tamasaḥ parastāt. (8.09)*

(*yaḥ*) The one who (*anusmaret*) meditates on Brahman, (*kaviṁ*) the omniscient, (*purāṇaṁ*) the oldest, (*anuśāsitāraṁ*) the controller, (*aṇoraṇiyānsaṁ*) smaller than the smallest [and bigger than the biggest], (*dhātā*) the sustainer of (*sarvasya*) everything, (*achintyaṁ*) the inconceivable, (*āditya-varṇaṁ*) the self-luminous like the sun, (*tamasaḥ parastāt*) and beyond darkness of moha (delusion);

प्रयाणकाले मनसाऽचलेन भक्त्या युक्तो योगबलेन चैव।
भ्रुवोर्मध्ये प्राणमावेश्य सम्यक् स तं परं पुरुषमुपैति दिव्यम्॥ ८.१०॥
*prayāṇa-kāle manasācalena,*
*bhaktyā yukto yoga-balena caiva.*
*bhruvor madhye prāṇam āveśya samyak,*
*sa taṁ paraṁ puruṣam upaiti divyam. (8.10)*

And at the time of death with steadfast mind, devotion and power of yoga; making the flow of prāṇic impulse rise up [to the middle of the two eye brows] and holding there; he/she attains the Supreme spirit. (See also 4.29, 5.27, and 6.13).

यदक्षरं वेदविदो वदन्ति विशन्ति यद्यतयो वीतरागाः।
यदिच्छन्तो ब्रह्मचर्यं चरन्ति तत्ते पदं संग्रहेण प्रवक्ष्ये॥ ८.११॥
*yadakṣaraṁ vedavido vadanti,*
*viśanti yadyatayo vītarāgāḥ.*
*yadicchanto brahmacaryaṁ caranti,*
*tatte padaṁ saṅgraheṇa pravakṣye. (8.11)*

I shall briefly explain to you the word, known by the Vedic scholars and actualized by the ascetics freed from attachment and desire, to know which seeker leads a life of Brahmacharya under the guidance of a Guru.

सर्वद्वाराणि संयम्य मनो हृदि निरुध्य च।
मूर्ध्न्याधायात्मनः प्राणमास्थितो योगधारणाम्॥ ८.१२॥
*sarvadvārāṇi sañyamya mano hṛdi nirudhya ca,*
*mūrdhnyādhāyātmanaḥ prāṇam-āsthito yogadhāraṇām.*

Controlling all the gates of sense organs in the body,

focusing the mind on the heart and shifting the focus of the mind from the heart to the brain through the arteries connecting the heart with the brain, and thus establishing the prāṇa in the cerebrum, a seeker attains Supreme path engaging in yogic practice;

ओमित्येकाक्षरं ब्रह्म व्याहरन्मामनुस्मरन्।
यः प्रयाति त्यजन्देहं स याति परमां गतिम्॥ ८.१३॥
*Om ityekākṣaraṁ brahma vyāharan mām anusmaran,*
*yaḥ prayāti tyajan dehaṁ sa yāti paramāṁ gatim. (8.13)*

Keeping in mind almighty Brahman, one who leaves the body while uttering Om attains the supreme goal called mokṣa.

अनन्यचेताः सततं यो मां स्मरति नित्यशः।
तस्याहं सुलभः पार्थ नित्ययुक्तस्य योगिनः॥ ८.१४॥
*ananya cetāḥ satataṁ yo māṁ smarati nityaśaḥ,*
*tasyāhaṁ sulabhaḥ Pārtha nitya-yuktasya yoginaḥ (8.14)*

The steadfast yogī, who constantly meditates upon Brahman without deflecting his mind on other objects, easily approaches Brahman, O son of Pṛthā.

मामुपेत्य पुनर्जन्म दुःखालयमशाश्वतम्।
नाप्नुवन्ति महात्मानः संसिद्धिं परमां गताः॥ ८.१५॥
*mām upetya punarjanma duḥkhālayam aśāśvatam,*
*nāpnuvanti mahātmānaḥ sansidhiṁ paramāṁ gatāḥ. (8.15)*

Attaining Brahman, the great souls do not incur rebirth, the impermanent home of misery, because they have attained the highest perfection (*mokṣa*).

आब्रह्मभुवनाल्लोकाः पुनरावर्तिनोऽर्जुन।
मामुपेत्य तु कौन्तेय पुनर्जन्म न विद्यते॥ ८.१६॥
*ābrahma bhuvanāllokāḥ punarāvartino'rjuna,*
*mām upetya tu Kaunteya punarjanma na vidyate. (8.16)*

All worlds (*lokas*), starting from the Brahma-loka, are

meant for returning. One who realises Brahman, O Arjuna, does not retake birth till the end of present creation cycle. (See also 9.25)

सहस्रयुगपर्यन्तमहर्यद् ब्रह्मणो विदुः ।
रात्रिं युगसहस्रान्तां तेऽहोरात्रविदो जनाः ॥ ८.१७ ॥
*sahasra-yuga-paryantam ahar yad brahmaṇo viduḥ,*
*rātriṁ yuga sahasrāntāṁ te'horātravido janāḥ. (8.17)*

The yogis, who know the measurement of time, know that the day of Brahmā [period of Kalpa] lasts for one thousand Yugas [4.32 billion years] and that his night also lasts for one thousand Yugas [4.32 billion years]. As such, different lokas have a time limit, so the residents of all lokas have to cycle back into this world. Only emancipated people do not come back to life till the end of one creation cycle.

अव्यक्ताद् व्यक्तयः सर्वाः प्रभवन्त्यहरागमे ।
रात्र्यागमे प्रलीयन्ते तत्रैवाव्यक्तसंज्ञके ॥ ८.१८ ॥
*avyaktād vyaktayaḥ sarvāḥ prabhavanty ahar āgame,*
*rātryāgame pralīyante tatraivāvyaktasañjñake. (8.18)*

All living and non-living manifestations take place at the time of Brahmā's day, and they again cease to occur at Brahmā's night.

भूतग्रामः स एवायं भूत्वा भूत्वा प्रलीयते ।
रात्र्यागमेऽवशः पार्थ प्रभवत्यहरागमे ॥ ८.१९ ॥
*bhūtagrāmaḥ sa evāyaṁ bhūtvā pralīyate,*
*ratryāgame'vaśḥ pārtha prabhavatyaharāgame. (8.19)*

The multitude of five bhūtas [evolutes of prakṛti] come into existence again and again and is dissolved. At the approach of Brahmā's night, it dies down and at the arrival of the day it rises.

परस्तस्मात्तु भावोऽन्योऽव्यक्तोऽव्यक्तात्सनातनः ।

यः स सर्वेषु भूतेषु नश्यत्सु न विनश्यति ॥ ८.२० ॥
*paras tasmāt tu bhāvo'nyo'vyakto'vyaktāt sanātanaḥ,*
*yaḥ sa sarveṣu bhūteṣu naśyatsu na vinaśyati. (8.20)*

There is another eternal unmanifest state [Brahman] higher than the already stated unmanifest Prakṛti that does not perish at the time of decreation when all beings perish.

अव्यक्तोऽक्षर इत्युक्तस्तमाहुः परमां गतिम्।
यं प्राप्य न निवर्तन्ते तद्धाम परमं मम ॥ ८.२१ ॥
*avyakto'kṣara ityuktas tam āhuḥ paramāṁ gatim.*
*yaṁ prāpya na nivartante taddhāma paramaṁ mama.(8.21)*

This unmanifest state is called the imperishable or Brahman. This is said to be the ultimate destination. Those who reach the abode of Supreme Brahman do not return (or take rebirth) till the end of current creation cycle.

पुरुषः स परः पार्थ भक्त्या लभ्यस्त्वनन्यया।
यस्यान्तःस्थानि भूतानि येन सर्वमिदं ततम् ॥ ८.२२ ॥
*puruṣaḥ sa paraḥ Pārtha bhaktyā labhyastvananyayā,*
*yasyāntaḥsthāni bhūtāni yena sarvam idaṁ tatam. (8.22)*

This Supreme Brahman, within whom all five-bhūtas [evolutes of prakṛti] and beings exist [because the effect always locates in its cause], and who pervades the entire universe, is attainable by unswerving devotion, O son of Pṛthā. (See also 9.4 and 11.55)

यत्र काले त्वनावृत्तिमावृत्तिं चैव योगिनः।
प्रयाता यान्ति तं कालं वक्ष्यामि भरतर्षभ ॥ ८.२३ ॥
*yatra kāletvanāvṛttim āvṛttiṁ caiva yoginaḥ,*
*prayātā yānti taṁ kālaṁ vakṣyāmi Bharatarṣabha. (8.23)*

O Best of Bharatas, now I shall describe you different departing times which determine whether a particular yogī has attained mokṣa or not.

अग्निर्ज्योतिरहः शुक्लः षण्मासा उत्तरायणम् ।
तत्र प्रयाता गच्छन्ति ब्रह्म ब्रह्मविदो जनाः ॥ ८.२४ ॥
*agnir jyotir ahaḥ śuklaḥ ṣaṇmāsā uttarāyaṇam,*
*tatra prayātā gacchanti Brahma brahmavido janāḥ. (8.24)*

If a yogī departs during the period of enlightenment (Brahma-realisation) represented or characterised by agni (fire), jyoti (light), day time, brightness and uttarāyaṇa, he/she attains mokṣa.

धूमो रात्रिस्तथा कृष्णः षण्मासा दक्षिणायनम् ।
तत्र चान्द्रमसं ज्योतिर्योगी प्राप्य निवर्तते ॥ ८.२५ ॥
*dhūmo rātristathā kṛṣṇa ṣaṇmāsā dakṣiṇāyanam,*
*Tatra cāndramasaṁ jyotiryogī prāpya nivartate. (8.25)*

If a yogī departs during any day when he/she is unable to attain enlightenment (Brahma-realisation) represented / characterized by dhūma (smoke), night, dark-half, and dakṣiṇāyaṇa, he/she does not attain mokṣa but takes rebirth.

NB: It may be noted here that the above method to find out whether a yogī has attained mokṣa or not applies only to yogīs and not to any laymen in the society since there is no chance for a layman achieving mokṣa.

शुक्लकृष्णे गती ह्येते जगतः शाश्वते मते ।
एकया यात्यनावृत्तिमन्ययावर्तते पुनः ॥ ८.२६ ॥
*śuklakṛṣṇe gatī hyete jagataḥ śāśvate mate,*
*Ekayāyātyanāvṛttim anyayāvartate punaḥ. (8.26)*

The brightness [realisation of Brahman] and darkness [absence Brahma-realisation] are the two eternal phases of life. The former leads to mokṣa and the latter leads to rebirth.

नैते सृती पार्थ जानन्योगी मुह्यति कश्चन।
तस्मात्सर्वेषु कालेषु योगयुक्तो भवार्जुन॥ ८.२७॥
*naite sṛti Pārtha jānanyogī muhyati kaścana,*
*tasmāt sarveṣu kāleṣu yoga-yukto bhavārjuna. (8.27)*

(*jānan*) Knowing (*ete*) these (*sṛtī*) two phases of creation, O son of Pṛthā, a yogī is not (*muhyati*) deluded (*kaśchan*) at all. Therefore, O Arjuna, (*yogayuktaḥ*) conduct samādhi yoga (*sarveṣu kāḷeṣu*) all times.

वेदेषु यज्ञेषु तपःसु चैव
दानेषु यत्पुण्यफलं प्रदिष्टम्।
अत्येति तत्सर्वमिदं विदित्वा
योगी परं स्थानमुपैति चाद्यम्॥ ८.२८॥
*vedeṣu yajñeṣu tapaḥsu caiva,*
*dāneṣu yat puṇya-phalaṁ pradiṣṭam.*
*atyeti tat-sarvam idaṁ viditvā,*
*yogī paraṁ sthānam upaiti cādyam. (8.28)*

The yogī attains all that has been described in the Vedas through his yogic powers, all that is attainable through the performance of yajñas, austerities, and charities. He attains the foremost Supreme Brahman.

ॐ तत्सदिति श्रीमद् भगवद्गीतासूपनिषत्सु ब्रह्मविद्यायां योगशास्त्रे श्रीकृष्णार्जुनसंवादे अक्षरब्रह्मयोगो नाम अष्टमोऽध्यायः॥ ८ ॥

Here ends the eighth chapter, named Akṣara Brahma yoga in the *Bhagvadgitā*, dealing with the Brahmavidyā as propounded in the Upaniṣad and Yogaśāstra in the form of dialogue between Śri Krishna and Arjuna.

# अथ नवमोऽध्याय:

## राजविद्याराजगुह्ययोग:

# Chapter 9

[Supreme Knowledge and the Supreme Mystery]

In this chapter, Śri Krishna tells confused Arjuna about the supreme knowledge of Brahman with the method of Brahma-realisation. The words used here are jñāna and vijñāna. In the Vedic terminology, jñāna signifies correct knowledge/information of a subject, and vijñāna signifies the realisation of the subject information. For example, the information of Brahman is jñāna, and the realisation of Brahman through samādhi becomes vijñāna. That is why the *Chhāndogya Upanishad* says: 'vijñānam ānandam Brahma'. That is, when the Brahman is realised, a yogī experiences ecstatic bliss. According to Śri Krishna, Brahman can be realised through the path of samādhi. He also defines ahaṁkāra as the root behind the worldly creation. The distinct identities of various living beings and non-living things are due to ahaṅkāra. According to the Sāṅkhya system of philosophy, ahaṅkāra is created from Prakṛti [inactive energy] in the course of creation immediately after mahat [intelligence]. Ahaṅkāra [the notion of individuation] gives a sense of individuality to all living beings, whereas sanskāras acts as the seed of the creation of living beings. Due to ahaṅkāra, everybody identifies himself/herself as a distinct identity from others and feels that he/she is doing this and that. The feeling of I, my, me is the contribution of ahaṅkāra among living beings. Ahaṅkāra is the main factor that does not let you achieve emancipation. Once the sanskāra of ahaṅkāra is eliminated, a person becomes very humble and down to the earth, and this type of person is eligible to achieve emancipation.

श्री कृष्ण उवाच

Śri Krishna said

इदं तु ते गुह्यतमं प्रवक्ष्याम्यनसूयवे।
ज्ञानं विज्ञानसहितं यज्ज्ञात्वा मोक्ष्यसेऽशुभात्॥ ९.१॥
*idaṁ tu te guhya-tamaṁ pravakṣyāmyanasūyave,*
*jñānaṁ vijñāna-sahitaṁ yajjñātvā mokṣyase'śubhāt. (9.1)*

Śri Krishna said— I shall reveal to you, who is devoid of fault-finding and backbiting tendency, the most profound knowledge of Brahman and its realisation technique. Having realised the same, you will be (*mokṣyase*) freed (*aśubhāt*) from the world's bondage.

राजविद्या राजगुह्यं पवित्रमिदमुत्तमम्।
प्रत्यक्षावगमं धर्म्यं सुसुखं कर्तुमव्ययम्॥ ९.२॥
*rājavidyā rājaguhyaṁ pavitram idam uttamam,*
*pratyakṣāvagamaṁ dharmyaṁ susukhaṁ kartumavyayam.*

This Brahma-vidyā or Brahma-jñāna (Brahma-realisation) is the king of all knowledge (supreme knowledge); it is the king of all secrets (supreme secret); it is the purifier of all good or bad kārmic sanskāras accumulated in previous lives, and of highest nature. It can be realised directly like happiness and sorrow. It conforms to dharma, which is very easy to practice, and its fruit is imperishable.

Note: Fruit of other karmas is perishable or going to end, but the fruit of Brahma-realisation is imperishable.

अश्रद्दधानाः पुरुषा धर्मस्यास्य परंतप।
अप्राप्य मां निवर्तन्ते मृत्युसंसारवर्त्मनि॥ ९.३॥

*aśraddadhānāḥ puruṣā dharmasyāsya parantapa,*
*aprāpya māṁ nivartante mṛtyu-sansāra-vartmani. (9.3)*

O destroyer of enemies, those who are not positive about this knowledge cannot attain its (dharma) fruit of Brahma-realisation, rather undergo the cycle of birth and death, which is the characteristics of the mundane world.

मया ततमिदं सर्वं जगदव्यक्तमूर्तिना।
मत्स्थानि सर्वभूतानि न चाहं तेष्ववस्थितः ॥ ९.४ ॥
*mayā tatamidaṁ sarvaṁ jagada-vyakta-mūrtinā,*
*matsthāni sarvabhūtāni na cāhaṁ teṣvavasthitaḥ. (9.4)*

All bhūtas (evolutes of prakṛti) are pervaded by Brahman, Who is of un-manifest nature. All bhūtas are located in Brahman, but Brahman is located in them [He pervades them].

According to the Sāṅkhya system of philosophy, the creation is the manifestation of Prakṛti (inactive energy) agitated by the will of Brahman. In the process of creation, Prakṛti disintegrates into Mahat (intelligence). Mahat gives rise to ahaṅkāra (individual identity), followed by the creation of subtle tanmātras and gross bhūtas.

न च मत्स्थानि भूतानि पश्य मे योगमैश्वरम्।
भूतभृन्न च भूतस्थो ममात्मा भूतभावनः ॥ ९.५ ॥
*na ca matsthāni bhūtāni paśya me yogam-aiśvaram,*
*bhūta-bhṛnna ca bhūtastho mamātmā bhūta-bhāvanaḥ.*

Look at the miracle of Brahman or understand the reality of Brahman. Brahman is not the material cause of five bhūtas [five evolutes of Prakṛti]; instead, Prakṛti is their material cause. Similarly, Brahman sustains all bhūtas, but not sustained by them. (*mamātmā*) It is a pure spiritual element (*bhūtabhāvanaḥ*) that creates and sustains all the material world.

यथाकाशस्थितो नित्यं वायुः सर्वत्रगो महान्।
तथा सर्वाणि भूतानि मत्स्थानीत्युपधारय॥ ९.६॥
*yathākāśa-sthito nityaṁ vāyuḥ sarvatra-go mahān,*
*tathā sarvāṇi bhūtāni matsthāni ityupadhāraya. (9.6)*

Just as the mighty wind is located in the space and moves all around without being attached to it. Similarly, all living beings and non-living things are located in Brahman [space of Brahman] without being attached to it.

सर्वभूतानि कौन्तेय प्रकृतिं यान्ति मामिकाम्।
कल्पक्षये पुनस्तानि कल्पादौ विसृजाम्यहम्॥ ९.७॥
*sarvabhūtāni Kaunteya prakṛtiṁ yānti māmikām,*
*kalpa-kṣaye punastāni kalpādau visṛjāmyaham. (9.7)*

All living beings merge into Brahman and non-living things [active energy] convert into prakṛti [inactive energy] contained in the space of Brahman at the end of a Kalpa-cycle [a kalpa is equal to 4.32 billion years and kalpa-cycle ends in 311 trillion years], O son of Kuntī. They are released again by Brahman at the beginning of the next Kalpa-cycle.

प्रकृतिं स्वामवष्टभ्य विसृजामि पुनः पुनः।
भूतग्राममिमं कृत्स्नमवशं प्रकृतेर्वशात्॥ ९.८॥
*prakṛtiṁ svām avaṣṭabhya visṛjāmi punaḥ punaḥ,*
*Bhūta-grāmam-imaṁ kṛtsnam avaśaṁ prakṛtervaśāt. (9.8)*

(*avaṣṭabhya*) Controlling (*svāṁ*) His basic (*prakṛtiṁ*) nature, Brahman (*vsṛjāmi*) creates (*bhūtagrāmaṁ*) entire multitude of bhūtas (*punaḥ punaḥ*) time and again, these bhūtas are (*avaśaṁ*) helpless in the matter of birth and death, being under the control of their respective prakṛtis and sanskāras /karmas.

न च मां तानि कर्माणि निबध्नन्ति धनंजय।
उदासीनवदासीनमसक्तं तेषु कर्मसु॥ ९.९॥
*na ca māṁ tāni karmāṇi nibadhnanti dhanañjaya,*
*udāsīna-vad-āsinam-asaktaṁ teṣu karmasu. (9.9)*

These karmas (acts) of creation do not affect Brahman O Dhanañjaya, as He remains indifferent and unattached to these acts.

Here it is said that karma of creation impresses no sanskāra of life and death on Brahman like the karmas of living beings are impressed upon thier minds in the form of sanskāras of life and death.

मयाध्यक्षेण प्रकृतिः सूयते सचराचरम्।
हेतुनानेन कौन्तेय जगद्विपरिवर्तते॥ ९.१०॥
*mayādhyakṣeṇa prakṛti sūyate sacarācaram,*
*hetunānena kaunteya jagad viparivartate. (9.10)*

Presided over [governed] by Brahman, the whole world of animate and inanimate objects is created from prakṛti which is of the nature of avidyā [matter] and due to this reason, the world undergoes different changes, O son of Pṛthā. (See also 14.03).

Nature of prakṛti is called avidyā, as it is devoid of the power of knowing and understanding.

अवजानन्ति मां मूढा मानुषीं तनुमाश्रितम्।
परं भावमजानन्तो मम भूतमहेश्वरम्॥ ९.११॥
*avajānanti māṁ mūḍhā mānuṣiṁ tanumāśritam,*
*paraṁ bhāvamajānanto mama bhūta-maheśvaram. (9.11)*

The deluded ones, insult Brahman by considering him taking birth in the form of human-body. They do not understand the supreme nature [spiritual nature] of Brahman, who is the supreme Governor of entire creation.

मोघाशा मोघकर्माणो मोघज्ञाना विचेतसः ।
राक्षसीमासुरीं चैव प्रकृतिं मोहिनीं श्रिताः ॥ ९.१२ ॥
*moghāśā mogha-karmāṇo mogha-jñānā vicetasaḥ,*
*rākṣasim-āsuriṁ caiva prakṛtiṁ mohinīm śritāḥ. (9.12)*

A person who insults Brahman by considering him taking birth in the form of a human being becomes hopeless, gains no fruit of the karmas like Agnihotra performed by him; his knowledge becomes useless or bears no fruit; he is devoid of discriminating and rational power of intellect. He is led by Rākṣasī [grabbing others' property by terror and corrupt means] and Āsurī [materialistic] tendencies and takes his (*prakṛtiṁ mohinīṁ*) body for the soul.

महात्मानस्तु मां पार्थ दैवीं प्रकृतिमाश्रिताः ।
भजन्त्यनन्यमनसो ज्ञात्वा भूतादिमव्ययम् ॥ ९.१३ ॥
*mahātmānas tu māṁ pārtha daivīṁ prakṛtim āśritāḥ,*
*bhajantyananya-manaso jñātvā bhūtādim avyayam. (9.13)*

But great souls, O Arjuna, take Brahman as daivī-prakṛti [pure spiritual element] (See 16.01-03). They worship Brahman as the (*bhūtādi*) primary or efficient cause of creation with a (*ananya-manasaḥ*) concentrated mind.

सततं कीर्तयन्तो मां यतन्तश्च दृढव्रताः ।
नमस्यन्तश्च मां भक्त्या नित्ययुक्ता उपासते ॥ ९.१४ ॥
*satataṁ kīrtayanto māṁ yatantaśca dṛḍha vratāḥ,*
*namasyantaśca māṁ bhaktyā nitya-yuktā upāsate. (9.14)*

Persons of firm resolve continuously eulogize Brahman. They bow to Him with devotion and meditate on Him with steadfast mind.

ज्ञानयज्ञेन चाप्यन्ये यजन्तो मामुपासते ।
एकत्वेन पृथक्त्वेन बहुधा विश्वतोमुखम् ॥ ९.१५ ॥

*jñānayajñena cāpyanye yajanto mām upāsate,*
*ekatvena pṛthaktvena bahudhā viśvatomukham. (9.15)*

Others who are doing jñāna yajña [studies of Vedas and Śāstras) also worship Him as one Brahman, and still others worship him by various names as Agni, Vāyu, Āditya, Viṣṇu, etc.

अहं क्रतुरहं यज्ञः स्वधाहमहमौषधम्।
मन्त्रोऽहमहमेवाज्यमहमग्निरहं हुतम्॥ ९.१६॥
*ahaṁ kratur ahaṁ yajñaḥ svadhāhamahamauṣadham,*
*mantro'ham ahamevājyam ahamagnir-ahaṁ hutam. (9.16)*

Insofar as the rituals of the (*kratu*) -Śrauta Yajñas [described in Vedic texts expounding various aspects of creation] (*yajña*) and Smārta Yajñas [described in Smṛti-texts expounding social, political, economic, ethical codes and sanskāras for the transformation of human beings], (*svadhā*) giving food to living beings, (*auṣdham*) administering medicine to the ill, (*mantra*) chanting of mantras, (*ājyāṁ*) oblation of ghee in Agnihotra, (*agniḥ*) kindling the fire of yajña, and (*hutaṁ*) the act of Agnihotra are concerned, (*aham*) Brahman is always addressed there as the subject of worship. (See also 4.24)

पिताहमस्य जगतो माता धाता पितामहः।
वेद्यं पवित्रमोंकार ऋक्साम यजुरेव च॥ ९.१७॥
*pitāham asya jagato mātā dhātā pitāmahaḥ,*
*vedyaṁ pavitram oṅkāra ṛk-sāma-yajureva ca. (9.17)*

Brahman is the protector of this world like a father, creator like a mother (*dhātā*), giver of the fruits of karmas to all living beings, and sustains this creation like the grandsire. In this world, only Brahman is worth knowing; He is holy and called as Om; His knowledge exits in the form of the Ṛg, the Yajuḥ, and the Sāmaveda.

Here Śri Krishna wants to advise Arjuna not to waste his energy in matters other than Brahman and the Vedas. Only Brahman and Vedas, the knowledge of His creation, are worth knowing.

गतिर्भर्ता प्रभुः साक्षी निवासः शरणं सुहृत्।
प्रभवः प्रलयः स्थानं निधानं बीजमव्ययम्॥ ९.१८॥
*gatir bhartā prabhuḥ sākṣī nivāsaḥ śaraṇaṁ suhṛt,*
*prabhavaḥ pralayaḥ sthānaṁ nidhānaṁ bijamavyayam.*

Brahman is the (*gatiḥ*) ultimate destination and (*bhartā*) sustainer of this world. (*sākṣī*) He is the lone witness of our deeds. (*Nivāśaḥ*) He is our rehabilitator, (śaraṇam) shelter, and (*suhṛt*) friend. He is (*prabhavaḥ*) the origin, (*pralayaḥ*) dissolution, (*sthānṁ*) foundation, (*nidhānaṁ*) substratum, and (*avyayam*) imperishable (*bijaṁ*) efficient cause of the whole creation. (See also 7.10 and 10.39)

तपाम्यहमहं वर्षं निगृह्णाम्युत्सृजामि च।
अमृतं चैव मृत्युश्च सदसच्चाहमर्जुन॥ ९.१९॥
*tapāmyaham ahaṁ varṣaṁ nigṛhṇāmyutsṛjāmi ca,*
*amṛtaṁ caiva mṛtyuśca sad asaccāham arjuna. (9.19)*

Brahman observes tapa (*saṅkalpa*) for creation. (*varṣaṁ utsṛjāmi*) He creates and (*ngṛhṇāmi*) decreates the worlds. (*amṛtam*) Emancipation and (*mṛtuḥ*) cycle of life and death are due to him. He is both sat (present for knowers) and also asat (absent for ignorants), O Arjuna.

त्रैविद्या मां सोमपाः पूतपापा यज्ञैरिष्ट्वा स्वर्गतिं प्रार्थयन्ते।
ते पुण्यमासाद्य सुरेन्द्रलोकं अश्नन्ति दिव्यान्दिवि देवभोगान्॥ ९.२०॥
*traividyā māṁ somapāḥ pūtapāpā,*
*yajñairiṣtvā svargatiṁ prārthayante.*
*te puṇyam āsādya surendralokam,*
*aśnanti divyān divi deva-bhogān.* (9.20)

The knowers of the three vidyās [Ṛg, Yajuḥ and Sāma] and the drinkers of Soma [enjoyers of spiritual experience as well as knowledge], who have come out of a negative and destructive attitude, who seek permanent light of emancipation by performing yajñas, they, having accumulated (*puṇyaṁ*) good sanskāras as a result of their good karmas, (*āsādya*) reach (*surendralokaṁ*) the space of Brahman and (aśnanti) enjoy (*divyān deva-bhogān*) spiritual divinity (*divi*) in mokṣa.

ते तं भुक्त्वा स्वर्गलोकं विशालं क्षीणे पुण्ये मर्त्यलोकं विशन्ति।
एवं त्रयीधर्ममनुप्रपन्ना गतागतं कामकामा लभन्ते॥ ९.२१॥

*te taṁ bhuktvā svargalokaṁ viśālaṁ,*
*kṣīṇe puṇye martya-lokaṁ viśanti.*
*evaṁ trayī-dharmam anuprapannā,*
*gatāgataṁ kāmakāmā labhante. (9.21)*

Here, Śri Krishna wants to tell that the state of mokṣa [emancipation] is not permanent. Swami Dayananda has also pointed out this fact. A yogī in mokṣa has to revert to the mundane world in the subsequent creation cycle after completing one current cycle of 311 trillion years. In the next creation cycle when Brahman relases all ātmans, an ātman in mokṣa is also released. After taking birth, it may againgo to mokṣa. Thus, a yogī remains in mokṣa till the maximum period of 311 trillion years.

Śri Krishna says (*taṁ viśālaṁ svargalokaṁ bhuktvā*) having enjoyed the state of emancipation for long period, the yogīs (*viśanti*) return to the (*mṛtya-lokaṁ*) mortal world (*kṣiṇe*) upon exhaustion of (*puṇye*) the sanskāras of good Karma (*puṇyas*) in the subsequent creation cycle. (*evam*) Thus (*anuprapannā*), we know through the injunctions of (*trayī-dharmam*) three Vedas, (*gatāgatam*) that the cycle of birth and death of human beings (*labhante*) is acquired by them (*kāma-kāmā*) as per their sanskāras or unfulfilled desires. If they want the fulfilment of their unfulfilled desires, they will take birth to fulfil their unfulfilled desires.

अनन्याश्चिन्तयन्तो मां ये जना: पर्युपासते।
तेषां नित्याभियुक्तानां योगक्षेमं वहाम्यहम्॥ ९.२२॥
*ananyāś cintayanto māṁ ye janāḥ paryupāsate,*
*teṣāṁ nityābhiyuktānāṁ yoga-kṣemaṁ vahāmyaham.*

(*ye janāḥ*) Seekers who are (*nityābhiyuktānāṁ*) totally (*paryupāsate*) devoted to (*māṁ*) Brahman (*ananyāḥ chintayantaḥ*) without thinking about anybody or anything else except Brahman, their yoga-kṣema [wellbeing or mokṣa] is (*vahāmi*) safeguarded\guaranteed by Brahman Himself.

Yoga means achieving what has not been achieved, and kṣema means safeguarding the things that have been achieved so that they may not slip out of the hands of achievers. Mokṣa is a thing or state to be achieved by everybody. So, here, Śri Krishna talks about the method of attainment of mokṣa and its safeguard.

येऽप्यन्यदेवताभक्ता यजन्ते श्रद्धयान्विता:।
तेऽपि मामेव कौन्तेय यजन्त्यविधिपूर्वकम्॥ ९.२३॥
*ye'pyanya-devatā bhaktā yajante śraddhayānvitāḥ,*
*te'pi māmeva kaunteya yajantyavidhipūrvakam. (9.23)*

The seekers who worship other Vedic deities with a positive attitude in the name of Brahman also worship Brahman indirectly, although their path of worship is different.

Here, we must understand that all Vedic deities represent different characteristics of Brahman, because they represent Brahman partially. They are secondary names of Brahman. As such, if we worship them, we would do worship of Brahman by his secondary names.

In this stanza, Śri Krishna wants to say that worship of Brahman if done with a positive attitude, irrespective of names, yields fruit. He differentiates between the worship of Almighty Brahman and deities with different names. Śri Krishna is a propagator of the worship of the ultimate Brahman. However, he wants to tell Arjuna that even those seekers who worship Vedic deities representing some characteristics of Brahman with a positive attitude, too, worship Brahman indirectly, although their path of worship is improper.

The above stanza implies that direct worship [worship by primary name] of the Almighty Brahman is the proper worship. The worship of deities, representing some or other characteristics of Brahman, mentioned in the Vedas are secondary names of Brahman. Here, it may be reminded that Swami Dayananda Saraswati also emphasised that all Vedic deities represent some characteristics of Brahman, so they may also be considered as the secondary names of Brahman. However, Brahman needs to be worshipped by his primary name [Om].

अहं हि सर्वयज्ञानां भोक्ता च प्रभुरेव च ।
न तु मामभिजानन्ति तत्त्वेनातश्च्यवन्ति ते ॥ ९.२४ ॥
*ahaṁ hi sarva-yajñānāṁ bhoktā ca prabhureva ca,*
*na tu mām-abhijānanti tattvenātaś cyavanti te. (9.24)*

Brahman is the only deity addressed in all Śrauta and Smārta-yañjas by different names. He is presiding deity and receiver of all types of oblations. But, people who do not know this reality fall into lower species.

यान्ति देवव्रता देवान्पितॄन्यान्ति पितृव्रताः ।
भूतानि यान्ति भूतेज्या यान्ति मद्याजिनोऽपि माम् ॥ ९.२५ ॥
*yānti devavratā devān pitṛn yānti pitṛvratāḥ,*
*bhūtāni yānti bhūtejyā yānti mad-yājino'pi mām. (9.25)*

Persons who have taken saṅkalpa of divinity are uplifted to divinehood. Those who have developed love for their elders are born in their houses in the next life. Those who worship creatures of lower species and lifeless things like stones and trees go to the lower species that look lifeless, like trees and plants. However, those who meditate upon Almighty Brahman achieve mokṣa. (See also 8.16)

पत्रं पुष्पं फलं तोयं यो मे भक्त्या प्रयच्छति ।
तदहं भक्त्युपहृतमश्नामि प्रयतात्मनः ॥ ९.२६ ॥
*patraṁ puṣpaṁ phalaṁ toyaṁ yo me bhaktyā prayacchati,*
*Tad ahaṁ bhaktyuphṛtam aśnāmi prayatātmanaḥ. (9.26)*

Whosoever gifts Brahman a leaf, a flower, a fruit, or water with love, He accepts the same with happiness from the pure-hearted one.

यत्करोषि यदश्नासि यज्जुहोषि ददासि यत् ।
यत्तपस्यसि कौन्तेय तत्कुरुष्व मदर्पणम् ॥ ९.२७ ॥
*yat-karoṣi yad-aśnāsi yajjuhoṣi dadāsi yat,*
*yattapasyasi kaunteya tatkuruṣva madarpaṇam. (9.27)*

O Arjuna, whatever you do, whatever you eat, whatever you offer as oblation to the fire of yajña, whatever charity you do, whatever austerity you observe, surrender all to Brahman [or do all as the servant of Brahman in the name of Brahman]. (See also 12.10, 18.46)

शुभाशुभफलैरेवं मोक्ष्यसे कर्मबन्धनैः ।
संन्यासयोगयुक्तात्मा विमुक्तो मामुपैष्यसि ॥ ९.२८ ॥

*śubhāśubha-phalair evaṁ mokṣyase karma-bandhanaiḥ,*
*Saṁnyāsa-yoga-yukt-ātmā vimukto mām upaiṣyasi. (9.28)*

By this attitude of complete surrender to Brahman, you shall be freed from the bondage of karmas resulting in good or bad results. You shall be liberated and merged with Brahman having renunciated kāmya (acts for fulfilment of selfish desires), naimittika (actions done on account of some occasion) and niṣiddha karmas [actions prohibited by Śāstras] and by establishing yourself in Brahman through samādhi.

समोऽहं सर्वभूतेषु न मे द्वेष्योऽस्ति न प्रियः ।
ये भजन्ति तु मां भक्त्या मयि ते तेषु चाप्यहम् ॥ ९.२९ ॥
*samo'haṁ sarva-bhūteṣu na me deveṣyo'sti na priyaḥ,*
*ye bhajanti tu māṁ bhaktyā mayi te teṣu cāpyaham. (9.29)*

Brahman treat all beings equally. He neither hates nor loves anybody. But, those who meditate upon Him devoutly merge with Him and He pervades them, i.e. both become one. (See also 7.18)

अपि चेत्सुदुराचारो भजते मामनन्यभाक् ।
साधुरेव स मन्तव्यः सम्यग्व्यवसितो हि सः ॥ ९.३० ॥
*api cetsudurācāro bhajate mām-ananyabhāk,*
*sādhureva sa mantavyaḥ samyag vyavasito hi saḥ. (9.30)*

Even if the most criminal person resolves to meditate upon Brahman alone, such a person should no more be regarded as a cruel person, as he has made a right decision/resolution to take recourse to the right path.

क्षिप्रं भवति धर्मात्मा शश्वच्छान्तिं निगच्छति ।
कौन्तेय प्रतिजानीहि न मे भक्तः प्रणश्यति ॥ ९.३१ ॥
*kṣipraṁ bhavati dharmātmā śaśvac-chāntiṁ nigacchati,*
*kaunteya pratijānīhi na me bhaktaḥ praṇaśyati. (9.31)*

Such a person soon becomes endowed with dharma

and attains everlasting peace. Be aware, O Arjuna, devotees of Brahman are never downgraded.

मां हि पार्थ व्यपाश्रित्य येऽपि स्युः पापयोनयः।
स्त्रियो वैश्यास्तथा शूद्रास्तेऽपि यान्ति परां गतिम्॥ ९.३२॥
*māṁ hi pārtha vyapāśritya ye'pi syuḥ pāpayonayaḥ.*
*striyo vaiśyāstathā śūdrās te'pi yānti parāṁ gatim. (9.32)*

Anybody, including women, traders or manufacturers or producers, illetrate persons and even the evil-minded persons can attain the supreme goal by just meditating upon Brahman, O Arjuna. (See also 18.66)

किं पुनर्ब्राह्मणाः पुण्या भक्ता राजर्षयस्तथा।
अनित्यमसुखं लोकमिमं प्राप्य भजस्व माम्॥ ९.३३॥
*kiṁ punar brāhmaṇāḥ puṇyā bhaktā rājarṣayas tathā,*
*anityam asukhaṁ lokam-imaṁ prāpya bhajasva mām.*

Śri Krishna says that even the wicked persons are emancipated by devotion to Brahman, then there should be no doubt about the emancipation of the pious learned persons and devout royal sages who meditate upon him. Therefore, having obtained this joyless and transient human life, one should always meditate upon Brahman so he may not waver from the right path.

मन्मना भव मद्भक्तो मद्याजी मां नमस्कुरु।
मामेवैष्यसि युक्त्वैवमात्मानं मत्परायणः॥ ९.३४॥
*man-manā bhava mad-bhakto mad-yājī māṁ namaskuru,*
*māṁ evaiṣyasi yuktvaivaṁ ātmānaṁ mat-parāyaṇaḥ. (9.34)*

Fix your mind upon Brahman, have faith in Him, do all works with Him in mind and eulogize Him. Thus having eastablished yourself in Brahman with full faith in Him, you will also attain Him.

ॐ तत्सदिति श्रीमद् भगवद्गीतासूपनिषत्सु ब्रह्मविद्यायां योगशास्त्रे श्रीकृष्णार्जुनसंवादे राजविद्याराजगुह्ययोगोनामनवमोऽध्यायः॥९॥

Here ends the ninth chapter named Rājavidyā-rājaguhya-yoga in the *Bhagvadgitā* dealing with the Brahmavidyā as propounded in the Upaniṣad and Yogaśāstra in the form of dialogue between Śri Krishna and Arjuna.

# अथ दशमोऽध्यायः

## विभूतियोगः

# Chapter 10

[Powers of Brahman]

The Gītā is based upon the philosophy of Sāṅkhya and Yoga. This has already been explained by the author. Ahaṁ, and all its declined forms denote ahaṅkāra. It is a technical term that has no synonym in English. It and its declensions do not mean "I" in Gītā at the places that refer to the creation or origin of the worlds or living beings. For example, I quote Charaka Saṁhiā (1.66). It says: *jāyate buddhir avyaktād buddhayā aham iti.* In the above line, 'aham' is used to denote 'ahaṅkāra' and not "I". According to Saṅkhya, due to the Saṅkalpa of Brahman, prakṛti is agitated, and the state of equilibrium of prakṛti gets disturbed (*Sāṅkhya*, 1.143). The first evolute of prakṛti is called mahat [intelligence] (*Saṅkhya*, 1.71), which is generated by a preponderance of sattva. This is the earliest state of the embodiment of a soul.

This mahat-tattva is further modified into the sattva dominant mahat, rajas dominant mahat, and tamas dominant mahat. Mahat evolves into ahaṅkara (*Saṅkhya*, 1.72). That part of ahaṅkāra where tamas subdues sattva and rajas is called the tāmasika-ahaṅkāra or bhūtādi, and it produces the mass-energy. The second part, where rajas subdue sattva and tamas, is called the rājasika ahaṅkāra, and it gives rise to the tanmātras. Finally, the part of ahaṅkāra where sattva subdues rajas and tamas is called the vaikārika-ahaṅkāra. This vaikārika-ahaṅkāra is sendriya since it produces five sense organs, five motor organs and a mind, while the former two ahaṅkāras are nirindriyas since they do not produce sense organs. Ahaṁ in Gītā, on the one hand, points out the aham/ahaṅkāra element of Sāṅkhya, which is behind the origin of the entire living world. Ahaṅkāra provides a distinct identity to the jīvas [embodied beings]. It has been used here in the sense of distinct identity, identifier, and essence and in the meaning of pride (A person feels pride when he feels something different from others).

On the other hand, aham in Gītā also signifies Brahman. This fact has been corroborated by the following statement of Vedānta sūtra in the context of Indra calling himself prāṇa [Brahman] to Viśvāmitra. Vedānta sūtra states:

न वक्तुरात्मोपदेशादिति चेदध्यात्मसंबन्धभूमा ह्यस्मिन् । 1.1.29 ।

*na vakturātmōpadēśāditi cēdadhyātmasambandha-bhūmā hyasmin*

If it is said that Brahman is (न) not referred here by prāṇa (वक्तुरात्मोपदेशादिति) on account of the speaker [Indra] declaring himself 'prāṇa', this is not correct. (चेत् अध्यात्मसंबन्धभूमा हि) The reply is that this type of declaration shows the abundance of the soul's relationship with Brahman in this passage.

The above-sūtra points out that the Ātman in the body of a living being is only receptor or reflector of Brahman. Brahman cannot be realized until an ātman can erase its aham [individuality]. After the individuality of the soul is eliminated, a person realises Brahman. This condition has been described in the above Vedānta sūtra as 'adhyātma'. Here, adhyātma means 'establishment of ātman in Brahman'. Brahman is everywhere, but it can be received or realized by ātman through samādhi-yoga. When ātman receives it, this phenomenon is called adhyātma. In this condition, whatever is said by ātman, that is said by it as the representative of Brahman. Hence, all such statements where somebody declares himself or herself like the qualities of Brahman are the declaration of Brahman through the Ātman of that person. It does not mean that a person making such a declaration is Brahman. We find several instances in the Bhagvadgitā where Yogīrāja Krishna declares himself through the first person pronoun as if he is Brahman. According to the present Vedānta sūtra under reference above, all those statements should be considered as Brahman's statement through the soul of Śri Krishna. We also have similar examples from Upaniṣads:

प्राणोऽस्मि प्रज्ञात्मा तं मामायुरमृतमित्युपास्स्व ।

[Meaning] I am pṛāṇa, the all-knowing Brahman. So meditate upon me, the imperishable.

As such at all such places, as per Vedānta sūtra under reference above, it is the declaration of Brahman through that ātman and not the declaration of ātman.

To sum up, aham has four meanings— 1. ahaṅkāra 2. specific identity 3. individual soul if refering to an individual person 4. Brahman if refering to Brahman.

Moreover, Brahman is the first person of this universe, so first person pronoun [aham (I), mama (my). mām (me)] is used for Him, if it relates to creation, or creator, etc.

श्री कृष्ण उवाच
Śri Krishna said

भूय एव महाबाहो श्रृणु मे परमं वचः ।

यत्तेऽहं प्रीयमाणाय वक्ष्यामि हितकाम्यया ॥ १०.१ ॥
*bhūya eva mahābāho śṛṇu me paramaṁ vacaḥ,*
*yatte'haṁ prīyamāṇāya vakṣyāmi hita-kāmyayā. (10.01)*

Śri Krishna said— O Long-armed Arjuna, listen once again to my most important words that I shall speak to you, my dear, for your welfare.

न मे विदुः सुरगणाः प्रभवं न महर्षयः ।
अहमादिर्हि देवानां महर्षीणां च सर्वशः ॥ १०.२ ॥
*na me viduḥ suragaṇāḥ prabhavaṁ na maharṣayaḥ,*
*aham ādir hi devānāṁ maharṣīṇāṁ ca sarvaśaḥ. (10.02)*

Neither the devas [enlightened scholars] nor the Maharṣis [greatest seers] know the origin of Brahman, because He existed first of all. All these Ṛṣis and Maharṣis were born very late in the process of creation.

यो मामजमनादिं च वेत्ति लोकमहेश्वरम् ।
असंमूढः स मर्त्येषु सर्वपापैः प्रमुच्यते ॥ १०.३ ॥
*yo mām ajam anādiṁ ca vetti loka-maheśvaram,*
*asammūḍhaḥ sa martyeṣu sarva pāpāiḥ pramucyate. (10.03)*

One who knows Brahman as unborn, beginning-less and the supreme Governor of all, is considered wise [undelued] among the mortals. He will not commit any mistake in life.

बुद्धिर्ज्ञानमसंमोहः क्षमा सत्यं दमः शमः ।
सुखं दुःखं भवोऽभावो भयं चाभयमेव च ॥ १०.४ ॥
*buddhir-jñānam-asammohaḥ kṣamā satyaṁ damaḥ śamaḥ,*
*sukhaṁ duḥkhaṁ bhavo'bhāvo bhayaṁ cābhayameva ca. (10.04)*

(*Buddhi*) Power to comprehend the minutest things, (*Jñāna*) proper information of various elements of nature and Brahman, (*asaṁmoha*) developing rational love for comprehensible objects, (*kṣmā*) undisturbed mind even when abused or denigrated by someone, (*satya*) truthfulness, (*damaḥ, śamaḥ*) control over the mind and senses, pleasure, pain, birth, death, fear, fearlessness;

अहिंसा समता तुष्टिस्तपो दानं यशोऽयशः ।
भवन्ति भावा भूतानां मत्त एव पृथग्विधाः ॥ १०.५ ॥
*ahiṁsā samatā tuṣṭis tapo dānaṁ yaśo'yaśaḥ,*
*bhavanti bhāvā bhūtānāṁ matta eva pṛthagavidhāḥ. (10.05)*

Nonviolence, equanimity, contentment, austerity keeping the mind restrained, charity as per one's capacity, fame on account of dharma [righteous acts], and ill-fame on account of adharma [unrighteous acts]; all these diverse qualities in human beings arise due to their kārmic sanskāras as ordained by Brahman.

महर्षयः सप्त पूर्वे चत्वारो मनवस्तथा ।
मद्भावा मानसा जाता येषां लोक इमाः प्रजाः ॥ १०.६ ॥
*maharṣayaḥ sapta pūrve catvāro manavas tathā,*
*madbhāvā mānasā jātā yeṣāṁ loka imāḥ prajāḥ. (10.06)*

Seven great seers like Buddhi [intellect], mind and five sense organs[1] perform various functions of the mind. The four classes of manavas or jīvas [creatures]— Jeraja [viviparous], Aṇḍaja [oviparous], Svedaja [aquatic] and Udbhija [plants] are born in this world due to the various sanskāras of mind.

एतां विभूतिं योगं च मम यो वेत्ति तत्त्वतः ।
सोऽविकम्पेन योगेन युज्यते नात्र संशयः ॥ १०.७ ॥
*etāṁ vibhūtiṁ yogaṁ ca mama yo vetti tattvataḥ,*
*so'vikampena yogena yujyate nātra saṁśayaḥ. (10.07)*

One who understands this stratification (*vibhutiṁ*) of jīvās into various categories by Brahman and the power

---

[1] They are known as great seers, as they help the living beings in seeing or perceiving.

of yoga [to liberate from this worldly network] will engage himself in yoga.

अहं सर्वस्य प्रभवो मत्तः सर्वं प्रवर्तते ।
इति मत्वा भजन्ते मां बुधा भावसमन्विताः ॥ १०.८ ॥
*ahaṁ sarvasya prabhavo mattaḥ sarvaṁ pravartate,*
*iti matvā bhajante māṁ budhā bhāva-samanvitāḥ. (10.08)*

Brahman is the efficient cause of the origin of all. The whole network has been set in motion by Him. Understanding this fact, the wise ones meditate upon Him with love and devotion.

मच्चित्ता मद्गतप्राणा बोधयन्तः परस्परम् ।
कथयन्तश्च मां नित्यं तुष्यन्ति च रमन्ति च ॥ १०.९ ॥
*maccittā madgata-prāṇā bodhayantaḥ parasparam,*
*kathayantaś ca māṁ nityaṁ tuṣyanti ca ramanti ca. (10.09)*

With their minds absorbed in Brahman, with their lives surrendered unto Him, always enlightening each other by talking about Him, such persons remain ever content and delighted in meditating upon Him.

तेषां सततयुक्तानां भजतां प्रीतिपूर्वकम् ।
ददामि बुद्धियोगं तं येन मामुपयान्ति ते ॥ १०.१० ॥
*teṣāṁ satata-yuktānāṁ bhajatāṁ prīti-pūrvakam,*
*dadāmi buddhi-yogaṁ taṁ yena mām upayānti te. (10.10)*

Those who are constantly engaged in yoga and enjoy the bliss of Brahman with love, He gave them buddhi-yoga [indifferent mind to pleasures and pains], which helps them attain Him.

तेषामेवानुकम्पार्थमहमज्ञानजं तमः ।
नाशयाम्यात्मभावस्थो ज्ञानदीपेन भास्वता ॥ १०.११ ॥
*teṣām evānukampārthamajñānajaṁ tamaḥ,*
*nāśayāmyātmabhāvastho jñānadīpena bhāsvatā. (10.11)*

Out of compassion for them, Brahman, who dwell

within their hearts, destroy the darkness born of attachment to material world by the shining lamp of knowledge [right information].

अर्जुन उवाच

Arjuna said

परं ब्रह्म परं धाम पवित्रं परमं भवान्।
पुरुषं शाश्वतं दिव्यमादिदेवमजं विभुम्॥ १०.१२॥
आहुस्त्वामृषयः सर्वे देवर्षिर्नारदस्तथा।
असितो देवलो व्यासः स्वयं चैव ब्रवीषि मे॥ १०.१३॥
*paraṁ brahma paraṁ dhāma pavitraṁ paramaṁ bhavān,*
*puruṣaṁ śāśvataṁ divyam ādi-devam ajaṁ vibhum. (10.12)*
*āhus tvām ṛṣayaḥ sarve devarṣir nāradastathā,*
*asito devalo vyāsaḥ savayaṁ caiva bravīṣi me. (10.13)*

Arjuna said— For me, you have merged in Supreme Brahman, Who is the supreme resting place, the supreme purifier; Who is Eternal, Divine, First one, Unborn and All prevalent one. You have been acclaimed so by the sages like Nārada, Asita, Devala, Vyāsa, and your personality speaks of you.

सर्वमेतदृतं मन्ये यन्मां वदसि केशव।
न हि ते भगवन्व्यक्तिं विदुर्देवा न दानवाः॥ १०.१४॥
*sarvam etad ṛtaṁ manye yanmāṁ vadasi keśava,*
*na hi te bhagavan vyaktiṁ vidur devā na dānavāḥ. (10.14)*

O Keshava, I believe all that you have told me to be true. O Blessed one, neither the Devas [people from the northern hemisphere of Earth] nor the Danavas [people from the southern hemisphere of Earth] fully understand your (*vyaktim*) intention. (See also 4.06)

स्वयमेवात्मनात्मानं वेत्थ त्वं पुरुषोत्तम।
भूतभावन भूतेश देवदेव जगत्पते॥ १०.१५॥
*svayamevātmanātmānaṁ vettha tvaṁ puruṣottama,*
*bhūtabhāvana bhūteśa devadeva jagatpate. (10.15)*

O Best of all human beings, guide of all, real king, scholar of scholars, and protector of this world; through your soul you have realized Brahman.

वक्तुमर्हस्यशेषेण दिव्या ह्यात्मविभूतय: ।
याभिर्विभूतिभिर्लोकानिमांस्त्वं व्याप्य तिष्ठसि ॥ १०.१६ ॥
*vaktum arhasyaśeṣeṇa divyā hyātma-vibhūtayaḥ,*
*yābhir vibhūtibhir lokān imān stvaṁ vyāpya tiṣṭhasi. (10.16)*

(Therefore), you alone are able to fully describe the powers of Brahman. You have merged in Brahman and pervades the whole universe along with Him and His powers.

कथं विद्यामहं योगिंस्त्वां सदा परिचिन्तयन् ।
केषु केषु च भावेषु चिन्त्योऽसि भगवन्मया ॥ १०.१७ ॥
*kathaṁ vidhām ahaṁ yogins tvāṁ sadā paricintayan,*
*keṣu keṣu ca bhāveṣu cintyo'si bhagavan mayā. (10.17)*

How may I know you, O yogī [merged in Brahman] by constant contemplation on your teachings? In what forms, [Guru, Friend, Relative, etc.] are you to be taken by me, O blessed one?

विस्तरेणात्मनो योगं विभूतिं च जनार्दन ।
भूय: कथय तृप्तिर्हि श्रृण्वतो नास्ति मेऽमृतम् ॥ १०.१८ ॥
*vistareṇ ātmano yogaṁ vibhūtiñ ca janārdana,*
*bhūyaḥ kathaya tṛptir hi śṛṇvato nāsti me'mṛtam. (10.18)*

O Janārdana, explain to me again in detail (*ātmanaḥ*) your yoga [state of merging with Brahman] and powers gained by you as a consequence thereof; because, I am not able to withhold myself from listening to your nectar-like words.

श्री कृष्ण उवाच
Śri Krishna said

हन्त ते कथयिष्यामि दिव्या ह्यात्मविभूतय: ।

प्राधान्यत: कुरुश्रेष्ठ नास्त्यन्तो विस्तरस्य मे ॥ १०.१९ ॥
*hanta te kathayiṣyāmi divyā hyātmavibhūtayaḥ,*
*prādhānyataḥ kuruśreṣtha nāstyanto vistarasya me. (10.19)*

Śri Krishna said— O Arjuna, now I shall explain to you the main powers of Brahman, because there is no end of His powers.

अहमात्मा गुडाकेश सर्वभूताशयस्थित: ।
अहमादिश्च मध्यं च भूतानामन्त एव च ॥ १०.२० ॥
*aham ātmā guḍākeśa sarva-bhūtāśayasthitaḥ,*
*aham ādiśca madhyaṁ ca bhūtānāmanta eva ca. (10.20)*

The Brahman is abiding in the heart of all beings, O conqueror of sleep. He is the efficient cause of (*ādi*) birth, (*sthithi*) organisation and (*anta*) destruction of this material world and living beings.

आदित्यानामहं विष्णुर्ज्योतिषां रविरंशुमान् ।
मरीचिर्मरुतामस्मि नक्षत्राणामहं शशी ॥ १०.२१ ॥
*ādityānām ahaṁ viṣṇur jyotiṣāṁ ravir añśumān,*
*marīcir marutām asmi nakṣatrāṇām ahaṁ śaśī. (10.21)*

Viṣṇu [sustenance] is the specific identity of all the 12 āditya. [Note: The Sun's presence on Earth between 23.50 South and 23.50 North is known as Viṣṇu. This tropical movement causes twelve Rāśīs or twelve 12 months that are known as Ādityas. Together, these twelve months or 12 Ādityas are known as Viṣṇu because they contribute to the creation on the Earth]. The illuminating sun is the specific identity of stars. Marīci [flow] is the specific identity of Maruts [winds]. The moon is the specific identity of constellations [constellations are identified with the help of the moon]. The Vedic mantra says: *nakṣatrāṇām upasthe soma āhitaḥ*, i.e. the moon is sitting in the lap of constellations.

वेदानां सामवेदोऽस्मि देवानामस्मि वासवः ।
इन्द्रियाणां मनश्चास्मि भूतानामस्मि चेतना ॥ १०.२२ ॥
*vedānāṁ sāmavedo'smi devānām asmi vāsavaḥ,*
*indrayāṇāṁ manaś cāsmi bhūtānām asmi cetanā. (10.22)*

Sāmaveda is the specific identity of all the Vedas because it deals with upāsanā kāṇḍa; Indra [lightning in clouds or cosmic electric force saving the universe from contraction] is the specific identity of the devas [natural forces]; the mind is the specific identity of senses [when a person goes lunatic, his sense-organs stop working]; consciousness is the specific identity of living beings.

रुद्राणां शङ्करश्चास्मि वित्तेशो यक्षरक्षसाम् ।
वसूनां पावकश्चास्मि मेरुः शिखरिणामहम् ॥ १०.२३ ॥
*rudrāṇāṁ śaṅkaraś cāsmi vitteśo yakṣa-rakṣasām,*
*vasūnāṁ pāvakaś cāsmi meruḥ śikhariṇām aham. (10.23)*

(*śiva*) The soul is the specific identity of the Rudras [five senses, five vital forces known as prāṇās and mind make together 11 rudras. They are functional as long as the soul dwells in the body]. (*vitteśa*) The wealthiest person is the specific identity of (*yakṣas*), the persons who want to hoard material things and (*rakṣasas*), the persons who are custodians of the material wealth; (*pāvaka*) Agni [fire, geothermal and solar energy] is the specific identity of the 8 Vasus [earth, water, fire, air, space, moon, sun and stars, since without fire, geothermal and solar energies there can be no life and Vasus are meant for life in the universe]; and Sumeru [North pole] is the specific identity of mountains.

Note: North pole of the earth is called Sumeru, and the South pole is called Kumeru.

पुरोधसां च मुख्यं मां विद्धि पार्थ बृहस्पतिम् ।
सेनानीनामहं स्कन्दः सरसामस्मि सागरः ॥ १०.२४ ॥

*purodhasāṁ ca mukhyaṁ māṁ viddhi pārtha bṛhaspatim,*
*senāninām ahaṁ skandaḥ sarasām asmi sāgaraḥ. (10.24)*

(*bṛhaspati*) The vision is the specific identity of leaders, O son of Pṛthā. (*Skanda*) The power is the specific identity of generals; the ocean is the specific identity of the rivers.

महर्षीणां भृगुरहं गिरामस्म्येकमक्षरम् ।
यज्ञानां जपयज्ञोऽस्मि स्थावराणां हिमालयः ॥ १०.२५ ॥
*maharṣīṇāṁ bhṛgur ahaṁ girām asmyekamakṣram,*
*yajñānāṁ japayajño'smi sthāvarāṇāṁ himālayaḥ. (10.25)*

(*bhṛgu*) The aura/shining on face is the specific identity of great sages. Monosyllabic Om [cosmic sound] is the specific identity of all speech sounds; (*japa yajña*) mantra chanting is the specific identity of all the yajñas [without mantra chanting a yajñā is incomplete]; and Himalaya is the specific identity of all hills.

अश्वत्थः सर्ववृक्षाणां देवर्षीणां च नारदः ।
गन्धर्वाणां चित्ररथः सिद्धानां कपिलो मुनिः ॥ १०.२६ ॥
*aśvatthaḥ sarvavṛkṣāṇāṁ devarṣiṇāṁ ca nāradaḥ,*
*gandharvāṇāṁ citrarathaḥ sidthānāṅ kapilo muniḥ. (10.26)*

The pīpal tree is specific among all the trees [as it emits oxygen day and night whereas other trees emit oxygen only during the day time]; Nārada is distinguished personality among (*devarṣis*) enlightened persons who had visualisation of the mantras; (*chitra-ratha*) sun is the particular identity of (*gandharvas*) solar radiation, and sage Kapila is distinct among the siddhas [experts of specific field or those scholars who have inborn divine powers due to previous life sanskāras]

उच्चैःश्रवसमश्वानां विद्धि माममृतोद्भवम् ।
ऐरावतं गजेन्द्राणां नराणां च नराधिपम् ॥ १०.२७ ॥

*uaccaiḥ śravasam aśvānāṁ viddhi mām amṛtodbhavam,*
*airāvataṁ gajendrāṇāṁ narāṇāṁ ca narādhipam. (10.27)*

(*uchchaiḥśravā*) The sun born during the process of ocean churning [rotation of the Earth around its axis] is the specific identity of (*aśvas*) sun-rays; (*Airāvata*) Milky Way is the particular identity of the (*gajendras*) galaxies, and the King is the specific identity of men.

Note: Ocean churning is nothing but the Earth's rotation around its axis. Space is known as the ocean in Vedas, and churning is done by the rotating Earth. It takes place daily. During this process, fourteen things originated. One among them is the Uccaiḥśravā horse, which is nothing but the sun. In the Vedas, amṛta has been equated with light, and mṛtyu has been correlated with darkness. Airāvata path has been described in astronomical treatises as our galaxy or the Milky Way. Galaxies are the biggest body in the universe, and Gaja [elephant] is the biggest body on the Earth, so Gaja has been used to denote Galaxies in the astronomical sense.

आयुधानामहं वज्रं धेनूनामस्मि कामधुक्।
प्रजनश्चास्मि कन्दर्पः सर्पाणामस्मि वासुकिः ॥ १०.२८ ॥
*āyudhānām ahaṁ vajraṁ dhenūnām asmi kāmadhuk,*
*prajanaścāsmi kandarpaḥ sarpāṇāmasmi vāsukīḥ. (10.28)*

The Thunderbolt is the specific identity of weapons operated by electric current. [This shows that electric weapons were in currency during the time of Mahābhārata war], Kāmadhenu [the earth is called kāmadhenu because it caters to all the needs of all beings] is the specific identity of all (*gaus*) planets in our solar system. Sexual desire is central to the creation of living beings. Vāsukī nāga [equatorial zone of the earth] is the centre of sarpas [various spiral zones of the earth, like tropical, arid and frigid zones, etc.].

अनन्तश्चास्मि नागानां वरुणो यादसामहम्।
पितॄणामर्यमा चास्मि यम: संयमतामहम्॥ १०.२९॥
*anantaścāsmi nāgānāṁ varuṇo yādasām-aham,*
*pitṛṇām-aryamā cāsmi yamaḥ saṁyamatām-aham. (10.29)*

(*anantaḥ*) Śeṣanāga [molten lava] is the specific identity of the Nāgas [volcanic mountains], (*varuṇa*) water is the specific identity of water bodies, (*aryamā*) Uttaraphalguni Nakṣtra or Leonis is specific identity of all Pitara-constellations starting from U. Phalgunī to Jyeṣṭhā forming the period of Śarada Ṛtu. (*yama*) Social discipline is central to law and order.

प्रह्लादश्चास्मि दैत्यानां काल: कलयतामहम्।
मृगाणां च मृगेन्द्रोऽहं वैनतेयश्च पक्षिणाम्॥ १०.३०॥
*prahalādaś cāsmi daityānāṅ kālaḥ kalayatām aham,*
*mṛgāṇāṁ ca mṛgendro'haṁ vainateyaśca pakṣiṇām. (10.30)*

Prahlāda [lover of Brahman] is superior to Daityas [lovers of money], time is central to astronomers [time reckoners], the lion is foremost among all beasts, and the (*vaintaeya*) falcon is foremost among all the birds.

पवन: पवतामस्मि राम: शस्त्रभृतामहम्।
झषाणां मकरश्चास्मि स्रोतसामस्मि जाह्नवी॥ १०.३१॥
*pavanaḥ pavatām asmi rāmaḥ śastra-bhṛtām aham,*
*jhaṣāṇāṁ makaraś cāsmi srotsām asmi jāhnavī. (10.31)*

The wind is the specific purifier, and Rāma is the superior among all warriors. The crocodile is distinct among the fishes, and the ganges is typical among all rivers (flowing waters).

सर्गाणामादिरन्तश्च मध्यं चैवाहमर्जुन।
अध्यात्मविद्या विद्यानां वाद: प्रवदतामहम्॥ १०.३२॥
*sargāṇāmādirantaśca madhyaṁ caivāhamarjuna,*

*adhyātmavidhā vidhānāṁ vādaḥ pravadatāmaham. (10.32)*

Brahman is in the beginning, middle, and end of the creation, O Arjuna. Spiritual education is supreme of all education. Logic is central to arguers.

अक्षराणामकारोऽस्मि द्वन्द्वः सामासिकस्य च।
अहमेवाक्षयः कालो धाताऽहं विश्वतोमुखः ॥ १०.३३ ॥
*akṣarāṇām akāro'smi dvandvaḥ sāmāsikasya ca,*
*aham evākṣayaḥ kālo dhātāhaṁ viśvatomukhaḥ. (10.33)*

The letter "A" is the basis of alphabets, Dual compound is specific among all compounds [2], imperishability is the specific identity of time, dhātā [galactic centre] is the distinct identity of our universe facing all directions.

मृत्युः सर्वहरश्चाहमुद्भवश्च भविष्यताम्।
कीर्तिः श्रीर्वा नारीणां स्मृतिर्मेधा धृतिः क्षमा ॥ १०.३४ ॥
*mṛtyuḥ sarvaharaścāham udbhavaśca bhaviṣyatām,*
*kīrtiḥ śrirvāk ca nāriṇāṁ smṛtirmedhā dhṛtiḥ kṣamā.*

Death is a specific identity of devourers; origin is the specific identity of future existence. [If the process of origin ceases to occur, the concept of the future will be lost]. Seven great ladies named Kirti, Śri, Vāk, Smṛti, Medhā, Dhṛti, Kṣamā are the specific identities of ladies.

बृहत्साम तथा साम्नां गायत्री छन्दसामहम्।
मासानां मार्गशीर्षोऽहमृतूनां कुसुमाकरः ॥ १०.३५ ॥
*bṛhatsāma tathā sāmnāṁ gāyatri chandasāmaham,*
*māsānāṁ mārgaśīrṣo'ham ṛtūnāṁ kusumākaraḥ. (10.35)*

(*bṛhatsāma*) Our solar system is a specific identity of

---

[2] Note: In a compound, all compounded words lose their individual identity and are reduced to one word, but in the dual compound, all words retain their individual identity.

all the (*sāmans*) solar systems in visible space. Gāyatrī is the particular identity of chhandas, and Mārgaśīrṣa is the distinct identity of the months [the months used to begin with Mārgaśīrṣa during the Mahābhārata period]. Spring is a particular identity of seasons [seasons used to start with spring season as the first one].

Note: The above description shows that during the Mahābhārata period, the spring season used to commence with Mārgaśīrṣa Saṅkrānti. These days, the Vasanta season starts on 18th Feb., and Mārgaśīrṣa Sankranti starts on 22nd Nov. So there is a precession of 88 days. If we multiply 88 by 72 [rate of precession per day], it shows that around 6336 years ago, the Vasanta season used to fall with Mārgaśīrṣa Saṅkrānti. It happened till 4176 years ago, i.e. 2156 B.C. Afterwards, the Vasanta season started with Pauṣa Saṅkrānti. In 4 AD, the Vasanta season started with Māgha Saṅkrānti. In 2016, it started occurring with Phālguna Saṅkrānti.

द्युतं छलयतामस्मि तेजस्तेजस्विनामहम्।
जयोऽस्मि व्यवसायोऽस्मि सत्त्वं सत्त्ववतामहम्॥ १०.३६॥
*dyūtaṁ chalayatām asmi tejas tejasvinām aham,*
*jayo'smi vyavasāyo'smi sattvaṁ sattvavatām aham. (10.36)*

Gambling is a specific identity of the act of cheating; splendour is central to or basis of splendid; victory is central to victorious; resolution is central to the resolute; sattva is the basis of sāttvikas.

वृष्णीनां वासुदेवोऽस्मि पाण्डवानां धनंजयः।
मुनीनामप्यहं व्यासः कवीनामुशना कविः॥ १०.३७॥
*vṛṣṇīnāṁ vāsudevo'smi pāṇḍavānāṁ dhanañjayaḥ,*
*munīnām apyahaṁ vyāsaḥ kavinām uśaṇā kaviḥ. (10.37)*

Vāsudeva is representative of Vṛṣṇis; Arjuna is representative of the Pāṇḍavas; Vyāsa is representative of all munis; Uśanā, being the first one, represents all Kavis [who were able to transcend or see beyond time].

दण्डो दमयतामस्मि नीतिरस्मि जिगीषताम्।
मौनं चैवास्मि गुह्यानां ज्ञानं ज्ञानवतामहम्॥ १०.३८॥
*daṇḍo damayatāṁ asmi nītir asmi jigiṣatām,*
*maunaṁ caivāsmi guhyānāṁ jñānaṁ jñānavatāṁ aham. (10.38)*

Power is the specific identity of rulers, statesmanship is a particular identity of the seekers of victory, silence is a distinct identity of the secrets, and wisdom is a specific identity of wise men.

यच्चापि सर्वभूतानां बीजं तदहमर्जुन।
न तदस्ति विना यत्स्यान्मया भूतं चराचरम्॥ १०.३९॥
*yaccāpi sarvabhūtānāṁ bījaṁ tad aham arjuna,*
*na tad asti vinā yatsyān mayā bhūtaṁ carācaram. (10.39)*

Aham [individuality] is the original identity of all beings, O Arjuna. No animate being or inanimate thing can exist without a specific identity. (See also 7.10 and 9.18)

नान्तोऽस्ति मम दिव्यानां विभूतीनां परंतप।
एष तूद्देशतः प्रोक्तो विभूतेर्विस्तरो मया॥ १०.४०॥
*nānto'sti mama divyānāṁ vibhūtīnāṁ parantapa,*
*eṣa tūddeśataḥ prokto vibhūtervistaro mayā. (10.40)*

There is no end to the expansion of the divine powers of Brahman, O destroyer of enemies. This expansion is (*uddeśataḥ*) briefly described by me.

यद्यद्विभूतिमत्सत्त्वं श्रीमदूर्जितमेव वा।
तत्तदेवावगच्छ त्वं मम तेजोंशसंभवम्॥ १०.४१॥
*yad yad vibhūtimat sattvaṁ śrimad ūrjitameva vā,*
*tat tadevāvagaccha tvaṁ mama tejoñ'śa-sambhavam. (10.41)*

Whatever is endowed with divinity, sāttavika guṇas, brilliance and power, know that to be part of Brahman.

अथवा बहुनैतेन किं ज्ञातेन तवार्जुन।
विष्टभ्याहमिदं कृत्स्नमेकांशेन स्थितो जगत्॥ १०.४२॥
*athavā bahunaitena kiṁ jñātena tavārjuna,*
*viṣṭabhyāham idaṁ kṛtsnam ekāñśena sthito jagat. (10.42)*

There is no need for you to know all this in detail, O Arjuna, except that Brahman has (*viṣṭabhya*) bounded this complete bhūtākāśa where this material expansion or creation takes place to the quarter part of His space. [In other words, 25% energy (*prakṛti*) is active in the bhūtākāśa to give birth to creation]. Taittirīya Āraṇyaka (3.12) also corroborates this fact as *pādo'sya viśvā bhūtāni*, i.e. the entire creation of the Bhūtākāśa is made up of the quarter part of the total energy existing in the Chidākāśa.

ॐ तत्सदिति श्रीमद् भगवद्गीतासूपनिषत्सु ब्रह्मविद्यायां योगशास्त्रे श्रीकृष्णार्जुनसंवादे विभूतियोगोनाम दशमोऽध्याय:॥ १०॥

Here ends the tenth chapter, named Vibhūti yoga in the *Bhagvadgitā*, dealing with the Brahmavidyā as propounded in the Upaniṣad and Yogaśāstra in the form of dialogue between Śri Krishna and Arjuna.

# अथैकादशोऽध्यायः

## विश्वरूपदर्शनयोगः

# Chapter 11

[Universal form of Paramātman]

In this chapter, Śri Krishna reveals to Arjuna the mystery of the universal form of Brahman. Brahman becomes manifest during creation [as His presence is known through His act of creation], and He remains unmanifest during decreation. During creation period, this Brahmāṇḍa [the universe] appears as His Viṛāṭ [universal form]. According to Śri Krishna, Brahman manifests Himself in all the living beings of the world. Śri Krishna tells Arjuna that Brahman is present in all the warriors on the battlefield.

अर्जुन उवाच

Arjuna said

मदनुग्रहाय परमं गुह्यमध्यात्मसंज्ञितम्।
यत्त्वयोक्तं वचस्तेन मोहोऽयं विगतो मम॥ ११.१॥

*madanugrahāyaparamaṁ guhyamadhyātmasañjñitam,*
*yattavayoktaṁ vacastena moho'yaṁ vigato mama (11.01)*

Arjuna said—(*mohaḥ*) My delusion (*vigataḥ*) is dispelled by (*vachaḥ*) your profound words, (*yat tvayā uktaṁ*) which you spoke (*mad anugrahāya*) out of compassion towards me, (*guhyam*) about the supreme secret (*adhyātma sañjitam*) involving the subject of the Universal self, Parmātman.

भवाप्ययौ हि भूतानां श्रुतौ विस्तरशो मया।
त्वत्तः कमलपत्राक्ष माहात्म्यमपि चाव्ययम्॥ ११.२॥

*bhavāpyayau hi būtānāṁ śrutau vistaraśo mayā,*
*tvattaḥ kamala-patrākṣa māhātmyamapi cāvyayam. (11.02)*

(*kamala-patrākṣa*) O Lotus-eyed one, (*mayā*) I (*śrutau*) have heard (*tvattaḥ*) from you (*vistaraśaḥ*) in detail about (*bhava*) the origin and (*apyaya*) dissolution of beings, (*api*) and (*mahātmyam*) the glory of (*avyayam*) imperishable Paramātman.

एवमेतद्यथात्थ त्वमात्मानं परमेश्वर।
द्रष्टुमिच्छामि ते रूपमैश्वरं पुरुषोत्तम॥ ११.३॥
*evam etad yathāttha tvam ātmānaṁ parameśvara,*
*draṣṭum icchāmi te rūpaṁ aiśvaraṁ puruṣottama. (11.03)*

O Parameśavara [Krishna merged in Brahman], (*yathā āttha*) whatever you have said (*ātmānam*) about you enjoying the powers of Brahman (*evam etat*) that is true. (*puruṣottam*) O Super human-being, (*icchhāmi*) I wish (*draṣṭum*) to see (*te*) your (*aiśvaraṁ*) universal (*rūpam*) form (after you have merged in Brahman).

मन्यसे यदि तच्छक्यं मया द्रष्टुमिति प्रभो।
योगेश्वर ततो मे त्वं दर्शयात्मानमव्ययम्॥ ११.४॥
*manyase yadi tacchakyaṁ mayā draṣtum iti prabho,*
*yogeśvara tato me tvaṁ darśayātmānamavyayam. (11.04)*

(*manyase*) If you think (*yadi*) that (*tat śakyam*) it is possible (*mayā*) for me (*draṣṭum*) to see your universal form, (*prabho*) O capable of doing everything, (*tataḥ*) then (*yogeśavara*) O master of the yogis, (*darśaya*) show (*me*) me (*ātmānam*) your (*avyayam*) imperishable form manifested/pervaded in universal objects.

श्री कृष्ण उवाच
Śri Krishna said

पश्य मे पार्थ रूपाणि शतशोऽथ सहस्रशः।
नानाविधानि दिव्यानि नानावर्णाकृतीनि च॥ ११.५॥
*paśya me pārtha rūpāṇi śataśo'tha sahasraśaḥ,*
*nānāvidhāni divyāni nānāvarṇākṛtīni ca. (11.05)*

Here Krishna shows Arjuna his universally manifested/ pervaded ātman (after merging with Brahman). He says, "O Arjuna, behold the hundreds and thousands of various colours and shapes manifested/ pervaded by me after merging with Brahman".

पश्यादित्यान्वसून्रुद्रानश्विनौ मरुतस्तथा।
बहून्यदृष्टपूर्वाणि पश्याश्चर्याणि भारत॥ ११.६॥
*paśyādityān vasūn rudrānaśvinau marutastathā,*
*bahūnyadṛṣṭapūrvāṇi paśyāścaryāṇi bhārata. (11.06)*

"See the Ādityas (twelve solar months), the eight Vasus, the eleven Rudras, the two Aśvins (inhalations and exhalations in spiritual sense, and +ve and -ve forces in astronomical sense), and the Maruts (49 pressure belts on earth, atmosphere, and interplanetary space) are all manifested by me after merging with Brahman. Behold, O Bhārata, this wonder that you have never seen from this angle".

Here Sri Krishna wants to say that ātman that has merged with Brahman also pervades or manifests everything in the company of Brahman.

इहैकस्थं जगत्कृत्स्नं पश्याद्य सचराचरम्।
मम देहे गुडाकेश यच्चान्यद् द्रष्टुमिच्छसि॥ ११.७॥
*ihaikasthaṁ jagat kṛtsnaṁ paśyādya sacarācaram,*
*mama dehe guḍākeśa yaccānyad draṣṭum icchasi. (11.07)*

(*Guḍākeśa*) O conqueror of sleep, (*adya*) now (*paśya*) behold (*kṛtsnam*) the entire (*jagat*) creation; (sacharācharam) animate, inanimate, (*cha*) and (*yat anyat*) whatever else you see; (*ekasthaṁ*) all at one place (*iha*) in (*mama dehe*) in my universalized soul.

न तु मां शक्यसे द्रष्टुमनेनैव स्वचक्षुषा।
दिव्यं ददामि ते चक्षुः पश्य मे योगमैश्वरम्॥ ११.८॥

*na tu māṁ śakyase draṣṭum anenaiva svacakṣuṣā,*
*divyaṁ dadāmi te cakṣuḥ paśya me yogam aiśvaram. (11.08)*

But, you are not able to see my universalized soul with your physical eyes; therefore, I give you the divine eyes to see my (*yogam aiśvaram*) merging with Iśvara or univesalisation.

संजय उवाच

Sañjaya said

एवमुक्त्वा ततो राजन्महायोगेश्वरो हरिः ।
दर्शयामास पार्थाय परमं रूपमैश्वरम् ॥ ११.९ ॥
*evam uktvā tato rājan mahāyogeśvaro hariḥ,*
*darśayāmāsa pārthāya paramaṁ rūpam āiśvaram. (11.09)*

Sañjaya Said: O King, having said this, Śri Krishna, the great master of yoga, revealed to Arjuna his universalized form. According to Vedānta, Brahman manifested/pervaded in the universe is known as Īśvara and unmanifest Brahman is known as Brahman. In other words, Brahman during creation is called Iśvara, and without creation is called Brahman. Why He is called Īśvara? Because after His act of creation, His majestic power [aiśvarya] becomes known.

अनेकवक्त्रनयनमनेकाद्भुतदर्शनम् ।
अनेकदिव्याभरणं दिव्यानेकोद्यतायुधम् ॥ ११.१० ॥
*anekavaktra nayanam anekādbhutadarśanam.*
*anekadivyābharaṇaṁ divyānekodyat āyudham. (11.10)*

Arjuna could visualize a marvelous form of Krishna pervaded in (*aneka*) various (*udyata āyudham*) armed soldiers on the battlefield. (*aneka vaktram*) There were many mouths and (*nayanam*) eyes. There were (*aneka*) many (*adbhuta darśanam*) strange faces. There were (*aneka*) many soldiers with (*divya*) divine ornaments like

Karṇa, and (*aneka*) many were holding (*divya*) divine weapons.

दिव्यमाल्याम्बरधरं दिव्यगन्धानुलेपनम् ।
सर्वाश्चर्यमयं देवमनन्तं विश्वतोमुखम् ॥ ११.११ ॥
*divya-mālyāmbaradharaṁ divya-gandhānulepanam,*
*sarvāścarya-mayaṁ devam anantaṁ viśvatomukham. (11.11)*

Many wore divine garlands and apparel, anointed with excellent perfumes. It was all wonderful to see the divine presence of Krishna in limitless faces all around in the army.

दिवि सूर्यसहस्रस्य भवेद्युगपदुत्थिता ।
यदि भा: सदृशी सा स्याद्भासस्तस्य महात्मन: ॥ ११.१२ ॥
*divi sūrya-sahasrasya bhaved-yugapadutthitā,*
*yadi bhāḥ sadṛśī sā syād bhāsas-tasya mahātmanaḥ. (11.12)*

(*bhāḥ*) The splendour of (*sūrya-sahasrasya*) thousands of suns (*yugapad-utthitā*) were to blaze forth all at once (*divi*) in the sky, (*yadi*) I am not sure that (*sadṛśī*) even that would resemble (*bhāsaḥ*) the splendour (*tasya*) of that (*mahātmanaḥ*) Great Ātman [Śri Krishna].

तत्रैकस्थं जगत्कृत्स्नं प्रविभक्तमनेकधा ।
अपश्यद्देवदेवस्य शरीरे पाण्डवस्तदा ॥ ११.१३ ॥
*tatraikasathaṁ jagat kṛtsnaṁ pravibhaktamanekadhā,*
*apaśyaddeva-devasya śarīre pāṇḍavas tadā. (11.13)*

The son of Pāṇḍu, Arjuna, watched that the entire universe with manifold divisions is located in one place: within the Super Being, who is the God of gods.

तत: स विस्मयाविष्टो हृष्टरोमा धनंजय: ।
प्रणम्य शिरसा देवं कृताञ्जलिरभाषत ॥ ११.१४ ॥
*tataḥ sa vismayāviṣṭo hṛṣṭa-romā dhanañjayaḥ,*
*praṇamya śirasā devaṁ kṛtāñjalir abhāṣata. (11.14)*

(*tataḥ*) Then (*Dhanañjaya*) Arjuna, (*vismayāviṣṭaḥ*)

filled with wonder and (*hṛṣṭaromā*) elevated with happiness, (*praṇamya śirasā*) saluted (*devaṁ*) the divinity of Śri Krishna and (*abhāṣat*) prayed (*kṛtāñjali*) with folded hands.

अर्जुन उवाच

Arjuna said

पश्यामि देवांस्तव देव देहे सर्वांस्तथा भूतविशेषसङ्घान्।
ब्रह्माणमीशं कमलासनस्थं ऋषींश्च सर्वानुरगांश्च दिव्यान्॥ ११.१५॥

*paśyāmi devān stava deva dehe,*
*sarvāns tathā bhūtaviśeṣa-saṅghān.*
*brahmāṇam īśaṁ kamalāsanastham,*
*riṣīñśca sarvān uragāñśca divyān. (11.15)*

(*Deva*) O Divine power, (*paśyāmi*) I see in (*tava*) your (*dehe*) universalized soul (*sarvān devān*) all the gods [natural forces] and (*bhūta-viśeṣa-saṅghān*) the multitude of beings, (*brahmāṇam*) Brahmā [the first created human being in this world] born on the lotus-shaped earth [the earth was four-petalled like the petals of a lotus at the beginning of its origin], (*ṛṣin*) all sages, (*cha*) and (*divyān*) celestial (*uragān*) spiral bodies like galaxies.

अनेकबाहूदरवक्त्रनेत्रं पश्यामि त्वां सर्वतोऽनन्तरूपम्।
नान्तं न मध्यं न पुनस्तवादिं पश्यामि विश्वेश्वर विश्वरूप॥ ११.१६॥

*anekabāhūdara vaktra netraṁ,*
*paśyāmi tvāṁ sarvato'nantarūpam.*
*nāntaṁ na madhyaṁ napunastavādiṁ,*
*paśyāmi viśveśvarupa viśvarūpa. (11.16)*

(*Viśveśvara*) O, Master of the universe, *(paśyāmi)* I see (*tvām*) you (*viśvarūpam*) as universalized soul (*ananta-rūpam*) with infinite forms, (*aneka*) possessing many (*bāhū*) arms, (*udara*) stomachs, (*vaktra*) faces, (*netram*) and eyes. (*na*) Neither do *(paśyāmi)* I see (*tava*) your (*ādim*) beginning, (*na madhyam*) middle (*na antaṁ*) nor the end O (*viśvarūpa*) universalized soul.

किरीटिनं गदिनं चक्रिणं च तेजोराशिं सर्वतो दीप्तिमन्तम्।
पश्यामि त्वां दुर्निरीक्ष्यं समन्ताद् दीप्तानलार्कद्युतिमप्रमेयम्॥ ११.१७॥
*kirīṭinaṁ gadinaṁ cakriṇaṁ ca,*
*tejorāśiṁ sarvato dīptimantam.*
*paśyāmi tvāṁ durnirīkṣyaṁ samantād,*
*dīptānalārka-dyutim-aprameyam. (11.17)*

*(paśyāmī)* I watch (*tvām*) you (*kirīṭinaṁ*) wearing a crown, (*gadinaṁ*) holding a mace, (*cha*) and (*chakriṇaṁ*) Chakra [literally meaning discus, a kind of weapon that was able to pierce through the enemy and aeroplanes when operated]. I watch you as the (*tejorāśiṁ*) mass of radiance, (*diptimantam*) shining (*sarvataḥ*) all around, (*durnirīkṣyam*) difficult to behold (*samantāt*) from all sides, (*aprameyam*) with immeasurable (*dyutim*) brilliance (*arka*) of the sun and (*dīpta anala*) the blazing cosmic fire.

त्वमक्षरं परमं वेदितव्यं त्वमस्य विश्वस्य परं निधानम्।
त्वमव्ययः शाश्वतधर्मगोप्ता सनातनस्त्वं पुरुषो मतो मे॥ ११.१८॥
*tvam akṣaraṁ paramaṁ veditavyaṁ,*
*tvam asya viśvasya paraṁ nidhānam.*
*tvamavyayaḥ śāśvata dharma-goptā,*
*sanātanas tvaṁ puruṣo mato me. (11.18)*

You have become one with imperishable and Supreme to be realized. You have become one with the ultimate resort of this universe. You have become one with the unchangeable and protector of the eternal laws of creation. You have become one with the eternal Puruṣa.

अनादिमध्यान्तमनन्तवीर्यमनन्तबाहुं शशिसूर्यनेत्रम्।
पश्यामि त्वां दीप्तहुताशवक्त्रं स्वतेजसा विश्वमिदं तपन्तम्॥ ११.१९॥
*anādi-madhayāntam-anantavīryam,*

*anantabāhuṁ śaśi-sūrya-netram.*
*paśyāmi tvāṁ dīpta-hutāśa-vaktraṁ,*
*svatejasā viśvam idaṁ tapantam. (11.19)*

I watch you without beginning, middle, or end; with infinite power, with enumerable arms [represented by human beings on the earth], with the sun and the moon as your eyes, with cosmic blazing fire as your face whose brilliance is illuminating the entire universe.

द्यावापृथिव्योरिदमन्तरं हि व्याप्तं त्वयैकेन दिशश्च सर्वाः ।
दृष्ट्वाद्भुतं रूपमुग्रं तवेदं लोकत्रयं प्रव्यथितं महात्मन् ॥ ११.२० ॥
*dyāvāpṛthivyor idam-antaraṁ hi,*
*vyāptaṁ tvayaikena diśaśca sarvāḥ.*
*dṛṣṭvādbhutaṁ rūpam ugraṁ tavedaṁ,*
*loka-trayaṁ pravyathitaṁ mahātman. (11.20)*

The entire space between heaven and earth is pervaded by you alone in all directions. I am watching your effulgent form never seen before, (*loka-trayam*) all the three worlds will be (*pravyathitam*) fearful and blinded, [what to say of me], O great Ātman.

Note: Here '*pravyathita*' means (*bhita*) fearful and (*prachalita* or *vichalita*) means blinded.

अमी हि त्वां सुरसङ्घा विशन्ति
केचिद्भीताः प्राञ्जलयो गृणन्ति ।
स्वस्तीत्युक्त्वा महर्षिसिद्धसङ्घाः
स्तुवन्ति त्वां स्तुतिभिः पुष्कलाभिः ॥ ११.२१ ॥
*amī hi tvāṁ sura-saṅghā viśanti,*
*kecid bhītāḥ prāñjalayo gṛṇanti.*
*svastītyuktvā maharṣi-siddha-saṅghāḥ,*
*stuvanti tvāṁstutibhiḥ puṣkalābhiḥ. (11.21)*

The (*sura-saṅghāḥ*) hosts of divine people appeared to have been (*viśanti*) located in you. (*Kechid*) Some people (*bhitāḥ*) with the fear of your power (*gṛṇanti*) sing your glories (*prāñjalayaḥ*) with folded hands. (*Maharṣi-siddha-saṅghāḥ*) A multitude of Maharṣis and Siddhas (stuvanti) hail and adore You (*svasti-iti-uktvā*) with Svastivāchana mantras and (*stutibhiḥ*) hymns (*puṣkalābhiḥ*) abounding in praise for you.

रुद्रादित्या वसवो ये च साध्या विश्वेश्विनौ मरुतश्चोष्मपाश्च ।
गन्धर्वयक्षासुरसिद्धसङ्घा वीक्षन्ते त्वां विस्मिताश्चैव सर्वे ॥ ११.२२ ॥
*rudrādityā vasavo ye ca sādhyā,*
*viśve'śvināu marutaścoṣmapāśca.*
*gandharvayakṣāsurasiddhasaṅghā,*
*vīkṣante tvāṁ vismitāścaiva sarve. (11.22)*

Rudras, Ādityas, Vasus, Sādhyas [who have attained perfection in their present lives], Viśvedevas [divine people of the whole universe], Aśvinis (*Aśvinī-kumāras*), Maruts [people living on air], Uśmapās [living on heat of sun], Gandharvas [expert in classical dances], Yakṣas [rich people], Asuras [materialistic people], and Siddhas [born experts]; they all gaze you amazingly.

रूपं महत्ते बहुवक्त्रनेत्रं महाबाहो बहुबाहूरुपादम् ।
बहूदरं बहुदंष्ट्राकरालं दृष्ट्वा लोकाः प्रव्यथितास्तथाहम् ॥ ११.२३ ॥
*rūpaṁ mahatte bahu-vaktra-netraṁ,*
*mahābāho bahubāhūrupādam.*
*bahūdaraṁ bahudaṇṣṭrā-karālaṁ,*
*dṛṣṭvā lokāḥ pra-vyathitās tathāham. (11.23)*

Seeing your Virāṭa form [Bhūtākāśa] represented by many faces, eyes, arms, thighs, feet, stomachs, and many devouring teeth, myself and other people are bewildered, O mighty God.

नभःस्पृशं दीप्तमनेकवर्णं
व्यात्ताननं दीप्तविशालनेत्रम् ।
दृष्ट्वा हि त्वां प्रव्यथितान्तरात्मा
धृतिं न विन्दामि शमं च विष्णो ॥ ११.२४ ॥

*nabhaḥspṛśaṁ dīptam-anekavarṇaṁ,*
*vyāttānanaṁ dīptaviśāla-netram.*
*dṛṣṭvā hi tvāṁ pravyathitāntarātmā,*
*dhṛtiṁ na vindāmi śamaṁ ca viṣṇo. (11.24)*

Having seen your form (*nabhaḥ-spṛśam*) touching the sky, (*dīptam*) radiating (*aneka-varṇam*) many colours (*vyātta*) with a wide-open (*ānanam*) mouth [in the form of interstellar space] and (*dīpta-viśāla-netram*) large shining eyes [in the form of stars]; (*pravyathita+antarātmā*) I have become bewildered. (*dhṛtim*) My patience (*na vindāmi*) has lost, and (*na śama*) I feel restless, (*viṣṇo*) O All-Pervading One.

दंष्ट्राकरालानि च ते मुखानि दृष्ट्वैव कालानलसन्निभानि।
दिशो न जाने न लभे च शर्म प्रसीद देवेश जगन्निवास॥ ११.२५॥
*daṁṣṭrākarālāni ca te mukhāni,*
*dṛṣṭaiva kālānalasannibhāni.*
*diśo na jāne na labhe ca śarma,*
*prasīda deveśa jagannivāsa. (11.25)*

(*dṛṣṭvā+eva*) When I view (*te*) Your (*mukhāni*) mouths (*dansṭrā-karālani)* with devouring teeth (*sannibhāni)* resembling (*kālānala*) the blazing cosmic fire, I am baffled and (*na jāne)* have no knowledge (*diśaḥ*) of directions and (*na labhe*) find no (*śarma*) resort to rest upon myself. (*deveśa*) O God of gods! (*jagannivāsa*) O God of the universe! (*prasīda*) be pleased.

अमी च त्वां धृतराष्ट्रस्य पुत्राः सर्वे सहैवावनिपालसङ्घैः।
भीष्मो द्रोणः सूतपुत्रस्तथासौ सहास्मदीयैरपि योधमुख्यैः॥ ११.२६॥
वक्त्राणि ते त्वरमाणा विशन्ति दंष्ट्राकरालानि भयानकानि।
केचिद्विलग्ना दशनान्तरेषु संदृश्यन्ते चूर्णितैरुत्तमाङ्गैः॥ ११.२७॥
*amī ca tvāṁ dhṛtarāṣṭrasya putrāḥ,*
*sarve sahaivāva-nipālasaṅghaiḥ.*

*bhīṣmo droṇaḥ sūta putrastathāsau,*
*sahāsmadīyair api yodhamukhyaiḥ. (11.26)*
*vaktrāṇi te tvaramāṇā viśanti,*
*daṇṣṭrākarālāni bhayānakāni.*
*kecid vilagnā daśanāntareṣu,*
*sandṛśyante cūrṇitair uttmāṅgaiḥ. (11.27)*

I see the sons of Dhṛtarāṣṭra along with the hosts of kings, Bhīshma, Droṇa, and Karṇa, together with the chief warriors on our side entering speedily in your mouths appearing fearsome due to the devouring teeth. I can also see the crushed heads of some warriors sticking to your teeth.

यथा नदीनां बहवोऽम्बुवेगाः
समुद्रमेवाभिमुखा द्रवन्ति ।
तथा तवामी नरलोकवीरा
विशन्ति वक्त्राण्यभिविज्वलन्ति ॥ ११.२८ ॥
*yathā nadīnāṁ bahavo'mbuvegāḥ,*
*samudram evābhimukhā dravanti.*
*tathā tavāmī naralokavīrā,*
*viśanti vaktrāṇyabhijvalanti. (11.28)*

As many torrents of the rivers rush toward the ocean, similarly, those warriors of the mortal world are entering your blazing mouths.

यथा प्रदीप्तं ज्वलनं पतङ्गा
विशन्ति नाशाय समृद्धवेगाः ।
तथैव नाशाय विशन्ति लोकाः
तवापि वक्त्राणि समृद्धवेगाः ॥ ११.२९ ॥
*yathā pradīptaṁ jvalanaṁ pataṅgā,*
*viśanti nāśāya samṛddhavegāḥ.*
*tathaiva nāśāya viśanti lokās,*
*tavāpi vaktrāṇi samṛddhavegāḥ. (11.29)*

As moths rush with great speed into the blazing flame

for destruction, similarly, all these people are rapidly rushing into your mouth for destruction.

लेलिह्यसे ग्रसमान: समन्तात्
लोकान्समग्रान्वदनैर्ज्वलद्भिः ।
तेजोभिरापूर्य जगत्समग्रं
भासस्तवोग्राः प्रतपन्ति विष्णो ॥ ११.३० ॥

*lelihyase grasamānaḥ samantāt,*
*lokān samagrān vadanair jvaladbhiḥ.*
*tejobhirāpūrya jagatsamagraṁ,*
*bhāsastavogrāḥ pratapanti viṣṇo. (11.30)*

(*lelihyase*) You are licking up (*samagrān*) all (*lokān*) the worlds with Your (*jvaladbhiḥ*) flaming (*vadanaiḥ*) mouths, (*grasamānaḥ*) swallowing them (*samantāt*) from all sides. (*tava*) Your (*ugrāḥ*) powerful (*bhāsaḥ*) radiance (*pratapanti*) is burning (*samagram*) the entire (*jagat*) universe and (*āpūrya*) filling it (*tejobhīḥ*) with splendor, (*Viṣṇo*) O All-Pervading One.

आख्याहि मे को भवानुग्ररूपो
नमोऽस्तु ते देववर प्रसीद ।
विज्ञातुमिच्छामि भवन्तमाद्यं
न हि प्रजानामि तव प्रवृत्तिम् ॥ ११.३१ ॥

*ākhyāhi me ko bhavānugrarūpo,*
*namo'stu te devavara prasīda.*
*vijñātum icchāmi bhavantam ādyaṁ,*
*na hi prajānāmi tava pravṛttim. (11.31)*

Tell me, who are you in such a luminous form? My salutations to you, O best of gods, be pleased! I wish to understand you, the Primal Being, because I do not know your purpose.

श्री कृष्ण उवाच
Śri Krishna said

कालोऽस्मि लोकक्षयकृत्प्रवृद्धो

लोकान्समाहर्तुमिह प्रवृत्तः ।
ऋतेऽपि त्वां न भविष्यन्ति सर्वे
येऽवस्थिताः प्रत्यनीकेषु योधाः ॥ ११.३२ ॥

*kālo'smi loka-kṣayakṛt pravṛddho*
*lokān samāhartum iha pravṛttaḥ.*
*ṛte'pi tvāṁ na bhaviṣyanti sarve*
*ye'vasthitāḥ pratyanīkeṣu yodhāḥ. (11.32)*

*(kālaḥ asmi)* I am the death (*loka-kṣaya-kṛt*), the destroyer of worlds. I am here for the destruction of worlds. (*ṛte*) Even without (*tvām*) your participation in the war, (*sarve*) all the (*yodhāḥ*) warriors (*avasthitāḥ*) standing in (*pratyanīkeṣu*) the armies (*na bhaviṣyanti*) shall cease to exist.

Note: This śloka of Bhagavad Gitā ran through the mind of J. Robert Oppenheimer as he witnessed the first detonation of a nuclear weapon on July 16, 1945. He said, "Now I am become Death, the destroyer of worlds."

तस्मात्त्वमुत्तिष्ठ यशो लभस्व
जित्वा शत्रून् भुङ्क्ष्व राज्यं समृद्धम् ।
मयैवैते निहताः पूर्वमेव
निमित्तमात्रं भव सव्यसाचिन् ॥ ११.३३ ॥

*tasmāt tvam uttiṣṭha yaśo labhasva,*
*jitvā śatrūn bhuṅkṣva rājyaṁ samṛddham.*
*mayaivaite nihatāḥ pūrvameva,*
*nimitta-mātraṁ bhava savyasācin. (11.33)*

Therefore, you get up and take credit. Conquer your enemies and enjoy a prosperous kingdom. All these [warriors] already stand eliminated by the law of Brahman. You are only an instrument, O Savyasāchī Arjuna.

Note: Arjuna was called Savyasāchī as he had the

equal practice of operating arrows with the left hand as he did with his right hand.

द्रोणं च भीष्मं च जयद्रथं च
कर्णं तथान्यानपि योधवीरान्।
मया हतांस्त्वं जहि माव्यथिष्ठा
युध्यस्व जेतासि रणे सपत्नान्॥ ११.३४॥

*droṇaṁ ca bhīṣmaṁ ca jayadrathaṁ,*
*ca karṇaṁ tathānyānapi yodhavīrān.*
*mayā hatānstvaṁ jahi mā vyathiṣṭhā,*
*yudhyasva jetāsi raṇe sapatnān. (11.34)*

(*tvaṁ jahi*) Kill Droṇa, Bhīṣma, Jayadratha, Karṇa, and other great warriors (*mayā hatān*) who have already been killed by the law of Brahman. (*mā vyathiṣṭhāḥ*) Do not fear. (*jetāsi*) You will undoubtedly conquer (*sapatnān*) the enemies (*raṇe*) in the battle-field (*yudhyasva*); therefore, fight!

संजय उवाच
Sañjaya said

एतच्छ्रुत्वा वचनं केशवस्य
कृताञ्जलिर्वेपमानः किरीटी।
नमस्कृत्वा भूय एवाह कृष्णं
सगद्गदं भीतभीतः प्रणम्य॥ ११.३५॥

*etacchrutvā vacanaṁ keśavasya,*
*kṛtāñjalir-vepamānaḥ kirīṭī.*
*namaskṛtvā bhūya evāha kṛṣṇaṁ,*
*sagadgadaṁ bhīta-bhītaḥ praṇamya. (11.35)*

Sañjaya Said—(*śrutvā*) Having heard (*etat*) these (*vachanam*) words (*Keśvasya*) of Keśava; (*Kirīṭī*) the crowned Arjuna, (*vepamānaḥ*) trembling (*kṛtāñjaliḥ*) with folded hands, (*namaskṛtvā*) saluted (*bhitabhitaḥ*) with fear and having (*praṇamya*) bowed down and (*āha*) spoke (*bhūya*) again (*Kṛṣṇam*) to Krishna (*sa-gadgadam*) in a choked voice.

अर्जुन उवाच
Arjuna said

स्थाने हृषीकेश तव प्रकीर्त्या जगत्प्रहृष्यत्यनुरज्यते च।
रक्षांसि भीतानि दिशो द्रवन्ति सर्वे नमस्यन्ति च सिद्धसङ्घाः ॥ ११.३६ ॥
*sthāne hṛṣīkeśa tava prakīrtyā,*
*jagat prahṛṣyatyanurajyate ca.*
*rakṣānsi bhītāni diśo dravanti,*
*sarve namasyanti ca siddhasaṅghāḥ. (11.36)*

Arjuna said—(*Hṛṣīkeśa*) O Krishna, (*sthane*) now I can understand why the (*jagat*) world (*prahṛṣyati*) delights (*cha*) and (*anurajyate*) rejoices (*tava*) at your (*prakīrtyā*) name and fame. (*bhītāni*) Terrified (*rakṣānsi*) ultras (*dravanti*) flee (*diśaḥ*) in all directions. (*sarbe*) All (*siddha-saṅghāḥ*) groups of Siddhas (*namasyanti*) bow to you in respect.

Note: Siddha means born yogīs or experts of a particular field.

कस्माच्च ते न नमेरन्महात्मन् गरीयसे ब्रह्मणोऽप्यादिकर्त्रे।
अनन्त देवेश जगन्निवास त्वमक्षरं सदसत्तत्परं यत् ॥ ११.३७ ॥
*kasmācca te na nameran-mahātman,*
*garīyase bramaṇo'pyādikartre.*
*ananta deveśa jagannivāsa,*
*tvamakṣaraṁ sad-asat-tatparaṁ yat. (11.37)*

(*kasmāt cha*) Why should they not, (*mahātman*) O Universal Soul! (*nameran*) bow to you (*ādikartre*), who is the efficient cause of (*brahmaṇaḥ*) of Brahmā, the first progenitor? (*ananata*) O, infinite soul! (*deveśa*) O governor of divine souls, (*jagannivāsa*) the abode of the universe and (*akṣaraṁ*) imperishable, (*sat*) you are (*Sat*) present for enlightened yogīs, and (*Asat*) absent for ignorants. You are beyond the definition and ambit of 'sat' and 'asat', because a soul, time and prakṛti are also sat, but the Universal soul is beyond them.

Note: Having seen the Virāṭ form of Brahman through Śri Krishna, Arjuna also had the realisation of true form of Brahman.

त्वमादिदेवः पुरुषः पुराणः त्वमस्य विश्वस्य परं निधानम्।
वेत्तासि वेद्यं च परं च धाम त्वया ततं विश्वमनन्तरूप॥ ११.३८॥

*tvam ādidevaḥ puruṣaḥ purāṇaḥ,*
*tvam asya viśvasya paraṁ nidhānam.*
*vettāsi vedyaṁ ca paraṁ ca dhāma,*
*tvayā tataṁ viśvam-ananta rūpa. (11.38)*

(*ādidevaḥ*) You are the beginning of all, (*puruṣaḥ*) you pervade the entire creation, and (*purāṇaḥ*) you are eternal. (*tvam*) You are (*param*) the ultimate (*nidhānam*) shelter of (*asya viśvasya*) this world. (*vettāsi*) You are all-knowing and (*vedyam*) knowable (*cha*), and you are also (*param*) the supreme place. (*viśvam*) This world (*ananta-rūpam*) with infinite forms (*tatm*) is pervaded (*tvayā*) by you.

वायुर्यमोऽग्निर्वरुणः शशाङ्कः प्रजापतिस्त्वं प्रपितामहश्च।
नमो नमस्तेऽस्तु सहस्रकृत्वः पुनश्च भूयोऽपि नमो नमस्ते॥ ११.३९॥

*vāyur-yamo'gnir-varuṇaḥ śaśāṅkaḥ,*
*prajāpatis tvaṁ prapitāmahaśca.*
*namo namaste'stu sahasra-kṛtvaḥ,*
*punaśca bhūyo'pi namo namaste. (11.39)*

You are known as Vāyu, Yama, Agni, Varuṇa, Śaśāṅka, and Prajāpati. You are the father of Brahmā. Salutations to you a thousand times, and again and again salutations to you.

नमः पुरस्तादथ पृष्ठतस्ते नमोऽस्तु ते सर्वत एव सर्व।
अनन्तवीर्यामितविक्रमस्त्वं सर्वं समाप्नोषि ततोऽसि सर्वः॥ ११.४०॥

*namaḥ purastād atha pṛṣṭhataste,*
*namo'stu te sarvata eva sarva.*
*ananta-vīryāmit-avikramas-tvaṁ,*
*sarvaṁ samāpnoṣi tato'si sarvaḥ. (11.40)*

I salute you not only from my front side but also from my backside. O (*Sarva*) Existing everywhere, I salute you from all sides. (*tvam*) You have (ananta) infinite (vīrya) valour or energy and (*amita*) boundless (*vikrama*) prowess. (*samāpnoṣi*) You have pervaded (*sarvam*) everything. Therefore, you are known as 'Sarva'.

सखेति मत्वा प्रसभं यदुक्तं हे कृष्ण हे यादव हे सखेति।
अजानता महिमानं तवेदं मया प्रमादात्प्रणयेन वाऽपि॥ ११.४१॥
*sakheti matvā prasabhaṁ yad-uktaṁ,*
*he kṛṣṇa he yādava he sakheti.*
*ajānatā mahimānaṁ tavedaṁ,*
*mayā pramādāt praṇayena vāpi. (11.41)*

(*ajānatā*) Without knowing (tava) your (*mahimānam*) greatness (*matvā*), considering you as (*sakheti)* friend of the same age, out of affection or (*pramādāt*) carelessness, (*mayā*) I have (*yaduktam*) addressed (*tava*) you as O Krishna, O Yadava, O Friend of mine;

यच्चावहासार्थमसत्कृतोऽसि विहारशय्यासनभोजनेषु।
एकोऽथवाप्यच्युत तत्समक्षं तत्क्षामये त्वामहमप्रमेयम्॥ ११.४२॥
*yaccāvahāsārtham asatkṛto'si,*
*vihāraśayyāsanabhojaneṣu.*
*eko'thavāpyacyuta tat-samakṣaṁ,*
*tat kṣāmaye tvāmaham-aprameyam. (11.42)*

(*ahaṁ*) And if I might have *(asatkṛtaḥ asi)* disrespected (*tvām*) you *(avahāśārtham)* jokingly (*vihār*) while going for walks, (*śayyā)* sleep, (*āsana*) or sitting together, (*bhojaneṣu*) or at times of meals; (*ekaḥ*) alone, (*athavā api tat samakṣam*)) or in the company of others,

(*Achyuta*) O invincible! (*aprameyam*) beyond means of cognition, (*kśāmaye*) kindly forgive me (*tat*) for that.

पितासि लोकस्य चराचरस्य त्वमस्य पूज्यश्च गुरुर्गरीयान्।
न त्वत्समोऽस्त्यभ्यधिक: कुतोऽन्यो लोकत्रयेऽप्यप्रतिमप्रभाव॥ ११.४३॥
*pitāsi lokasya carācarasya,*
*tvam asya pūjyaśca gurur garīyān.*
*na tvatsamo'styabhyadhikaḥ kuto'nyo,*
*loka-traye'pyapratima-prabhāva. (11.43)*

You are the father of this animate and inanimate world. You are the greatest guru to be respected. No one is even equal to you; how can anyone greater than you be in the three worlds? O Krishna of incomparable power.

तस्मात्प्रणम्य प्रणिधाय कायं प्रसादये त्वामहमीशमीड्यम्।
पितेव पुत्रस्य सखेव सख्यु: प्रिय: प्रियायार्हसि देव सोढुम्॥ ११.४४॥
*tasmāt praṇamya praṇidhāya kāyaṁ,*
*prasādaye tvām-aham-iśam-īḍyam.*
*piteva putrasya sakheva sakhyuḥ,*
*priyaḥ priyāyārhasi deva soḍhum. (11.44)*

(*tasmāt*) Therefore, (*īḍyam*) O Respectable (*īśam*) Master, (*prasādaye*) I seek (*tvām*) your grace by (*praṇamya*) bowing down and (*praṇidhāya*) prostrating (*kāyam*) my body before you. (*Soḍhum*) Bear with me (*iva*) as (*pitā*) a father (*putrasy*) to his son, (*iva*) as (*sakhā*) a friend (*sakhyuḥ*) to a friend, and as a (*priya*) husband to (*priyāya*) his wife, (*Deva*) O Divine one.

अदृष्टपूर्वं हृषितोऽस्मि दृष्ट्वा भयेन च प्रव्यथितं मनो मे।
तदेव मे दर्शय देव रूपं प्रसीद देवेश जगन्निवास॥ ११.४५॥
*adṛṣṭapūrvaṁ hṛṣito'smi dṛṣṭvā,*
*bhayena ca pravyathitaṁ mano me.*
*tadeva me darśaya deva rūpaṁ,*
*prasīda deveśa jagannivāsa. (11.45)*

I am delighted by beholding that which has never been seen before, yet my mind is perturbed with fear. Show me the same normal form, O Deva, O Governor of enlightened persons, the Refuge of the World, be pleased!

किरीटिनं गदिनं चक्रहस्तं इच्छामि त्वां द्रष्टुमहं तथैव।
तेनैव रूपेण चतुर्भुजेन सहस्रबाहो भव विश्वमूर्ते॥ ११.४६॥
*kirīṭinaṁ gadinaṁ cakrahastam,*
*icchāmi tvāṁ draṣṭum ahaṁ tathaiva.*
*tenaiva rūpeṇa caturbhujena,*
*sahasrabāho bhava viśvamūrte. (11.46)*

(*aham*) I *(icchāmi)* wish (*draṣṭum*) to see (*tvām*) you (*kirīṭinam*) with a crown, (*gadinam*) holding mace and (*chakra-hastam*) discus in your hands (*tathā+iva*) as before. Let you come in *(tena+eva)*, the original form of (*chaturbhuja*) of a normal human being [two hands and two feet] from the present universal form O Sahasrabāhu! O Viśvamūrti!

Here, the term Chaturbhuja is generally translated by scholars as four-armed one, which is quite misleading. The actual meaning of Chaturbhuja is a cross-type of the human form. Here, it may also be pointed out that the symbol of the 'Cross' representing human beings originated in India in phrases like Chaturbhuja, used to symbolize human beings and transferred to foreign countries with the Indian immigrants in ancient times.

श्री कृष्ण उवाच
Śri Krishna said

मया प्रसन्नेन तवार्जुनेदं रूपं परं दर्शितमात्मयोगात्।
तेजोमयं विश्वमनन्तमाद्यं यन्मे त्वदन्येन न दृष्टपूर्वम्॥ ११.४७॥
*mayā prasannena tavārjunedaṁ,*
*rūpaṁ paraṁ darśitam ātmayogāt.*

*tejomayaṁ viśvam-anantam ādyaṁ,*
*yanme tvadanyena na dṛṣṭapūrvam. (11.47)*

Krishna said—O Arjuna, being pleased with you I have shown you, through My own yogic powers, this supreme form which is shining, universal, infinite, and primal one. It has never been seen by anyone else.

न वेद यज्ञाध्ययनैर्न दानैनर्न च क्रियाभिर्न तपोभिरुग्रैः।
एवं रूपः शक्य अहं नृलोके द्रष्टुं त्वदन्येन कुरुप्रवीर॥ ११.४८॥
*na veda-yajñādhyayanair-na dānira,*
*na ca kriyābhir na tapobhir ugraiḥ.*
*evaṁrūpaḥ śakya ahaṁ nṛloke,*
*drastuṁ tvad anyena kuru-pravīra. (11.48)*

Neither by study of the Vedas, nor by yajña, nor by charity, nor by rituals, nor by severe austerities, this universal form of a yogī like me who has merged in Brahman can be seen in this human world by none other than you, O Best of the Kurus.

मा ते व्यथा मा च विमूढभावो दृष्ट्वा रूपं घोरमीदृङ्ममेदम्।
व्यपेतभीः प्रीतमनाः पुनस्त्वं तदेव मे रूपमिदं प्रपश्य॥ ११.४९॥
*mā te vyathā mā ca vimūḍha-bhāvo,*
*dṛṣṭvā rūpaṁ ghoram-īdṛṅmamedam.*
*vyapeta bhīḥ prītamanāḥ punastvaṁ,*
*tadeva me rūpam idaṁ prapaśya. (11.49)*

Do not be perturbed and deluded by seeing this type of terrible form. (*vyapeta-bhīḥ*) With fearless and (*prītamanāḥ*) cheerful mind, (*punaḥ*) again (*prapaśya*) behold (*me*) my (*tat+eva*) same original (*rūpam*) form.

संजय उवाच
Sañjaya said
इत्यर्जुनं वासुदेवस्तथोक्त्वा स्वकं रूपं दर्शयामास भूयः।
आश्वासयामास च भीतमेनं भूत्वा पुनः सौम्यवपुर्महात्मा॥ ११.५०॥
*ityarjunaṁ vāsudevas tathoktvā,*

*svakaṁ rūpaṁ darśayāmāsa bhūyaḥ.*
*āśvāsayāmāsa ca bhītam enaṁ bhūtvā punaḥ,*
*saumya-vapur mahātmā. (11.50)*

Sañjaya said— O King, son of Vasudeva [Śri Krishna], having said this to Arjuna, showed him [Arjuna] again his original form. Then Mahātmā Krishna consoled terrified Arjuna (*saumya vapuḥ*) in a gentlemanly way.

अर्जुन उवाच
Arjuna said

दृष्ट्वेदं मानुषं रूपं तव सौम्यं जनार्दन।
इदानीमस्मि संवृत्तः सचेताः प्रकृतिं गतः॥ ११.५१॥
*dṛṣṭavedaṁ mānuṣaṁ rūpaṁ tava saumyaṁ janārdana,*
*idānīm-asmi saṁvṛttaḥ sacetāḥ prakṛtiṁ gataḥ. (11.51)*

Arjuna said— O Krishna, seeing this original gentle human form of yours, I have now (*saṁvṛttaḥ*) become (*sachetāḥ*) composed and (*prakṛtiṁ gataḥ*) I am normal again.

श्री कृष्ण उवाच
Śri Krishna said

सुदुर्दर्शमिदं रूपं दृष्टवानसि यन्मम।
देवा अप्यस्य रूपस्य नित्यं दर्शनकाङ्क्षिणः॥ ११.५२॥
*sudurdarśam idaṁ rūpaṁ dṛṣṭvān asi yan-mama,*
*devā apyasya rūpasya nityaṁ darśana-kāṅkṣiṇaḥ. (11.52)*

Śri Krishna said—Whatever form of Brahman you have seen is very very difficult to be seen. Even Devas [yogis endowed with divine powers] crave to see this form.

नाहं वेदैर्न तपसा न दानेन न चेज्यया।
शक्य एवंविधो द्रष्टुं दृष्टवानसि मां यथा॥ ११.५३॥
*nāhaṁ vedairna tapasā na dānena cejyayā,*
*śakya evaṁvidho draṣṭuṁ dṛṣṭavān asi māṁ yathā. (11.53)*

Neither by the study of the Vedas, nor by austerity, nor by charity, nor by ritual, can this form of Brahman (yogī merged in Brahman) be seen as you have seen.

भक्त्या त्वनन्यया शक्य अहमेवंविधोऽर्जुन।
ज्ञातुं द्रष्टुं च तत्वेन प्रवेष्टुं च परंतप॥ ११.५४॥
*bhaktyā tvananyayā śakya aham evaṁvidho'rjuna,*
*jñātuṁ draṣṭuṁ ca tattvena praveṣṭuṁ ca parantapa. (11.54)*

However, through (*ananyayā*) one-pointed (*bhaktyā*) samādhi alone, (*evam-vidhaḥ*) this universalized form (*aham*) of me or form of Brahman (*draṣṭum*) can be seen, (*jñātum*) known (*tatvena*) in essence, (*cha*) and (*praveṣṭum*) attained in mokṣa, (*Parantapaḥ*) O destroyer of enemies.

मत्कर्मकृन्मत्परमो मद्भक्तः सङ्गवर्जितः।
निर्वैरः सर्वभूतेषु यः स मामेति पाण्डव॥ ११.५५॥
*mat-karma-kṛn-mat-paramo mad-bhaktaḥ saṅga-varjitaḥ,*
*nirvairaḥ sarva-bhūteṣu yaḥ sa māmeti pāṇḍava. (11.55)*

Son of Pāṇḍu! The one who does all works according to my advice, who follows my instructions devotedly, who has no attachment and is free from enmity towards other beings, he attains Brahman as per me [following the path shown by me]. (See also 8.22)

ॐ तत्सदिति श्रीमद् भगवद्गीतासूपनिषत्सु ब्रह्मविद्यायां योगशास्त्रे श्रीकृष्णार्जुनसंवादे विश्वरूपदर्शनयोगोनाम एकादशोऽध्यायः॥११॥

Here ends the eleventh chapter, named Vibhūti yoga in the *Bhagvadgitā* dealing with the Brahmavidyā as propounded in the Upaniṣad and Yogaśāstra in the form of dialogue between Śri Krishna and Arjuna.

# अथ द्वादशोऽध्याय:

## भक्तियोग:

# Chapter 12

[Path of Devotion]

In this chapter, Śri Krishna tells Arjuna about the difference between yogīs who want to comprehend God on their own in samādhi without any help from an expert guide or Guru and those who seek the guidance of Śri Krishna in comprehending God. According to Śri Krishna, comprehending God at one's own level without guidance from an expert Guru is very difficult. The Guru makes it very easy. At the same time, Śri Krishna narrates here the qualifications of a seeker who can be guided by him and who is dear to him.

अर्जुन उवाच

Arjuna said

एवं सततयुक्ता ये भक्तास्त्वां पर्युपासते।
ये चाप्यक्षरमव्यक्तं तेषां के योगवित्तमा: ॥ १२.१ ॥

*evaṁ satata-yuktā ye bhaktās tvāṁ paryupāsate,*
*ye cāpyakṣaram avyaktaṁ teṣāṁ ke yoga-vittamāḥ. (12.1)*

Arjuna said— (*evam*) Thus (*ye*) those (*satata-yuktāḥ*) constantly (*bhaktāḥ*) devoted followers of yours (*tvāṁ pari+upāsate*) who follow your instructions by all means (*cha*) and (*ye*) those who follow the teachings of the (*akṣaram*) eternal (avyaktam) unmanifest (the formless) Brahman under samādhi at their own without your guidance, (*ke teṣām*) which of these is said to be the (*yogavittamāḥ*) best acquainted with yoga?

श्री कृष्ण उवाच

Śri Krishna said

मय्यावेश्य मनो ये मां नित्ययुक्ता उपासते ।
श्रद्धया परयोपेताः ते मे युक्ततमा मताः ॥ १२.२ ॥

*mayyāveśya mano ye māṁ nityayuktā upāsate,*
*śraddhayā parayopetās te me yuktatamā matāḥ. (12.2)*

Śri Krishna said— Those followers of mine *(nitya-yuktāḥ mām)* who follow my instructions *(parayā)* with supreme *(śradhayā upetāḥ)* faith *(mayi āveśya manaḥ)* by concentrating their mind in my instructions, *(me)* I (*matāḥ*) consider (*te*) them *(yukta-tamāḥ)* to be the best acquainted with yoga. (See also 6.47)

ये त्वक्षरमनिर्देश्यं अव्यक्तं पर्युपासते ।
सर्वत्रगमचिंत्यं च कूटस्थं अचलं ध्रुवम् ॥ १२.३ ॥

*ye tvakṣaram anirdeśyam avyaktaṁ paryupāsate,*
*Sarvatra-gam acintyañ ca kūṭastham acalan dhruvam. (12.3)*

(*tu*) But (*ye*) those (*pari+upāsate*) who meditate on their own upon (*akṣaram*) the imperishable, (*anirdeśyam*) the undefinable, (*avyaktam*) the unmanifest, (*sarvatragam*) the omnipresent, (*chintyam*) the unthinkable, (*kuṭastham*) the unchanging, (*achalam*) the immovable, and (*dhruvam*) the eternal Brahman;

संनियम्येन्द्रियग्रामं सर्वत्र समबुद्धयः ।
ते प्राप्नुवन्ति मामेव सर्वभूतहिते रताः ॥ १२.४ ॥

*sanniyamyendriya-grāmaṁ sarvatra sama-buddhayaḥ,*
*te prāpnuvanti māmeva sarvabhūta-hite ratāḥ. (12.4)*

(*saṁniyamya*) Restraining (*indriya-grāmam*) all the senses, (*samabuddhyaḥ*) even-minded (*sarvatra*) under all circumstances, (*sarva-bhūta-hite-ratāḥ*) engaged in the welfare of all creatures, (*te*) they (*prāpanuvanti*) (*eva*) surely attain (*mām*) Brahman.

This means there is no difference between the two, as my [Śri Krishna's] instructions also lead to samādhi.

क्लेशोऽधिकतरस्तेषां अव्यक्तासक्तचेतसाम् ॥
अव्यक्ता हि गतिर्दुःखं देहवद्भिरवाप्यते ॥ १२.५ ॥
*kleṣo'dhikataras teṣāṁ avyaktāsakta-cetasām,*
*avyaktā hi gatir duḥkhaṁ dehavadbhir avāpyate. (12.5)*

The only difference between the two is that those (*avyakta-āsakta-chetasām*) who meditate upon the formless Brahman on their own (*kleśaḥ adhikataraḥ teṣām*) get Him with difficulty compared to those who follow me. (*hi*) Because (*gatiḥ*) the comprehension of (*avyakta)* the unmanifest (*dehavadbhiḥ*) by an average embodied human being (*duḥkham*) is very difficult until and unless some expert guides him/her.

Meaning thereby— self-comprehension is difficult, whereas comprehension with the help of an expert Guru is very easy.

ये तु सर्वाणि कर्माणि मयि संन्यस्य मत्परः ।
अनन्येनैव योगेन मां ध्यायन्त उपासते ॥ १२.६ ॥
*ye tu sarvāṇi karmāṇi mayi sannyasya matparaḥ,*
*ananyenaiva yogena māṁ dhyāyanta upāsate. (12.6)*

But, (ye) to those who (*saṁnyasya*) leave (*sarvāṇi karmāṇi*) all their actions (*mayi*) unto me (*matparaḥ*) having complete faith in me [what I say], and (*dhyāyanti*) meditate upon (*mām*) Almighty Brahman (*ananyena+eva*) with the unique method of (*yogena*) yoga instructed by me.

तेषामहं समुद्धर्ता मृत्युसंसारसागरात् ।
भवामि न चिरात्पार्थ मय्यावेशितचेतसाम् ॥ १२.७ ॥
*teṣām ahaṁ samuddhartā mṛtyu-sansāra-sāgarāt,*
*bhavāmi na cirāt pārtha mayyāveśita-cetasām. (12.7)*

(*ahaṁ*) I (*bhavāmi*) become (*na chirāt*) instantly the cause for (*teṣām*) their (*samuddhartā*) deliverance (*mṛtyu-sansāra-sāgarāt*) from the birth and death cycle of this mundane world, (*mayi-āveśita-chetasām*) who have expressed their complete faith in me, (Pārtha!) O Son of Pṛthā. (12.7)

मय्येव मन आधत्स्व मयि बुद्धिं निवेशय।
निवसिष्यसि मय्येव अत ऊर्ध्वं न संशय: ॥ १२.८ ॥
*mayyeva mana ādhatsva mayi buddhiṁ niveśaya,*
*nivasiṣyasi mayyeva ata ūrdhvaṁ na sañśayaḥ. (12.8)*

Therefore, (*ādhatsva*) focus (*mana*) your mind (*mayi+eva*) on what I say and let (*buddhim*) your intellect (*niveśaya*) fix upon (*mayi*) my instructions. As such, (*nivasiṣyasi*) you will attain (*mayi+eva*) the same status as me, there is (*na*) no (*sañśaya*) doubt (*ata ūrdhvam*) about it.

अथचित्तं समाधातुं न शक्नोषि मयि स्थिरम्।
अभ्यासयोगेन ततो मामिच्छाप्तुं धनंजय ॥ १२.९ ॥
*atha cittaṁ samādhātuṁ na śaknoṣi mayi sthiram.*
*abhyāsayogena tato mām icchāptuṁ dhanañjaya. (12.9)*

(*atha*) If (*na śaknoṣi*) you are unable (*sthiram samādhātum*) to concentrate (*chittam*) your mind (*mayi*) upon my instructions, (*tataḥ*) then try to (*āptum*) attain (*mām*) Brahman (*abhyāsa yogena*) with the help of the practice of yoga (*Dhanañjaya*!) O Dhanañjaya.

अभ्यासेऽप्यसमर्थोऽसि मत्कर्मपरमो भव।
मदर्थमपि कर्माणि कुर्वन्सिद्धिमवाप्स्यसि ॥ १२.१० ॥
*abhyāse'pyasamartho'si mat-karma-paramo bhava,*
*Madartham api karmāṇi kurvan siddhim avāpsyasi. (12.10)*

(*api*) If (*asi*) you are (*asamarthaḥ*) unable (*abhyāse*) even to do the practice of yoga (*matkarma paramaḥ bhava*), then try to take other actions like jñāna yoga, karma yoga suitable for attaining Brahman. (*api*) If you (*karmāṇi kurvan*) do actions (*madartham*) suitable to attain Brahman, (*avāpsyasi*) you can also attain (*siddhi*) success in realisation of Brahman. (See also 9.27, 18.46)

अथैतदप्यशक्तोऽसि कर्तुंमद्योगमाश्रितः।
सर्वकर्मफलत्यागं ततः कुरु यतात्मवान्॥ १२.११॥
*athaitad apyaśakto'si kartuṁ mad-yogam āśritaḥ.*
*sarva-karma-phala-tyāgaṁ tataḥ kuru yatātmavān. (12.11)*

(*atha*) If *(asi)* you are (*aśaktaḥ*) unable (*kartum*) to take *(udyogam)* other actions (*āśritaḥ*) suitable for the realisation of Brahman, (*tataḥ*), then (*kuru sarva-karma-phala-tyāgaḥ*) do all such acts as do not require fruits or involve self-interest (*yata+ātmavān*) exercising control over your mind.

श्रेयो हि ज्ञानमभ्यासाज्ज्ञानाद्ध्यानं विशिष्यते।
ध्यानात्कर्मफलत्यागस्त्यागाच्छांतिरनन्तरम्॥ १२.१२॥
*śreyo hi jñānam abhyāsāj jnānād dhyānaṁ viśiṣyate,*
*dhyānāt karma-phala-tyāgas tyāgācchāntir anantaram.(12.12)*

Correct knowledge is better than wrong practice, meditation is better than knowledge, renunciation of the fruit of karmas is better than meditation, peace immediately follows the renunciation [the attachment to the fruit of karmas]. [See more on renunciation in Chapter 18].

अद्वेष्टा सर्वभूतानां मैत्रः करुण एव च।
निर्ममो निरहङ्कारः समदुःखसुखः क्षमी॥ १२.१३॥
*adveṣṭā sarva-bhūtānāṁ maitraḥ karuṇa eva ca,*
*nirmamo nirahaṅkāraḥ samaduḥkhasukhaḥ kṣamī. (12.13)*

One who does not hate any creature, who is friendly and compassionate, free from [the notion of] "I" and "my", even-minded in pain and pleasure, forgiving; and

संतुष्टः सततं योगी यतात्मा दृढनिश्चयः।
मय्यर्पितमनोबुद्धिर्यो मद्भक्तः स मे प्रियः॥ १२.१४॥
*santuṣṭaḥ satataṁ yogī yatātmā dṛḍhaniścayaḥ,*
*Mayyarpita-mano-buddhir yo madbhaktaḥ sa me priyaḥ.*

Who is ever content, (*satatam yogī*) who practices yoga continuously, (*yatātmā*) who has subdued the mind, (*dṛḍha-niśchayaḥ*) whose resolve is firm, (*yaḥ*) who has (*arpita*) fixed (*manaḥ*) his mind (*buddhiḥ*) and intellect (*mayi*) upon my advice, (*madbhaktaḥ*) who is my follower; (*saḥ me priyaḥ*) I like him to give advice.

यस्मान्नोद्विजते लोको लोकान्नोद्विजते च यः।
हर्षामर्षभयोद्वेगैर्मुक्तो यः स च मे प्रियः॥ १२.१५॥
*yasmān nodvijate loko lokān nodvijate ca yaḥ,*
*harṣāmarṣa-bhayod-vegair mukto yaḥ sa ca me priyaḥ.*

(*yasmāt*) The one by whom (*lokaḥ*) people are (*na*) not (*udvijate*) agitated, (*cha*) and (*yaḥ*) who (*na*) is not (*udvijate*) agitated (*lokāt*) by people; (*yah*) who is (*muktaḥ*) free from (*harṣa*) joy, (*āmarṣa*) envy, (*bhaya*) fear, and (*udvega*) anxiety; (*saḥ*) he is (*priyaḥ*) liked by (me) me.

अनपेक्षः शुचिर्दक्ष उदासीनो गतव्यथः।
सर्वारम्भपरित्यागी यो मद्भक्तः स मे प्रियः॥ १२.१६॥
*anapekṣaḥ śucir dakṣa udāsīno gata-vyathaḥ,*
*sarvārambha-parityāgī yo madbhaktaḥ sa me priyaḥ. (12.16)*

(*yaḥ*) One who is (*anapekṣaḥ*) free from expectations; (*śuchi*) who is pure, (*dakṣaḥ*) wise, (*udāsīnaḥ*) impartial, and (*gatavyathaḥ*) free from anxiety; (*parityāgī*) who has renounced (*sarvārambhaḥ*) all undertakings, (*madbhaktaḥ*) who trusts me, (*saḥ*) he is (*priyaḥ*) liked (*me*) by me.

यो न हृष्यति न द्वेष्टि न शोचति न काङ्क्षति।
शुभाशुभपरित्यागी भक्तिमान्यः स मे प्रियः ॥ १२.१७ ॥
*yo na hṛṣyati na dveṣṭi na śocati na kāṅkṣati,*
*śubhāśubha-parityāgī bhaktimān yaḥ sa me priyaḥ. (12.17)*

One who neither rejoices nor grieves, neither mourns the loss nor dislikes, who is unconcerned for both the good and the bad, and who is trustworthy, I like such a person.

समः शत्रौ च मित्रे च तथा मानापमानयोः।
शीतोष्णसुखदुःखेषु समः सङ्गविवर्जितः ॥ १२.१८ ॥
*samaḥ śatrau ca mitre ca tathā mānāpamānayoḥ,*
*śītoṣṇa-sukha-duḥkheṣu samaḥ saṅga-vivarjitaḥ*
*imān yaḥ sa me priyaḥ. (12.18)*

The one who is indifferent to a friend or a foe, honour or disgrace, heat or cold, pleasure or pain; who is free from attachment;

तुल्यनिन्दास्तुतिर्मौनी संतुष्टो येन केनचित्।
अनिकेतः स्थिरमतिर्भक्तिमान्मे प्रियो नरः ॥ १२.१९ ॥
*tulya-nindā-stutir maunī santuṣṭo yena kenacit,*
*aniketaḥ sthira-matir bhaktimān me priyo naraḥ. (12.19)*

The one who is indifferent or silent in censure or praise, content with anything, unattached to a place [country or house], equanimous, and full of trust; I like that person.

ये तु धर्म्यामृतमिदं यथोक्तं पर्युपासते।
श्रद्दधाना मत्परमा भक्तस्तेऽतीव मे प्रियाः ॥ १२.२० ॥
*ye tu dharmyāmṛtam idaṁ yathoktaṁ paryupāsate,*
*śraddadhānā matparamā bhaktāste'tīva me priyāḥ. (12.20)*

Those who sincerely try to develop the above-mentioned immortal virtues, who follow what I say, who have a positive attitude and complete faith in me, are very much liked by me.

ॐ तत्सदिति श्रीमद् भगवद्गीतासूपनिषत्सु ब्रह्मविद्यायां योगशास्त्रे श्रीकृष्णार्जुनसंवादे भक्तियोगोनाम द्वादशोऽध्याय: ॥१२ ॥

Here ends the 12th chapter named, Bhakti yoga in the *Bhagvadgitā* dealing with the Brahmavidyā as propounded in the Upaniṣad and Yogaśāstra in the form of dialogue between Śri Krishna and Arjuna.

# अथ त्रयोदशोऽध्यायः

## क्षेत्रक्षेत्रज्ञविभागयोगः

# Chapter 13

[Distinction between Body and Soul]

In this chapter, Śri Krishna tells Arjuna about the difference between kṣetra and kṣetrajña. The concept of kṣetra and kṣetrajña is nothing else but the Sāṁkhya concept of Prakṛti [body] and Puruṣa [soul]. Prakṛti [body] is like a kṣetra [field or house] where seeds can be sown. The soul is the kṣetrajña [knower of its body]. The soul is the owner of the body. An owner is supposed to know his/her house. If the owner does not know his/her house, He/she cannot use his/her house properly.

अर्जुन उवाच

Arjuna said

प्रकृतिं पुरुषं चैव क्षेत्रं क्षेत्रज्ञमेव च।
एतद्वेदितुमिच्छामि ज्ञानं ज्ञेयं च केवलम्॥ १३.१॥
*prakṛtiṁnpuruṣaṁ caiva kṣetraṁ kṣetrajñamevaca,*
*etatveditumicchāmi jñānaṁ jñeyaṁ ca keśava. (13.01)*

Arjuna said— I want to know about the prakṛti or keṣtra [field] and puruṣa or kṣetrajña [owner]; jñāna [knowledge] and jñeya [knowable].

श्री कृष्ण उवाच

Śri Krisna Said

इदं शरीरं कौन्तेय क्षेत्रमित्यभिधीयते।
एतद्यो वेत्ति तं प्राहुः क्षेत्रज्ञ इति तद्विदः॥ १३.२॥
*idaṁ śarīraṁ kāunteya kṣetram ityabhidhīyate,*
*etad yo vetti taṁ prāhuḥ kṣetrajña iti tadvidaḥ. (13.02)*

Śri Krishna said— O son of Kunti, this physical body may be called keṣtra. One who internalizes it is called the keṣtrajña [owner], the knower of this body.

Note: Just as the seeds sown in a field bear fruits in time according to their nature [information they contain], similarly, the seeds of karmic sanskāras sown in the body bear fruits in time.

क्षेत्रज्ञं चापि मां विद्धि सर्वक्षेत्रेषु भारत।
क्षेत्रक्षेत्रज्ञयोर्ज्ञानं यत्तज्ज्ञानं मतं मम॥ १३.३॥
*kṣetrajñaṁ cāpi māṁ viddhi sarvakṣetreṣu bhārata,*
*kṣetra-kṣetrajñayorjñānaṁ yattajjñānaṁ mataṁ mama.*

Śri Krishna said— (*mām*) This soul should be (*viddhi*) known as the keṣtrajña [knower of the body] (*sarva-kṣetreṣu*) for all the physical bodies, (*Bhārata*) O descendent of Bharatas. (*mama*) In my (*matam*) opinion, (*jñānam*) knowing the difference between (*keṣtra*) body and (*keṣtrajña*) soul is the real knowledge.

तत्क्षेत्रं यच्च यादृक् यद्विकारि यतश्च यत्।
स च यो यत्प्रभावश्च तत्समासेन मे शृणु॥ १३.४॥
*tat kṣetraṁ yacca yādṛk ca yadvikāri yataśca yat,*
*sa ca yo yatprabhāvaś ca tat samāsena me śṛṇu. (13.04)*

(*tat yachcha*) What is the physical body? (*yādṛk*) What is it like? (*yadvikārī*) What are its transformations? (*yataścha*) Whence it comes from? (*saḥ cha yaḥ*) Who is that soul? And (*yat*) what are (*prabhāvaḥ cha*) its powers? (*śṛṇū*) Hear (*tat*) all these (*samāsena*) briefly from (*me*) me.

ऋषिभिर्बहुधा गीतं छन्दोभिर्विविधैः पृथक्।
ब्रह्मसूत्रपदैश्चैव हेतुमद्भिर्विनिश्चितैः॥ १३.५॥
*ṛṣibhir-bahudhā gītaṁ chandobhirvividhaiḥ pṛthak,*
*brahma-sūtrapadaiś caiva hetumadbhirviniścitaiḥ. (13.05)*

This all has been described variously by seers in different Vedic hymns. This subject has also been dealt with the in a (*viniśchitaiḥ*) decisive and (*hetumadbhiḥ*) convincing manner in the verses of the Brahmasūtra.

महाभूतान्यहंकारो बुद्धिरव्यक्तमेव च।
इन्द्रियाणि दशैकं च पंच चेन्द्रियगोचरा: ॥ १३.६ ॥
*mahā-bhūtānyahankāro buddhir-avyaktameva ca,*
*indriyāṇi daśāikaṁ ca pañca cendriya-gocarāḥ. (13.06)*

The five mahābhūtas [evolutes], ahaṅkāra, the intellect, the unmanifest prakṛti [inactive energy], ten senses, mind, and five sensory objects; (See also 7.4)

इच्छा द्वेष: सुखं दु:खं संघातश्चेतना धृति:।
एतत्क्षेत्रं समासेन सविकारमुदाहृतम् ॥ १३.७ ॥
*icchā dveṣaḥ sukhaṁ duḥkhaṁ saṅghātaścetanā dhṛtiḥ,*
*etat kṣetraṁ samāsena savikāramudāhṛtam. (13.07)*

Desire, hatred, pleasure, pain, (*saṅghātaḥ*) physical body, (*chetanā*) consciousness, and (*dhṛti*) resolve— all these (*samāsena*) collectively are described as kṣetra [field] with its transformations.

अमानित्वमदम्भित्वमहिंसा क्षान्तिरार्जवम्।
आचार्योपासनं शौचं स्थैर्यमात्मविनिग्रह: ॥ १३.८ ॥
*amānitvam adambhitvam ahinsā kṣāntir ārjavam,*
*ācāryopāsanaṁ śaucaṁ sthairyam ātma-vinigrahaḥ. (13.8)*

(*amānitvam*) Humility [absence of self-worshipfulness], (*adambhitvam*) modesty [absence of self-glorification], (*ahinsā*) non-violence [non-harmfulness], (*kśāntiḥ*) forbearance [attitude of accommodation], (*ārjavam*) straight-forwardness, (*upāsanam*) service (*āchārya*) to Gurus, (*śaucham*) internal and external cleanliness [cleanliness of thought, word, and deed], (*sthairyam*) steadfastness, [ātma-vinigrahaḥ] self-control;

इन्द्रियार्थेषु वैराग्यमनहंकार एव च।

जन्ममृत्युजराव्याधिदुःखदोषानुदर्शनम् ॥ १३.९ ॥
*indriyārtheṣu vairāgyam-anahaṁkāra eva ca,*
*janma-mṛtyu-jarā-vyādhi-duḥkha-doṣānudarśanam. (13.9)*

(*vairāgyam*) State of dispassion (*indriyārtheṣu*) towards the objects of sense organs or the absence of compelling drive for worldly pleasures and possessions, (*anahṅkāram*) absence of ahaṅkāra [notion of I, my, me], (*anudarśanam*) seeking (*duḥkha*) agony, suffering (*doṣa*) and problems or harms inherent in (*janma*) birth, (*jarā*) old age, (*vyādhi*) disease, and (*mṛtyu*) death.

असक्तिरनभिष्वङ्गः पुत्रदारगृहादिषु ।
नित्यं च समचित्तत्वमिष्टानिष्टोपपत्तिषु ॥ १३.१० ॥
*asaktir-anabhiṣvaṅgaḥ putradāra-gṛhādiṣu,*
*nityaṁ ca samacittatvamiṣt-āniṣṭopapattiṣu. (13.10)*

(*āsaktiḥ*) Detachment, (*anabhiṣaṅgaḥ*) non-fondness with (*putra*) progeny, (*dāra*) wife, and (*gṛhādiṣu*) home; (*nityam*) unfailing (*samachittatvam*) equanimity (*upapattiṣu*) upon attainment of the (*iṣṭa*) desirable and the (*aniṣṭa*) undesirable; and

मयि चानन्ययोगेन भक्तिरव्यभिचारिणी ।
विविक्तदेशसेवित्वमरतिर्जनसंसदि ॥ १३.११ ॥
*mayi cānanya-yogena bhaktir avyabhicāriṇī,*
*Vivikta-deśa-sevitvam aratirjana-sansadi. (13.11)*

(*avyabhichāriṇī*) Unswerving (*bhaktiḥ*) faith (*mayī*) in my words (*ananya-yogena*) with complete devotion, (*sevitvam*) love (*vivikta-deśa*) for solitude, (*aratiḥ*) distaste for (*jana-sansadi*) social gatherings.

अध्यात्मज्ञाननित्यत्वं तत्त्वज्ञानार्थदर्शनम् ।
एतज्ज्ञानमिति प्रोक्तमज्ञानं यदतोऽन्यथा ॥ १३.१२ ॥
*adhyātma-jñāna-nityatvaṁ tattva-jñānārtha-darśanam,*
*etajjñānam iti proktam-ajñānaṁ yadato'nyathā. (13.12)*

(*nityatvam*) Constant absorption (*adhyātma-jñāna*) into spirituality (*darśanam*), seeking the (*tattva-jñāna*) essential knowledge, i.e. mokṣa or realisation of Brahman. (*etat*) This is (*proktam*) called (*jñānam*) knowledge; (*yad ataḥ*) contrary to it is ajñāna or avidyā.

ज्ञेयं यत्तत्प्रवक्ष्यामि यज्ज्ञात्वाऽमृतमश्नुते ।
अनादिमत्परं ब्रह्म न सत्तन्नासदुच्यते ॥ १३.१३ ॥
*jñeyaṁ yat-tat-pravakṣyāmi yajjñātvāmṛtam aśnute,*
*anādimat paraṁ brahma na sattannāsaducyate. (13.13)*

(*pravakṣyāmi*) I shall say (*yat*) what is (*jñeyam*) worth knowing, (*jñātvā*) by knowing (*yat*) that (*aśnute*) one attains (*amṛitam*) immortality. (*Param Brahma*) The Supreme Brahman is (*anādimat*) beginning-less. (*uchyate*) He is said to be (*na*) neither sat [because His presence is not known] nor asat [His existence cannot be denied, because he is indescribable] (See also 9.19).

सर्वत: पाणिपादं तत्सर्वतोऽक्षिशिरोमुखम् ।
सर्वत: श्रुतिमल्लोके सर्वमावृत्य तिष्ठति ॥ १३.१४ ॥
*sarvataḥ pāṇipādaṁ tat sarvato'kṣiśiromukham,*
*sarvataḥ śrutimalloke sarvam āvṛtya tiṣṭhati. (13.14)*

He has hands and feet everywhere. He has eyes, head, and face about. He has ears everywhere. He is sitting, having pervaded everything.

Note: In the above lines, the all-pervasiveness of God has been described. That is only a style of telling all-pervasiveness and never means that the formless God has many hands, feet, or eyes.

सर्वेन्द्रियगुणाभासं सर्वेन्द्रियविवर्जितम् ।
असक्तं सर्वभृच्चैव निर्गुणं गुणभोक्तृ च ॥ १३.१५ ॥
*sarvendriya-guṇābhāsaṁ sarvendriya-vivarjitam,*
*asaktaṁ sarva-bhṛccaiva nirguṇaṁ guṇabhoktṛ ca. (13.15)*

He is the (*ābhāsam*) perceiver of (*sarva-indriya*) all sensory (*guṇa*) objects (*sarva+indriya-vivarjitam*) without the sense organs. He is (*asaktam*) unattached, (*cha+eva*) yet (*sarva-bhṛt*) the sustainer of all. Although He is (*nirguṇam*) devoid of the physical body and bad qualities, (*cha*) yet He (*guṇa-bhoktṛ*) is endowed with all good qualities.

Note: Brahman is endowed with the following qualities. He is the All truth, All-knowing, All beatitude, Incorporeal, Almighty, Just, Merciful, Unbegotten, Beginningless, Incomparable, the Support and Master of all, All-pervading, Omniscient, Imperishable, Immortal, Fearless, Eternal, Holy and Cause of the Universe.

बहिरन्तश्च भूतानामचरं चरमेव च।
सूक्ष्मत्वात्तदविज्ञेयं दूरस्थं चान्तिके च तत्॥ १३.१६॥
*bahir antaśca bhūtānām acaraṁ carameva ca,*
*sūkṣmatvāt-tadavijñeyaṁ dūrasthaṁ cāntike ca tat. (13.16)*

He is inside and outside of all— animates and inanimates. He is (*avijñeyam*) incomprehensible (*sūkṣmatvāt*) because of His subtlety. He is very near [because of His All pervasiveness] and far away [because of His incomprehensibility].

अविभक्तं च भूतेषु विभक्तमिव च स्थितम्।
भूतभर्तृ च तज्ज्ञेयं ग्रसिष्णु प्रभविष्णु च॥ १३.१७॥
*avibhaktaṁ ca bhūteṣu vibhaktam iva ca sthitam,*
*bhūtabhartṛ ca tajjñeyaṁ grasiṣṇu prabhaviṣṇu ca. (13.17)*

Undivided [because of All pervasiveness] yet appears as if divided in beings [because of their different bodies); (*tat+jñeyam*) He should be known as the (*bhūtabhatṛt*) sustainer, (*grasiṣṇu*) destroyer, and (*prabhaviṣṇu*) creator of (all) beings.

ज्योतिषामपि तज्ज्योतिस्तमसः परमुच्यते।
ज्ञानं ज्ञेयं ज्ञानगम्यं हृदि सर्वस्य विष्ठितम्॥ १३.१८॥
*jyotiṣāmapi tajjyotis-tamasaḥ paramucyate,*
*jñānaṁ jñeyaṁ jñāna-gamyaṁ hṛdi sarvasya viṣṭhitam. (13.18)*

He is the light of all lights. He is said to be beyond darkness. He is the knowledge. He is worth knowing and can be realized through knowledge only. He exists in the (*hṛdi*) palpitations of all.

इति क्षेत्रं तथा ज्ञानं ज्ञेयं चोक्तं समासतः।
मद्भक्त एतद्विज्ञाय मद्भावायोपपद्यते॥ १३.१९॥
*iti kṣetraṁ tathā jñānaṁ jñeyaṁ coktaṁ samāsataḥ,*
*madbhakta etad vijñāya madbhāvāyopapadyate. (13.19)*

Thus the concept of kṣetra (field) and knowledge and worth knowing have been briefly described. (*etad-vijñāya*) Having known this reality (*madbhaktaḥ*), my follower (*upapadyate*) attains (*madbhāvāya*) what I intended to say, i.e. mokṣa.

प्रकृतिं पुरुषं चैव विद्ध्यनादी उभावपि।
विकारांश्च गुणांश्चैव विद्धि प्रकृतिसंभवान्॥ १३.२०॥
*prakṛtiṁ puruṣaṁ caiva viddhyanādī ubhāvapi,*
*vikārānśca guṇāñścaiva viddhi prakṛti-saṁbhavān. (13.20)*

(*viddhi*) Know that prakṛti [primordial energy/dark energy] and puruṣa [soul] are both beginningless; and also know that all the vikāras [evolutes of prakṛti like intellect, ahaṅkāra, mind, sense organs, motor organs, five subtle and five gross elements and guṇas —sattva, rajas and tamas] are born of the prakṛti.

Five subtle elements are: sound, touch, vision, taste, and smell. Five gross elements are: space, air, fire, water, and earth.

कार्यकरणकर्तृत्वे हेतुः प्रकृतिरुच्यते।

पुरुषः सुखदुःखानां भोक्तृत्वे हेतुरुच्यते ॥ १३.२१ ॥
*kārya-karaṇa-kartṛtve hetuḥ prakṛtir ucyate,*
*puruṣaḥ sukha-duḥkhānāṁ bhoktṛtve hetur ucyate. (13.21)*

The prakṛti is said to be the (*hetuḥ*) material cause of (*kartṛtve*) the origin of kārya [body made of five subtle elements and five gross elements] and karaṇas [three Antaḥkaraṇas like intellect, ahaṅkāra and mind, and ten Bāhya karaṇas— five sense organs and five motor organs]. The Puruṣa [or soul, i.e. individuated being] is said to be the (*hetuḥ*) cause of (*bhoktṛtve*) experiencing pleasures and pains.

पुरुषः प्रकृतिस्थो हि भुङ्क्ते प्रकृतिजान्गुणान् ।
कारणं गुणसङ्गोऽस्य सदसद्योनिजन्मसु ॥ १३.२२ ॥
*puruṣaḥ prakṛtistho hi bhuṅkte prakṛtijān guṇān,*
*kāraṇaṁ guṇasaṅgo'sya sad-asad-yoni-janmasu. (13.22)*

The Puruṣa [embodied soul or individuated soul] sitting in the body or, say, in association with prakṛti [body], enjoys the guṇas [sattva, rajas, and tamas] (*prakṛtijān*) born of prakṛti. (*guṇa-saṅgaḥ*) Attachment to the particular guṇas (*kāraṇam*) causes (*janmasu*) the birth of puruṣa (soul) in (*sat*) higher or (*asat*) lower species.

Note: In human species also, there are higher or lower categories as per their experiences.

For example, if the soul is attached to sattva guṇa, it goes to higher deva species; if connected with rajoguṇa, it occupies human species, and in case of attachment with tamoguṇa, it occupies lower species like animals, birds, plants, and insects. The verification of attachment of Puruṣa with a particular species can be done through the food habits of individual beings, their likings and behaviour, etc.

उपद्रष्टानुमन्ता च भर्ता भोक्ता महेश्वरः।
परमात्मेति चाप्युक्तो देहेऽस्मिन्पुरुषः परः॥ १३.२३॥
*upadraṣṭānumantā ca bhartā bhoktā maheśvaraḥ,*
*paramātmeti cāpyukto dehe'smin puruṣaḥ paraḥ. (13.23)*

Puruṣa [Jīvātmā or Jīva/embodied soul] is (*upadraṣṭā*) witness and experiencer of the fruits of the karmas. [It does not do any karma, but witnesses and experiences the fruits of the karmas done by intellect, ahaṅkāra, mind, sense and motor organs of the body]. (*anumantā*) It gives permission to the body-system for doing actions. (*bhartā*) It is the possessor of body, intellect, ahaṅkāra, mind, sense and motor organs. (*bhoktā*) It enjoys the bad or good fruits as per karmas and it is (*maheśvara*) the independent controller of this body. (*paraḥ*) The Supreme (*puruṣaḥ*) Being (*uktaḥ*) called (*paramātmā+iti*) Paramātma (*api*) also resides (*asmin*) in this (*dehe*) body.

य एवं वेत्ति पुरुषं प्रकृतिं च गुणैः सह।
सर्वथा वर्तमानोऽपि न स भूयोऽभिजायते॥ १३.२४॥
*ya evaṁ vetti puruṣaṁ prakṛtiṁ ca guṇaiḥ saha,*
*sarvathā vartamāno'pi na sa bhūyo'bhijāyate. (13.24)*

He who (*vetti*) identifies (*evam*) thus the true nature of (*puruṣam*) soul and knows himself dissociated with (*prakṛtim*) material body (*guṇaiḥ saha*) with its guṇas, (*saḥ*) he is (*na*) not (*abhijāyate*) born (*bhūyaḥ*) again after leaving this body (*sarvathā vartamānaḥ api*) regardless of all sort of social interactions in the present life.

Note: The fact is that the social interactions are the impediments on the way of mokṣa, but these impediments no longer act as impediments if an individual identifies His true nature and dissociates himself with the prakṛti [material world].

ध्यानेनात्मनि पश्यन्ति केचिदात्मानमात्मना।

अन्ये साङ्ख्येन योगेन कर्मयोगेन चापरे ॥ १३.२५ ॥
*dhyānenātmani paśyanti kecidātmānam-ātmanā,*
*anye sāṅkhyena yogena karmayogen cāpare. (13.25)*

There are many ways of realisation of Brahman. Some realise Brahman through concentrating mind on Him; others by self-meditation; and others through the method described in Sāṅkhya and Yoga, yet others through Karma-yoga [minimizing nitya karmas abandoning all kāmya, naimittika and prohibited karmas]. One may also engae in altruistic welfare activities without involving self-interest.

अन्ये त्वेवमजानन्तः श्रुत्वान्येभ्य उपासते ।
तेऽपि चातितरन्त्येव मृत्युं श्रुतिपरायणाः ॥ १३.२६ ॥
*anye tvevam ajānantaḥ śrutvānyebhya upāsate,*
*te'pi cātitarantyeva mṛtyuṁ śruti parāyaṇāḥ. (13.26)*

Some, however, are not able to realise Brahman following the options mentioned above, (*śrutvā*) so hear the experience of His realisation from (*anyebhyaḥ*) other Āchāryas and (*upāsate*) meditate upon Him, accordingly. They also transcend death due to their habit of hearing about Him from other expert Āchāryas.

यावत्संजायते किंचित्सत्त्वं स्थावरजङ्गमम् ।
क्षेत्रक्षेत्रज्ञसंयोगात्तद्विद्धि भरतर्षभ ॥ १३.२७ ॥
*yāvat sañjāyate kiñcit sattvaṁ sthāvara-jaṅgamam,*
*kṣetra-kṣetrajña-saṁyogāt tadviddhi bharatarṣabha. (13.27)*

(*yāvat kiñchit*) Whatever (*sattvam sthāvara-jaṅgamam*) creature— moving or unmoveable is (*sañjāyate*) born here, (*viddhi*) know that to be [born] of the (*sañyogāt*) union of the (*kṣetra*) field [prakṛti] and the (*kṣetrajña*) Puruṣa [knower of prakṛti], O Best of Bharatas. (See also 7.06)

समं सर्वेषु भूतेषु तिष्ठन्तं परमेश्वरम्
विनश्यत्स्वविनश्यन्तं यः पश्यति स पश्यति ॥ १३.२८ ॥
*samaṁ sarveṣu bhūteṣu tiṣṭhantaṁ parameśvaram,*
*vinaśyatsvavinaśyantaṁ yaḥ paśyati sa paśyati. (13.28)*

(*yaḥ*) He, who (*paśyati*) sees the (*avinaśyantam*) imperishable (*Parameśvaram*) Supreme God (*tiṣṭhantam*) pervading (*samam*) equally (*sarveṣu bhūteṣu*) all the perishable beings and things, (*saḥ paśyati*)) he has the right vision.

समं पश्यन्हि सर्वत्र समवस्थितमीश्वरम् ।
न हिनस्त्यात्मनात्मानं ततो याति परां गतिम् ॥ १३.२९ ॥
*samaṁ paśyan hi sarvatra samavasthitam īśvaram,*
*na hinastyātmanātmānaṁ tato yāti parāṁ gatim. (13.29)*

(*paśyan*) Seeing (*samam*) the same Īśvara (*samavasthitam*) equally existing (*sarvatra*) everywhere, one (*na*) does not (*hinasti*) kill (*ātmanā ātmānam*) one's own self, and (*tataḥ*) thereupon (*yāti*) attains (*parām gatim*) the Supreme goal.

Note: Killing one's own self means keeping oneself away from self-realisation.

प्रकृत्यैव च कर्माणि क्रियमाणानि सर्वशः ।
यः पश्यति तथात्मानमकर्तारं स पश्यति ॥ १३.३० ॥
*prakṛtyaiva ca karmāṇi kriyamāṇāni sarvaśaḥ,*
*yaḥ paśyati tathātmānam akartāraṁ sa paśyati. (13.30)*

He/she who perceives that all actions are done by the system of the body alone and does not see his/her [soul's] role as the doer, he/she truly understands the mystery. (See also 3.27, 5.9, and 14.19)

यदा भूतपृथग्भावमेकस्थमनुपश्यति ।
तत एव च विस्तारं ब्रह्म संपद्यते तदा ॥ १३.३१ ॥
*yadā bhūta-pṛthag bhāvam ekastham anupaśyati,*

*tata eva ca vistāraṁ brahma sampadyate tadā. (13.31)*

(*yadā*) When (*anupaśyati*) one perceives a (*pṛthagbhāvam*) diversity (*bhūta*) of beings and things (*ekastham*) existing in One Brahman and (*vistāram*) expansion of the whole universe (*tata eve cha*) exclusively due to Him, then one realises Brahman.

अनादित्वान्निर्गुणत्वात्परमात्मायमव्ययः ।
शरीरस्थोऽपि कौन्तेय न करोति न लिप्यते ॥ १३.३२ ॥
*anāditvān-nirguṇatvāt paramātmāyam avyayaḥ,*
*śarīrastho'pi kaunteya na karoti na lipyate. (13.32)*

What is the chacteristics of Parmātmā?

(*avyayam*) The imperishable (*Paramātmā*) Supreme Being, (*anāditvāt*) being beginningless and (*nirguṇatvāt*) devoid of bad guṇas and physical body, (*api*) though (*śarīrasthaḥ*) pervades the bodies, it (*na*) neither (*karoti*) does anything (*na*) nor (*lipyate*) gets tainted by the karmas of the bodies, O Son of Kunti.

Note: Parmātmā remains as a witness.

यथा सर्वगतं सौक्ष्म्यादाकाशं नोपलिप्यते ।
सर्वत्रावस्थितो देहे तथात्मा नोपलिप्यते ॥ १३.३३ ॥
*yathā sarvagataṁ saukṣmyāda ākāśaṁ nopalipyate,*
*sarvatrāvasthito dehe tathātmā nopalipayate. (13.33)*

As the all-pervading space is not contaminated because of its subtlety, similarly, the Supreme Self, pervading everybody, is not contaminated.

यथा प्रकाशयत्येकः कृत्स्नं लोकमिमं रविः ।
क्षेत्रं क्षेत्री तथा कृत्स्नं प्रकाशयति भारत ॥ १३.३४ ॥
*yathā prakāśayatyekaḥ kṛtsnaṁ lokam imaṁ raviḥ,*
*kṣetraṁ kṣetrī tathā kṛtsnaṁ prakāśayati bhārata. (13.34)*

O Arjuna, just as one sun illuminates this entire

universe, similarly (*kṣetrī*) Brahman illuminates (or gives life to) (*kṛtsnam*) the all (*kśetram*) universes.

क्षेत्रक्षेत्रज्ञयोरेवमन्तरं ज्ञानचक्षुषा ।
भूतप्रकृतिमोक्षं च ये विदुर्यान्ति ते परम् ॥ १३.३५ ॥
*kṣetra-kṣetrajñayor-evam-antaraṁ jñāna-cakṣuṣā,*
*bhūta-prakṛti-mokṣaṁ ca ye vidur yānti te param. (13.35)*

They, who can distinguish between (*kṣetra*) the body and (*kṣetrajña*) soul (*jñāna-chakṣusā*) through the eyes of self-realisation and know the (*mokṣam*) technique of liberation [of jīva] (*bhūtaprakṛti*) from the trap of body (*yānti*) attain the (*param*) Supreme.

ॐ तत्सदिति श्रीमद् भगवद्गीतासूपनिषत्सु ब्रह्मविद्यायां योगशास्त्रे श्रीकृष्णार्जुनसंवादे क्षेत्रक्षेत्रज्ञविभागयोगोनाम त्रयोदशोऽध्यायः ॥१३ ॥

Here ends the 13th chapter named, Kṣetra-kṣetrajña-vibhāga yoga, in the *Bhagvadgitā* dealing with the Brahmavidyā as propounded in the Upaniṣad and Yogaśāstra in the form of dialogue between Śri Krishna and Arjuna

# अथ चतुर्दशोऽध्याय:

## गुणत्रयविभागयोग:

# Chapter 14

[Yoga of Classification of Three Guṇas]

In this chapter, Śri Krishna tells Arjuna that matter [Prakṛti] is characterized by three qualities: Sattva, Rajas, and Tamas. When your intellectual power of distinguishing between real and unreal things increases, it should be known that Sattva is dominant. When you have the obsession to gather all sorts of material things, undertake activities and become restless; it is a sign of Rajas' dominance. The inability to distinguish between real and unreal the tendency of inaction for obligatory karmas and duties is the sign of Tamas' dominance. According to Śri Krishna, if an individual dies during the predominance of Sattva, he takes birth in a family of spiritual and enlightened human beings in the next life. When one dies during the dominance of Rajas, one is reborn as a human being attached to the mundane world. In Tamas conditions, one is reborn in lower species of birds, animals, insects, plants, etc., devoid of the ability to distinguish between real and unreal. Śri Krishna wants to tell Arjuna that if he wants to attain mokṣa, he would have to rise above the three guṇas and get rid of the doership. So long as a person performs the role of doership due to ahaṅkāra [the notion of 'I', 'my', 'me'], he shall have to reap the fruits of his actions, and so he will be born again and again. When a person realises that he is not the actual doer, actions are performed by the system of the body under the impression of three guṇas; he will try to rise above the body [characterized by the above-cited three guṇas] and will qualify for mokṣa. In the Gītā, Śri Krishna says that even the Vedas also deal with the world of three guṇas- *triguṇaviṣayo vedāḥ*. It clearly shows that according to the Gītā, Vedic knowledge deals with the creation and decreation of the universe at physical, astrophysical, and metaphysical levels. The Vedic yajña is also the process of creation. Śri Krishna advises that for mokṣa, one has to be above the triguṇas. *naistraiguṇyo bhavārjuna*. That is, O Arjuna, rise above the three guṇas.

श्री कृष्ण उवाच
Śri Krishna said

परं भूयः प्रवक्ष्यामि ज्ञानानां ज्ञानमुत्तमम् ।
यज्ज्ञात्वा मुनयः सर्वे परां सिद्धिमितो गताः ॥ १४.१ ॥
*paraṁ bhūyaḥ pravakṣyāmi jñānānāṁ jñānam uttamam,*
*yajjñātvā munayaḥ sarve parāṁ siddhimito gatāḥ. (14.01)*

I shall further explain to you that supreme knowledge is the best of all knowledge, knowing that all the sages have attained ultimate perfection (mokṣa) after this life.

According to the Sāṁkhya philosophy, mokṣa cannot be attained without knowledge. *ṛte jñānāt na mukti.*

इदं ज्ञानमुपाश्रित्य मम साधर्म्यमागताः ।
सर्गेऽपि नोपजायन्ते प्रलये न व्यथन्ति च ॥ १४.२ ॥
*idaṁ jñānam upāśritya mama sādharmyamāgatāḥ,*
*sarge'pi nopajāyante pralaye na vyathanti ca. (14.02)*

Having attained this knowledge, the individual practitioners will achieve a status similar to mine, and after that, they are not born during the time of current creation nor afflicted during the time of dissolution.

मम योनिर्महद् ब्रह्म तस्मिन्गर्भं दधाम्यहम् ।
संभवः सर्वभूतानां ततो भवति भारत ॥ १४.३ ॥

*mama yonir mahad brahma tasmin garbhaṁ dadhāmyaham,*
*sambhavaḥ sarvabhūtānāṁ tato bhavati bhārata. (14.03)*

O son of Bharatas, Almighty Brahman is the efficient cause of my origin; I have my womb in Brahman. Similarly, the origin of all other beings is caused by Him. (See also 9.10)

सर्वयोनिषु कौन्तेय मूर्तय: संभवन्ति या: ।
तासां ब्रह्म महद्योनिरहं बीजप्रद: पिता ॥ १४.४ ॥
*sarvayoniṣu kaunteya mūrtayaḥ sambhavanti yāḥ,*
*tāsāṁ brahma mahad-yonir ahaṁ bījapradaḥ pitā. (14.04)*

(*yāḥ*) Whatever (*mūrtayaḥ*) forms are (*sambhavanti*) created (*sarva-yoniṣu*) in different species, the Almighty Brahman is (*mahad*) the efficient (*yoniḥ*) cause of origin of all of them. The element of ahaṅkāra, present in them as sanskāra, acts as the seed of their origin.

The meaning is that every being takes birth due to their sanskāra of ahaṁ, but the efficient cause of their origin is the Almighty Brahman. He gives different beings different species according to their sanskāras.

Note: According to Vedānta philosopher -*sanskāra bījāt sṛṣṭi.* It implies that sanskāra acts as the seed for the next life.

सत्त्वं रजस्तम इति गुणा: प्रकृतिसम्भवा: ।
निबध्नन्ति महाबाहो देहे देहिनमव्ययम् ॥ १४.५ ॥
*sattvaṁ rajas tama iti guṇāḥ prakṛtisambhavāḥ,*
*nibadhnanti mahābāho dehe dehinam avyayam. (14.05)*

Now, Śri Krishna defines the nature of sanskāra in different beings. Sattva, Rajas, and Tamas— these three guṇas are born of prakṛti. They (*nibadhnanti*) bind the (*avyayam*) imperishable (*dehinam*) soul (*dehe*) in different bodies of different beings according to their sanskāras, O Large armed one!

तत्र सत्त्वं निर्मलत्वात्प्रकाशकमनामयम् ।
सुखसङ्गेन बध्नाति ज्ञानसङ्गेन चानघ ॥ १४.६ ॥
*tatra sattvaṁ nirmalatvāt prakāśakam anāmayam,*
*sukhasaṅgena badhnāti jñānasaṅgena cānagha. (14.06)*

Of these, sattva, is (*nirmala*) transparent like a crystal; it allows (*prakāśakam*) buddhi to function appropriately and creates (*anāmayam*) no disturbance in body function. However, the desire for pleasure, comfort and knowledge binds the embodied soul to the cycle of life and death, O Arjuna, free from all evils!

Pleasure-seeking and knowledge-gathering are the quality of the mind and not the soul. So, the desire for pleasure and knowledge binds the soul to the body. So long as desires are there, a being cannot come out of the life and death cycle of bondage. He shall take birth to fulfil his unfulfilled desires.

रजो रागात्मकं विद्धि तृष्णासङ्गसमुद्भवम् ।
तन्निबध्नाति कौन्तेय कर्मसङ्गेन देहिनम् ॥ १४.७ ॥
*rajo rāgātmakaṁ viddhi tṛṣṇāsaṅga-samudbhavam,*
*tannibadhnāti kaunteya karmasaṅgena dehinam. (14.07)*

O son of Kunti, (*viddhi*) know that Rajas is characterized by passions. (*samudbhavam*). It is born of tṛṣṇā [desire to achieve what has not yet been achieved] and āsaṅga [attachment to the achieved things]. (*tad*) These passions (*badhnāti*) bind (*dehinam*) jīva to (*karmasaṅgena*), the attachment of karmas of visible and invisible objectives.

The dominance of Rajas makes a being passionate. And these passions are the great cause of bondage leading to perform actions resulting in visible and invisible objectives. So a being has to get rid of his/her passions to climb the ladder of sattva dominance which is must for mokṣa.

तमस्त्वज्ञानजं विद्धि मोहनं सर्वदेहिनाम्।
प्रमादालस्यनिद्राभिस्तन्निबध्नाति भारत॥ १४.८॥
*tamastvajñānajaṁ viddhi mohanaṁ sarva-dehinām,*
*pramādālasyanidrābhis-tannibadhnāti bhārata. (14.08)*

O son of Bharatas, the tamas (*sarvadehinām*) pushes all jīvas (*mohanam*) towards inabilty to distinguish between real and unreal; it is born of ajñāna [considering unreal as real]. It (*nibadhnāti*) binds the jīva by pramāda [non-performance of obligatory karmas or duties], ālasya [laziness], and nidrā [unawareness].

सत्त्वं सुखे संजयति रजः कर्मणि भारत।
ज्ञानमावृत्य तु तमः प्रमादे संजयत्युत॥ १४.९॥
*sattvaṁ sukhe sañjayati rajaḥ karmaṇi bhārata,*
*jñānam āvṛtya tu tamaḥ pramāde sañjayatyuta. (14.09)*

O son of Bharatas, sattva (*sañjayati*) affiliate one with spiritual happiness, Rajas with action, and Tamas with non-performance.

रजस्तमश्चाभिभूय सत्त्वं भवति भारत।
रजः सत्त्वं तमश्चैव तमः सत्त्वं रजस्तथा॥ १४.१०॥
*rajas tamaś cābhibhūya sattvaṁ bhavati bhārata.*
*rajaḥ sattvaṁ tamaś caiva tamaḥ sattvaṁ rajas tathā. (14.10)*

Sattva dominates by suppressing Rajas and Tamas; Rajas dominates by suppressing Sattva and Tamas; and Tamas dominates by suppressing Sattva and Rajas, O Son of Bharatas.

सर्वद्वारेषु देहेऽस्मिन्प्रकाश उपजायते।
ज्ञानं यदा तदा विद्याद्विवृद्धं सत्त्वमित्युत॥ १४.११॥

*sarvadvāreṣu dehe'smin prakāśa upajāyate,*
*jñānaṁ yadā tadā vidyād vivṛddhaṁ sattvam ityuta. (14.11)*

How to identify the dominance of Sattva? When the body feels enlightened through all the senses, and the jñāna [understanding or taking real as real and unreal as unreal] gets over ajñāna [taking unreal for real], then it should be known that Sattva is predominant.

लोभ: प्रवृत्तिरारम्भ: कर्मणामशम: स्पृहा।
रजस्येतानि जायन्ते विवृद्धे भरतर्षभ ॥ १४.१२ ॥
*lobhaḥ pravṛttir ārambhaḥ karmaṇām aśamaḥ spṛhā,*
*rajasyetāni jāyante vivṛddhe bharatarṣabha. (14.12)*

Signs of Rajas' dominance? (*lobha*) Desire to grab material things, money or property; (*pravṛtti*) tendency to act; (*ārambhaḥ)* undertaking (*karmaṇām*) activities; (*aśamaḥ*) restlessness or switching one's mind from one to another thing (*spṛhā*), common desire for all mundane things is the signs of Rajas' dominance, O Best of Bharatas.

अप्रकाशोऽप्रवृत्तिश्च प्रमादो मोह एव च।
तमस्येतानि जायन्ते विवृद्धे कुरुनन्दन ॥ १४.१३ ॥
*aprakāśo'pravṛttiś ca pramādo moha eva ca,*
*tamasyetāni jāyante vivṛddhe kurunandana. (14.13)*

What are signs of predominance of Tamas?

(*aprakāsaḥ*) Non-functioning of buddhi, (*apravṛttiḥ*) inaction (*pramādaḥ*) non-performance of obligatory karmas or duties, (*mohaḥ*) inabilty to distinguish between real and unreal are the signs of (*vivṛddhe*) predominance of Tamas, O son of Kurus.

यदा सत्त्वे प्रवृद्धे तु प्रलयं याति देहभृत्।
तदोत्तमविदां लोकानमलान्प्रतिपद्यते ॥ १४.१४ ॥
*yadā sattve pravṛddhe tu pralayaṁ yāti dehabhṛt,*

*Tadottama-vidāṁ lokān-amalān pratipadyate. (14.14)*

If an individual dies during the predominance of Sattva, he is born in the houses of evil-free and enlightened human beings in the next life.

रजसि प्रलयं गत्वा कर्मसङ्गिषु जायते।
तथा प्रलीनस्तमसि मूढयोनिषु जायते॥ १४.१५॥
*rajasi pralayaṁ gatvā karma-saṅgiṣu jāyate,*
*tathā pralīnastamasi mūḍhayoniṣu jāyate. (14.15)*

When one dies during the predominance of Rajas, one is reborn in the families of those human beings who remain attached to the sakāma karmas or karmas with a desire to get some visible or invisible fruits; and dying in Tamas-predominance, one is reborn in lower species of birds, animals, insects, plants, etc. which are devoid of distinction between real and unreal.

कर्मण: सुकृतस्याहु: सात्त्विकं निर्मलं फलम्।
रजसस्तु फलं दु:खमज्ञानं तमस: फलम्॥ १४.१६॥
*karmaṇaḥ sukṛtasyāhuḥ sāttvikaṁ nirmalaṁ phalam,*
*rajasas tu phalaṁ duḥkham ajñānaṁ tamasaḥ phalam. (14.16)*

What are fruits of various actions? The fruit of sāttvika actions is said to be sāttvika and nirmala [creating no disturbance and evil], the fruit of rājasika actions is painful, and the fruit of tāmasika actions is ajñāna [misunderstanding that leads one away from reality].

सत्त्वात्संजायते ज्ञानं रजसो लोभ एव च।
प्रमादमोहौ तमसो भवतोऽज्ञानमेव च॥ १४.१७॥
*sattvāt sañjāyate jñānaṁ rajaso lobha eva ca,*
*pramāda-mohau tamaso bhavato'jñānameva ca. (14.17)*

Knowledge [proper understanding] develops due to sattva; lobha [desire to accumulate mundane things] arises from rajas; and the tendency of (*pramāda*) not performing obligatory karmas or duties and (*mohaḥ*) inability to distinguish between real and unreal develops owes to tamas.

ऊर्ध्वं गच्छन्ति सत्त्वस्था मध्ये तिष्ठन्ति राजसाः ।
जघन्यगुणवृत्तिस्था अधो गच्छन्ति तामसाः ॥ १४.१८ ॥
*ūrdhvaṁ gacchanti sattvasthā madhye tiṣṭhanti rājasāḥ,*
*jaghanya-guṇa-vṛttisthā adho gacchanti tāmasāḥ. (14.18)*

Those established in sattva go higher and higher to attain their supreme goal of mokṣa; rājasika persons remain at the middle stage or say they are reborn as human beings; and the tāmasika persons fall to the lower species. [or, say born as lower creatures].

नान्यं गुणेभ्यः कर्तारं यदा द्रष्टानुपश्यति ।
गुणेभ्यश्च परं वेत्ति मद्भावं सोऽधिगच्छति ॥ १४.१९ ॥
*nānyaṁ guṇebhyaḥ kartāraṁ yadā draṣṭānupaśyati,*
*guṇebhyaśca paraṁ vetti madbhāvaṁ so'dhigacchati. (14.19)*

When a visionary person or seeker identifies that there is no other doer than the set of three guṇas [body system is the set of three guṇas] and realises that ātman is above three guṇas, he attains the (*madbhāvam*) my status of nirvāṇa. (See also 3.27, 5.9, and 13.29)

गुणानेतानतीत्य त्रीन्देही देहसमुद्भवान् ।
जन्ममृत्युजरादुःखैर्विमुक्तोऽमृतमश्नुते ॥ १४.२० ॥
*guṇān etān atītya trīn dehī deha-samudbhavān,*
*janma-mṛtyu-jarā-duḥkhair vimukto'mṛatam aśnute.(14.20)*

When a (*dehi*) soul (*atītya*) transcends [or rises above] (*etān*) these (*trīn guṇān*) three guṇas (*deha samudbhavān*) that are the source of his/her embodiment; he is (*vimuktaḥ*) freed from (*duḥkhaiḥ*) pains of (*janma*) birth, (*mṛtyu*) death, (*jarā*) old age, (*amṛtam aśnute*) and attains nirvāṇa.

अर्जुन उवाच

Arjuna said

कैर्लिङ्गैस्त्रीन्गुणानेतानतीतो भवति प्रभो।
किमाचारः कथं चैतांस्त्रीन्गुणानतिवर्तते॥ १४.२१॥

*kāir liṅgais trīn guṇān etān atīto bhavati prabho,*
*kimācāraḥ kathaṁ caitāns trīn guṇān ativartate. (14.21)*

Arjuna said—(*kaiḥ liṅgaiḥ*) What are the symptoms or signs of those who have (*atītaḥ*) transcended (*etān*) these (*trīn guṇān*) three guṇas? (*kimāchāraḥ*) What is their conduct? How does one transcend these three guṇas, O my Master?

Note: Arjuna wants to know the signs or symptoms of *guṇātīta* person.

श्री कृष्ण उवाच

Śri Krishna said

प्रकाशं च प्रवृत्तिं च मोहमेव च पाण्डव।
न द्वेष्टि संप्रवृत्तानि न निवृत्तानि काङ्क्षति॥ १४.२२॥

*prakāśaṁ ca pravṛttiṁ ca mohameva ca pāṇḍava,*
*na dveṣṭi saṁpravṛttāni na nivṛttāni kāṅkṣati. (14.22)*

Śri Krishna Said—A person who rises above the triguṇas [three guṇas] neither develops hatred [get rid of them] when they (*saṁpravṛttāni*) are present and operate in him nor does he (*kāṅkṣati*) desires them when they are (*nivṛttāni*) absent from him.

उदासीनवदासीनो गुणैर्यो न विचाल्यते।
गुणा वर्तन्त इत्येव योऽवतिष्ठति नेङ्गते॥ १४.२३॥

*udāsīnavad āsīno guṇair yo na vicālyate,*
*guṇā vartanta ityeva yo'vatiṣṭhati neṅgate. (14.23)*

A person who (*āsīnaḥ*) sits (*udāsīnavat*) in an indifferent manner and is (*na*) not (*vichālyate*) affected (*guṇaiḥ*) by the guṇas, (*ityeva*) thinking that (*guṇāḥ*) the guṇas alone are (*vartante*) operating, (*yaḥ*) he (*avatiṣṭhati*) stands firm and (*iṅgate*) wavers (*na*) not.

समदु:खसुख: स्वस्थ: समलोष्टाश्मकांचन: ।
तुल्यप्रियाप्रियो धीरस्तुल्यनिन्दात्मसंस्तुति: ॥ १४.२४ ॥
*samaduḥkha-sukhaḥ savasthaḥ sama-loṣṭāśma-kāñcanaḥ,*
*tulya-priyā-priyo dhīras tulya-nindātma-sanstutiḥ. (14.24)*

(*svasthaḥ*) Who is happy in himself, (*samaduḥkha-sukhaḥ*) indifferent to pain and pleasure; to whom (*loṣṭa*) a clod, (*aśma*) a stone, and (*kāñchanaḥ*) gold are (*sama*) alike; to whom the (*priya*) dear and (*apriya*) unfriendly (*tulya*) are alike; (*dhiraḥ*) who is of firm mind; who is (*tulya*) calm (*nindā-sanstutiḥ*) in censure and in praise.

मानापमानयोस्तुल्यस्तुल्यो मित्रारिपक्षयो: ।
सर्वारम्भपरित्यागी गुणातीत: स उच्यते ॥ १४.२५ ॥
*mānāpamānayos tulyas tulyo mitrāri-pakṣayoḥ,*
*sarvārambha-parityāgī guṇātītaḥ sa ucyate. (14.25)*

Who is indifferent to honour and disgrace; who is the same to a friend and (*aripakṣa*) a foe; who has renounced the sense of doership in all undertakings or actions resulting into visible and invisible fruits, except those actions that are necessary to sustain body; he is said to have transcended the guṇas.

मां च योऽव्यभिचारेण भक्तियोगेन सेवते ।
स गुणान्समतीत्यैतान्ब्रह्मभूयाय कल्पते ॥ १४.२६ ॥
*māṁ ca yo'vyabhicāreṇa bhaktiyogena sevate,*
*sa guṇān samatītyaitān brahma-bhūyāya kalpate. (14.26)*

The one who takes delight in Brahman with (*avyabhichāreṇa*) unswerving (*bhaktiyogena*) devotion (*samatītya*), transcends (*guṇān*) the guṇas, and (*kalpate*) becomes fit (*brahma-bhūyāya*) for attaining Brahma-loka or mokṣa. (See also 7.14 and 15.19)

ब्रह्मणो हि प्रतिष्ठाहममृतस्याव्ययस्य च।
शाश्वतस्य च धर्मस्य सुखस्यैकान्तिकस्य च॥ १४.२७ ॥
*brahmaṇo hi pratiṣṭhāham amṛtasyāvyayasya ca,*
*śāśvatasya ca dharmasya sukhasyaikāntikasya ca. (14.27)*

(*hi*) Because (*pratiṣṭhā*) the knowledge of existence of (*Brahmaṇaḥ*) of Brahman, (*avyasya*) Who is eternal, (*śāśvatasya cha dharmasya*) source of eternal Dharma, (*cha*) and (*aikāntiksya sukhasya*) absolute can be achieved through (*ahaṁ*) ātman.

ॐ तत्सदिति श्रीमद् भगवद्गीतासूपनिषत्सु ब्रह्मविद्यायां योगशास्त्रे श्रीकृष्णार्जुनसंवादे गुणत्रयविभागयोगोनाम चतुर्दशोऽध्याय: ॥१४ ॥

*ॐ tatsaditi śrīmad bhagavadgītāsūpaniṣatsu brahmavidyāyāṁ yogaśāstre śrīkṛṣṇārjunasaṁvāde guṇatrayavibhāgayogonāma chaturdaśo'dhyāya: ॥14 ॥*

Here ends the 14th chapter named Guṇa-traya-vibhāga yoga in the *Bhagvadgitā* dealing with the Brahmavidyā as propounded in the Upaniṣad and Yogaśāstra in the form of dialogue between Śri Krishna and Arjuna.

# अथ पंचदशोऽध्याय:

## पुरुषोत्तमयोग

# Chapter 15

[Puruṣottama Yoga]

In this chapter, Śri Krishna describes the material world as an Aśvattha [Peepal] tree with its roots upward in the Chidākāśa [space of Brahman] and branches downward in the Bhūtākāśa [visible space]. In the Vedas, there is a concept of three lokas - Dyau loka [Chidākāsa], Antarikṣa loka [Intermediate space], and Pṛthivī loka [Bhūtākāśa]. Chidākāsa is the storehouse of inactive energy [prakṛti], and the entire creation takes place in the Bhūtākāsa when Brahman activates energy. Thus, the material world has its roots above in the Chidākāśa and its branches [the extension of creation] only below in the Bhūtākāśa [visible space]. This creation is unfathomable. The only weapon to win over this material world is the weapon of detachment. A person not involved in this material world and gaining actual knowledge can achieve Mokṣa. Mokṣa has been described as the supreme place [Param pada]. The physical body, soul, and Brahman have been variously described by the names of kṣara [perishable], akṣara [imperishable] and Uttama Puruṣa or Puruṣottama [Supreme Spirit] respectively. In this chapter, God has been signified with the pronominal address of Aham and its declensions like Mama, Māma, etc. Since God is Uttama Puruṣa [first person], he is addressed with Uttama Puruṣa [first person] pronoun. Veda [knowledge of Brahmāṇḍa] is described as the sole property of Brahman. Since Brahman is All-Knowing, knowledge is said to have existed in Him. That is why the authorship of Veda is also assigned to Brahman.

श्री कृष्ण उवाच

Śri Krishna said

ऊर्ध्वमूलमधःशाखमश्वत्थं प्राहुरव्ययम्।
छन्दांसि यस्य पर्णानि यस्तं वेद स वेदवित्॥ १५.१॥
*ūdhrvamūlam adhaḥ śākham aśvatthaṁ prāhur-*
*avyayam,*
*chandānsi yasya parṇāni yastaṁ veda sa vedavit. (15.01)*

Śri Krishna said— The Aśvattha tree [Bhutākāśa or material world] having its roots above [in the chidākāśa] and branches below [in the Bhūtākāśa] is said to be (*avyayam*) of eternal cycles. Vedas are its leaves. (*yaḥ*) One who (veda) understands (*tam*) this material world along with its root (*vedavit*) also knows the Veda [its process of creation].

Note: Here Śri Krishna wants to convey a message that Vedas are nothing else but the knowledge of Brahman and his creation.

अधश्चोर्ध्वं प्रसृतास्तस्य शाखा गुणप्रवृद्धा विषयप्रवालाः।
अधश्च मूलान्यनुसंततानि कर्मानुबन्धीनि मनुष्यलोके॥ १५.२॥
*adhaś cordhvaṁ prasṛtās-tasya śākhā,*
*guṇa-pravṛddhā viṣaya-pravālāḥ.*
*adhaś ca mūlānyanusantatāni,*
*karmānubandhīni manuṣyaloke. (15.02)*

(*śākhā*) The branches (*tasya*) of this material world (prasṛtā) spread (*adhaḥ*) below and (*ūrdhvam*) above [or all over the cosmos]. This material world is the (*guṇa-pravṛddhā*) network of the three guṇas [sattva, rajas, and tamas, since, according to the Sāṅkhya system of philosophy, the evolution of the cosmos resulted from the imbalance of three guṇas. So long as the guṇas remain in the balanced form, no creation can occur, and that stage is known as the stage of inactive or dark energy]. (*viṣaya*) The five sensory objects or stimuli [sound, form, taste, touch, and smell] are (*pravālāḥ*) its sprouts and (*manuṣyaloke*). This human world has its (*mūlāni*) roots (*santatāni*) widespread in *(katmānubandhini)* the karmic sanskāras. Humans owe their karmas for their further origin into different species. Conversely, the human beings take their next birth depending upon their karmic sanskāras.

न रूपमस्येह तथोपलभ्यते नान्तो न चादिर्न च संप्रतिष्ठा ।
अश्वत्थमेनं सुविरूढमूलं असङ्गशस्त्रेण दृढेन छित्त्वा ॥ १५.३ ॥

*na rūpam-asyeha tathopalabhyate,*
*nānto na cādir na ca sampratiṣthā.*
*aśvattham enaṁ suviruḍha-mūlam,*
*asaṅga-śastreṇa dṛḍhena chittvā. (15.03)*

(Asya) This tree [material world] (*na*) does not have a (*rūpam*) particular form or appearance (*iha*) here. (*na antaḥ*) No one is aware of its end (*na cha ādiḥ*), neither beginning (*na cha*) nor (*pratiṣṭhā*) existence. One can (chhitvā) cut [get rid of] (*enam*) this (*suvirūḍha-mūlam*) firmly rooted *(aśvattham)* tree of the material world with (*dṛḍhena*) the strong (*śastreṇa*) weapon of (*asaṅga*) detachment.

ततः पदं तत्परिमार्गितव्यं
यस्मिन्गता न निवर्तन्ति भूयः ।
तमेव चाद्यं पुरुषं प्रपद्ये ।
यतः प्रवृत्तिः प्रसृता पुराणी ॥ १५.४ ॥

*tataḥ padaṁ tatparimārgitavyaṁ,*
*yasmin gatā na nivartanti bhūyaḥ.*
*tameva cādyaṁ puruṣaṁ prapadye,*
*yataḥ pravṛttiḥ prasṛtā purāṇī. (15.04)*

(*parimārgitavyam*) Moreover, achieve (*tat*) that (*padam*) place [mokṣa] (*yasmin gatāḥ*) having reached there, one (*na*) does not (*bhūyaḥ nivartante*) come back in this material world till the next creation cycle. [One creation cycle is of 311 Trillion years]. I also (*prapadye*) attain [merge with] (*tameva*) that very (*ādyam puruṣam*) Primal Spirit [Almighty Brahman], (*yataḥ*) Who is the efficient cause of (*prasṛtā*) the expansion of this (*purāṇi*) eternal (*pravṛttiḥ*) creation.

निर्मानमोहा जितसङ्गदोषा
अध्यात्मनित्या विनिवृत्तकामाः ।
द्वन्द्वैर्विमुक्ताः सुखदुःखसंज्ञैर्
गच्छन्त्यमूढाः पदमव्ययं तत् ॥ १५.५ ॥
*nirmāna-mohā jita-saṅga-doṣā,*
*adhyātma-nityā vinivṛtta-kāmāḥ.*
*Dvandvair-vimuktāḥ sukha-duḥkha-sañjñair,*
*gacchantyamūḍhāḥ padam avyayaṁ tat. (15.05)*

Those who are (*nir*) free from (*māna*) pride and (*moha*) delusion, who have (*jita*) conquered the (*doṣa*) evil of (*saṅga*) attachment, who are *(nitya)* constantly engrossed in the meditation upon (*adhyātma*) Supreme Self with (*kāmas*) all desires (*vinivṛtta*) wholly stilled, who are (*vimuktā)* free from the (*dvandva*) dualities of (*sukha*) pleasure and (*duḥkha*) pain; such (*amūḍhāḥ)* undeluded seekers (*gacchanti*) achieve (*avyayam*) the eternal (*padam*) place [mokṣa].

न तद्भासयते सूर्यो न शशाङ्को न पावकः ।
यद्गत्वा न निवर्तंते तद्धाम परमं मम ॥ १५.६ ॥
*na tad bhāsayate sūryo na śaśāṅko na pāvakaḥ,*
*yad gatvā na nivartante taddhāma paramaṁ mama. (15.06)*

The (*sūryaḥ*) sun, (*śaśāṅkaḥ*) moon, or (*pāvakaḥ*) the fire are (*na*) not able to (*bhāsayate*) illuminate that place of (*mama*) Brahman [Brahmaloka]. (*Gatvā*) Having reached (*tad dhāma*) that supreme abode, (*na nivartante*) no one comes back [until the next creation cycle].

ममैवांशो जीवलोके जीवभूत: सनातन: ।
मन: षष्ठानीन्द्रियाणि प्रकृतिस्थानि कर्षति ॥ १५.७ ॥
*mamaivāñśo jīvaloke jīvabhūtaḥ sanātanaḥ,*
*manaḥ-ṣaṣthānīndriyāṇi prakṛtisthāni karṣati. (15.07)*

All the eternal individuated souls or Jīvātmās in the (*jīvaloke*) the world of living beings are the (*añśaḥ*) parts of Mama [Supreme Being]. [If they are the part of the Brahman, how do they come in this world and leave it? The answer is given]. These souls (*karṣati*) attract towards them (*indriyāṇi*) five sense organs and the *(manaḥ-ṣaṣṭha)* mind as the sixth one, which are (*prakṛtisthāni*) parts of prakṛti. [That is the reason for their coming into this world].

Note: here the word 'Mama' stands for the Paramātmā.

शरीरं यदवाप्नोति यच्चाप्युत्क्रामतीश्वर: ।
गृहित्वैतानि संयाति वायुर्गंधानिवाशयात् ॥ १५.८ ॥
*śarīraṁ yad avāpnoti yaccāpyutkrāmatīśvaraḥ,*
*gṛhītvaitāni sañyāti vāyur gandhān ivāśayāt. (15.08)*

(*iva*) As (*vāyuḥ*) the air takes away (*gandhān*) the aroma from (*āśayāt*) the source [like flower], similarly (*īśvaraḥ*) The master of body, Ātmā, (*grahitvā*) carries (*etāni*) the mind and the five sensory faculties [in the form of a subtle body] (*yat śarīram*) from the body (*utkrāmati*) it casts off [during death] (*yat*) to the body it (*avāpnoti*) acquires as per its sanskāras. (See also 2.13).

श्रोत्रं चक्षु: स्पर्शनं च रसनं घ्राणमेव च ।
अधिष्ठाय मनश्चायं विषयानुपसेवते ॥ १५.९ ॥

*śrotraṁ cakṣuḥ sparśanaṁ ca rasanaṁ ghrāṇam eva ca,*
*adhiṣṭhāya manaś cāyaṁ viṣayān upasevate. (15.09)*

The jīvātmā [soul] enjoys objects of sense organs [fruits of nature] (*adhiṣṭhāya*) by ruling the mind and five sensory faculties: hearing, touch, sight, taste, smell.

उत्क्रामन्तं स्थितं वाऽपि भुंजानं वा गुणान्वितम्।
विमूढा नानुपश्यन्ति पश्यन्ति ज्ञानचक्षुषः॥ १५.१०॥
*utkrāmantaṁ sthitaṁ vāpi bhuñjānaṁ vā guṇānvitam,*
*vimūḍhā nānupaśyanti paśyanti jñāna-cakṣuṣaḥ. (15.10)*

(*vimūḍhāḥ*) The ignorant (*na*) does not (*anupaśyanyi*) perceive (utkrāmantam) how jīvātmā [soul] departs from the body or (*sthitam*) dwells in the body; how it (*bhuñjānam*) enjoys objects of sense organs [fruits of nature]; (*guṇānvitam*) and how it experiences the pleasure [caused by sattva], pain [caused by rajas] and delusion [caused by tamas]. Only those (*jñāna-chakṣusaḥ*) with the eye of wisdom (*paśyanti)* see it.

यतन्तो योगिनश्चैनं पश्यन्त्यात्मन्यवस्थितम्।
यतन्तोऽप्यकृतात्मानो नैनं पश्यंत्यचेतसः॥ १५.११॥
*yatanto yoginaś cainaṁ paśyantyātmanyavasthitam,*
*yatanto'pyakṛtātmāno nainaṁ paśyantyacetasaḥ. (15.11)*

(*Yoginaḥ*) The yogis (*yatantaḥ*) through efforts in samādhi (*paśyanti*) behold (*enam*) ātmā (*avasthitam*) abiding (*ātmani*) in their intellect part of mind [Buddhi]; but (*achetasaḥ*) the persons who are unable to distinguish between real and unreal, (*akṛtātmānaḥ*) whose mind is full of tāmasika sanskāras, (*na*) do not (*paśyanti*) perceive (*enam*) this ātmā (*api*) despite (*yatantaḥ*) efforts.

यदादित्यगतं तेजो जगद्भासयतेऽखिलम्।
यच्चन्द्रमसि यच्चाग्नौ तत्तेजो विद्धि मामकम्॥ १५.१२॥
*yadādityagataṁ tejo jagad bhāsayate'khilam,*

*yaccandramasi yaccāgnau tattejo viddhi māmakam. (15.12)*

The light of the sun that illuminates the whole world; and the light which is in the moon, and in the fire; belongs to the Universal soul (*māmaka*). (See also 13.17 and 15.6).

गामाविश्य च भूतानि धारयाम्यहमोजसा।
पुष्णामि चौषधीः सर्वाः सोमो भूत्वा रसात्मकः ॥ १५.१३ ॥
*gāmāviśya ca bhūtāni dhārayāmyahamojasā,*
*puṣṇāmi cauṣadhīḥ sarvāḥ somo bhūtvā rasātmakaḥ. (15.13)*

The Universal soul by (*āviśya*) entering (*gām*) into the earth (*dhāryāmi*) provides a stable platform (*bhūtāni*) to all beings (*ojasā*) by His power. He (*puṣṇāmi*) provides taste and nutritional value to (*sarvāḥ*) all the (*auṣadhiḥ*) herbs, shrubs, and plants (*bhūtvā*) through the (*rasātmaka*) polarized light of (*somaḥ*) the moon.

Here, the positive effect of the polarized light of the moon on plants and their products, viz. fruits and vegetables, is cited. Earth and moon are vital for the emergence of life.

Note: The moon's light is polarized. Light polarization is a property of light waves that depicts the direction of their oscillations. A polarized light vibrates or oscillates in only one direction. It is in contrast to a non-polarized light that vibrates in many directions.

Gitā is the propounder of the theory of equilibrium (stability) instead of the theory of buoyancy or subsidence (sinking) due to the crustal plate's gravity towards the earth's core. According to the rule of buoyancy, if the buoyant force is greater than the object's weight, the object rises to the surface and floats. The object sinks if the buoyant force is less than the object's weight. If the buoyant force equals the object's weight, it can remain suspended at its depth.

The present śloka of Gītā is based on following mantras of the *Taittirīya Saṁhitā*:

येन द्यौरुग्रा पृथिवि च दृढा (४.१.७)
*yena dyaurugrā pṛthivi ca dṛḍhā (4.1.7)*

स दाधार पृथिविम् (४.१.८)
*sa dādhāra pṛthivim (4.1.8) etc.*

अहं वैश्वानरो भूत्वा प्राणिनां देहमाश्रितः ।
प्राणापानसमायुक्तः पचाम्यन्नं चतुर्विधम् ॥ १५.१४ ॥
*ahaṁ vaiśvānaro bhūtvā prāṇināṁ deham āśritaḥ,*
*prāṇāpāna-samāyuktaḥ pacāmyannaṁ caturvidham. (15.14)*

(*aham*) Brahman (*āśritaḥ*) resides (*deham*) into the bodies of (*prāṇinām*) the living beings (*bhūtvā*) in the form of the (*vaiśvānaraḥ*) power of digestion [or jaṭhrāgni]. With the help of the Prāṇa and Apāna, He helps the digestion of all the four types of foods.

The four types of foods are: Bhakṣya [that which require mastication or what may be eaten by chewing], Bhojya [that which is eaten without mastication i.e. by gulping or swallowing, e.g. powdered food or paste type], Lehya [that which is eaten by licking e.g. sauce type foods] and Choṣya [that which is eaten by sucking, i.e. liquid foods].

सर्वस्य चाहं हृदि सन्निविष्टो मत्तः स्मृतिर्ज्ञानमपोहनं च ।
वेदैश्च सर्वैरहमेव वेद्यो वेदान्तकृद्वेदविदेव चाहम् ॥ १५.१५ ॥
*sarvasya cāhaṁ hṛdi sanniviṣṭo,*
*mattaḥ smṛtir jñānam apohanaṁ ca.*
*vedaiś ca sarvair aham eva vedyo,*
*vedānta-kṛd veda-vid eva cāham. (15.15)*

(*Aham*) Brahman is (*sanniviśṭaḥ*) seated (*hṛdi*) in the

mind [Buddhi] (*sarvasya*) of all beings. The (*smṛti*) memory, (*jñāna*) knowledge, and (*apohanam*) their removal are caused by Him according to the sanskāras of the souls. (*Aham*) He is (*vedyaḥ*) knowable (*sarvaiḥ*) by all (*Vedaiḥ*) the Vedas. (*Aham*) He is, indeed, (*vedānta-kṛt*) the eliminator of knowledge by decreation, (*vedavit*) and the source of knowledge of creation.

Here, Śaṅkarācārya has defined hṛdaya as Buddhi and not as the heart. Knowledge is the property of Brahman and not of anyone else in the world. Since only Brahman is All-Knowing, it is said that Vedas [source of all knowledge] are the property of Brahman. That is why Brahman is said to be the creator of the Vedas or knowledge by creating the worlds, and he also puts an end to the knowledge by decreating the worlds. Buddhi is the abode of Brahman in living beings, and the heart is the abode of ātman (See also 6.39).

द्वाविमौ पुरुषौ लोके क्षरश्चाक्षर एव च ।
क्षरः सर्वाणि भूतानि कूटस्थोऽक्षर उच्यते ॥ १५.१६ ॥
*dvāvimau puruṣau loke kṣaraś cākṣara eva ca,*
*kṣaraḥ sarvāṇi bhūtāni kūṭastho'kṣara ucyate. (15.16)*

(*dvau imau*) There are two entities (*loke*) in this world— (*kṣara*) the perishable (*eva cha*) and (*akṣaraḥ*) the imperishable. (*sarvāṇi bhūtāni*) All bhūtās [The bodies of all beings] are (*kṣaraḥ*) perishable, and (*kūṭathaḥ*) the ātmā [individuated soul] is imperishable.

उत्तमः पुरुषस्त्वन्यः परमात्मेत्युधाहृतः ।
यो लोकत्रयमाविश्य बिभर्त्यव्यय ईश्वरः ॥ १५.१७ ॥
*uttamaḥ puruṣas tvanyaḥ paramātmetyudāhṛtaḥ,*
*yo lokatrayam āviśya bibhartyavyaya Īśvaraḥ. (15.17)*

(*uttamaḥ*) The Supreme or First (*puruṣaḥ*) being (*anyaḥ*) is different from the two. (*Udāhṛtaḥ*) He is called

(*Paramātmā iti*) Paramātmā (Supreme soul or Universal Soul). (*yaḥ*) He (*āviśya*) pervades (*lokatrayam*) the three worlds -Chidākāsa, intermediate space and Bhūtākāsa- and (*bibharti*) upholds them. He is (*avyayaḥ*) indestructible and (*Īśvaraḥ*) Governor of all.

Note: Here the individuated soul is called akṣara and Universal soul is called Avyaya.

यस्मात्क्षरमतीतोऽहमक्षरादपि चोत्तमः ।
अतोऽस्मि लोके वेदे च प्रथितः पुरुषोत्तमः ॥ १५.१८ ॥
*yasmāt kṣaram atīto'ham akṣarād api cottamaḥ,*
*ato'smi loke vede ca prathitaḥ puruṣottamaḥ. (15.18)*

(*Yasmāt*) Because (*Aham*) Brahman is (*atitaḥ*) beyond (*kṣaram*) the perishable body (*api*) and Supreme than (*kṣarāt*) the imperishable soul. So the Supreme soul [Paramātmā] (*prathitaḥ*) is known (*loke*) in this world and (*Vede*) in the Vedas Puruṣottama [the Supreme Spirit or the First one].

यो मामेवमसंमूढो जानातिपुरुषोत्तमम् ।
स सर्वविद्भजति मां सर्वभावेन भारत ॥ १५.१९ ॥
*yo mām evam asammūḍho jānāti puruṣottamam,*
*sa sarva-vid bhajati māṁ sarvabhāvena bhārata. (15.19)*

(*asaṁmuḍhaḥ*) The undeluded (*yaḥ*) one, when (*jānāti*) knows or realises (*mām*) Brahman as the Puruṣottama [Supreme Being or the First person], he (*sarvavit*) knows everything and (*bhajati*) worships (*mām*) Him (*sarvabhāvena*) in all respects wholeheartedly, O descendent of Bharatas. (See also 7.14, 14.26, and 18.66).

इति गुह्यतमं शास्त्रमिदमुक्तं मयाऽनघ ।
एतत्बुद्ध्वा बुद्धिमान्स्यात्कृतकृत्यश्च भारत ॥ १५.२० ॥
*iti guhyatamaṁ śāstram idam uktaṁ mayānagha,*

*etad buddhvā buddhimān syāt kṛta-kṛtyaś ca Bhārata.*

Thus, I have explained this most secret science, O Pure Soul. Having understood this, one becomes enlightened and (*kṛtakṛtyaḥ*) blessed, O son of Bharatas.

ॐ तत्सदिति श्रीमद् भगवद्गीतासूपनिषत्सु ब्रह्मविद्यायां योगशास्त्रे
श्रीकृष्णार्जुनसंवादे पुरुषोत्तमयोगोनाम पंचदशोऽध्याय: ॥१५॥

Here ends the 15th chapter, named Puruṣottama yoga in the *Bhagvadgitā*, dealing with the Brahmavidyā as propounded in the Upaniṣad and Yogaśāstra in the form of dialogue between Śri Krishna and Arjuna.

# अथ षोडशोऽध्यायः

## दैवासुरसंपद्विभागयोगः

# Chapter 16

[Distinction Between Spiritualistic and Materialistic Qualities]

In the ninth chapter, three types of tendencies, Mānuṣī [human], Āsurī or Rākṣasī [demoniac], and Daivī [Divine], have been described. In this chapter, the two tendencies—Daivi and Āsurī have been elucidated further. Śri Krishna tells Arjuna about the difference between (*daivī*) divine or spiritualistic and (*āsurī*) materialistic tendencies. Spiritualistic tendencies are meant for the upliftment of human beings, and materialistic tendencies are meant for Naraka or the downfall of human beings to the lower species. Once a person falls to the lower species, he cannot come out of it until he travels to the lowest one in the series, i.e. the trees and plants. Anger, lust, and greed are the three factors that lead a human being to the (*varaka*) lower species. So, one should not be overpowered by the above three causes of downfall. Śri Krishna also tells us that scriptures are there for our rescue. If there is a doubt about the status of doing or not doing a particular work, one can refer to the scriptures and perform the duty in one's field accordingly.

श्री कृष्ण उवाच

Śri Krishna said

अभयं सत्त्वसंशुद्धिर्ज्ञानयोगव्यवस्थितिः।
दानं दमश्च यज्ञश्च स्वाध्यायस्तप आर्जवम्॥ १६.१॥

*abhayaṁ sattva-sañśuddhir jñāna-yoga-vyavasthitiḥ,*
*dānaṁ damaśca yajñaśca svādhyāyas-tapa ārjavam. (16.1)*

Śri Krishna said— (*Abhaya*) Fearlessness, (*sattva-sañśuddhi)* the purity of mind leading to good conduct or gentlemanly behaviour in society, (*vyavasthiti*) perseverance in accomplishing (*jñāna*) knowledge and yoga, (*dānam*) charity, (*damaścha*) restraining sense organs, (*yajñaścha*) performing yajñas, (*svādhyāyaścha*) the study of scriptures, (*tapaḥ*) austerity at the level of body, speech and mind, and (*ārjavam*) simplicity,

अहिंसा सत्यमक्रोधस्त्यागः शान्तिरपैशुनम् ।
दया भूतेष्वलोलुप्त्वं मार्दवं ह्रीरचापलम् ॥ १६.२ ॥
*ahinsā satyam akrodhas-tyāgaḥ śāntir apaiśunam,*
*dayā bhūteṣvalolupatvaṁ mārdavaṁ hrīr acāpalam. (16.2)*

(*Ahiṁsā*) Nonviolence, (*satyam*) truthfulness, (*akrodhaḥ*) absence of anger, (*tyāgaḥ*) renunciation, (*śāntiḥ*) equanimity [mind free from information of external world], (*apaiśunam*) abstaining from fault-finding and backbiting, (*dayā)* compassion (*bhūteṣu*) for all creatures, (*alolupatvaṁ*) freedom from covetousness, (*mārdvam*) gentleness, (*hriḥ*) modesty, (*āchāpalam*) movement of body without purpose;

तेजः क्षमा धृतिः शौचमद्रोहो नातिमानिता ।
भवन्ति संपदं दैवीमभिजातस्य भारत ॥ १६.३ ॥
*tejaḥ kṣamā dhṛtiḥ śāucam adroho nātimānitā,*
*bhavanti sampadaṁ daivīm abhijātsya bhārata. (16.3)*

(*Tejaḥ*) Strong aura around the face and not the shining of skin (*kṣamā)* maintaining calmness even when one is insulted and abused, (*dhṛtiḥ*) free from the feeling of mental exertion, (śaucham) external and internal purity, (*adrohaḥ*) spirit of non-violence, and (*na+atimānitā*) absence of excessive pride; (*bhavanti*) these are the qualities of those who are (*abhijātasya*) born (*daivim sampadam*) with divine qualities, O Arjuna.

दम्भो दर्पोऽतिमानश्च क्रोध: पारुष्यमेव च।
अज्ञानं चाभिजातस्य पार्थ संपदमासुरीम्॥ १६.४॥
*dambho darpo'bhimānaśca krodhaḥ pāruṣyameva ca,*
*ajñānaṁ cābhijātasya pārtha sampadam-āsurīm. (16.4)*

(*dambhaḥ*) To show as if one is the only custodian of dharma; (*darpaḥ*) feel proud of one's wealth and progeny; (*atimānaḥ*) to consider oneself most respectable; (*krodhaḥ*) to get provocative on being humiliated; (*pāruṣyam*) use of harsh language like to call an ugly person beautiful, one-eyed having beautiful eyes; (*ajñānam*) to think contrary to the reality— these are the qualities of those who are (*abhijātasya*) born with (*āsurī*) materialistic qualities [properties], O son of Pṛthā.

दैवी संपद्विमोक्षाय निबन्धायासुरी मता।
मा शुच: संपदं दैवीमभिजातोऽसि पाण्डव॥ १६.५॥
*daivī sampad vimokṣāya nibandhāyāsurī matā,*
*mā śucaḥ sampadaṁ daivīm abhijāto'si pāṇḍava. (16.5)*

Divine qualities [properties] lead to (*mokṣa*) liberation, and materialistic tendencies lead to bondage. (*mā śuchaḥ*) Do not grieve, (Pāṇḍava) O son of Pāṇḍu, (*abhijātaḥ*) you are born with (*daivim*) divine (*sampadam*) qualities [properties].

द्वौ भूतसर्गौ लोकेऽस्मिन्दैव आसुर एव च।
दैवो विस्तरश: प्रोक्त आसुरं पार्थ मे शृणु॥ १६.६॥
*dvau bhūta-sargau loke'smin daiv-āsura eva ca,*
*daivo vistaraśaḥ prokta āsuraṁ pārtha me śṛṇu. (16.6)*

(*dvau*) There are two types of (*bhūta-sargau*) creations of human beings (*loke*) in this world: (*daiva*) divine or spiritualistic and (*āsura*) the materialistic. (*daivaḥ*) The spiritualistic creation (*proktaḥ*) has been described (*vistaraśaḥ*) at length; (*śṛṇu*) now listen to me (*āsuram*) about the materialistic creation, (Pārtha!) O son of Pṛthā.

Note: The *Bṛhadāraṇyaka Upaniṣad* (1.3.1) also classifies human beings into Devas (having spiritualistic tendencies) and asuras (endowed with materialistic tendencies).

द्वयो ह प्राजापत्या देवाश्च असुराश्च ॥
*dvayo ha prājāpatyā devāśca asurāśca.*

प्रवृत्तिं च निवृत्तिं च जना न विदुरासुराः ।
न शौचं नापि चाचारो न सत्यं तेषु विद्यते ॥ १६.७ ॥
*pravṛttiṁ ca nivṛttiṁ ca janā na vidur āsurāḥ,*
*na śāucaṁ nāpi cācāro na satyaṁ teṣu vidyate. (16.7)*

(*Asurāḥ janāḥ*) Persons of materialistic tendencies (*na vidhūḥ*) do not know (*pravṛttim*) what action is to be taken and (*nivṛttim*) what not to achieve the objective of human life. (*na śaucham*) They lack purity, (*na api cha+āchāraḥ*) good conduct, and (*satyam*) truthfulness.

असत्यमप्रतिष्ठं ते जगदाहुरनीश्वरम् ।
अपरस्परसंभूतं किमन्यत्कामहैतुकम् ॥ १६.८ ॥
*asatyam apratiṣṭhaṁ te jagad āhur anīśvaram,*
*aparaspara-sambhūtaṁ kim anyat kāma-haitukam. (16.8)*

(*te*) They [materialists] (*āhuḥ*) say that this world is (*asatyam*) full of falsehood [as they are] (*apratiṣṭham*) not based upon rules of dharma [so they also do not want to follow dharma in their day-to-day activities]. (*anīśvaram*) This world is not governed by any power that punishes or rewards humans per their bad or good karmas. (*sambhūtam*) It is a product of the (*aparaspara*) sexual union of male and female, and as such, it has (*kim anyat*) no creative force other than (*kāmahaitukam*) lust. According to this view, lust is the creatures' purpose and cause of origin. This philosophy is called Chārvaka [materialistic] philosophy. According to this philosophy, the body is the soul.

एतां दृष्टिमवष्टभ्य नष्टात्मानोऽल्पबुद्धयः ।
प्रभवन्त्युग्रकर्माणः क्षयाय जगतोऽहिताः ॥ १६.९ ॥
*etāṁ dṛṣṭim avaṣṭabhya naṣṭātmāno'lpabuddhayaḥ,*
*prabhavantyugra-karmāṇaḥ kṣayāya jagato'hitāḥ. (16.9)*

(*avaṣṭabhya*) Adhering to (*etāṁ dṛṣṭiṁ*) the above view [philosophy], people (*naṣṭātmānaḥ*) who do not identify their true nature [who think that they are body], (*alpabuddhayaḥ*) who are engaged in sensory pleasures and (*ugrakarmāṇaḥ*) violent acts, (*prabhavanti*) are born (*jagataḥ ahitāḥ*) to play havoc in this world and (*kṣayāya*) act for its destruction.

Note: The people who believe in this philosophy cannot think of the well-being of humanity at large. Their life is dedicated to terrorism, bloodshed and destruction of the world. This truth was unfolded by Śri Krishna 5,000 years ago.

काममाश्रित्य दुष्पूरं दम्भमानमदान्विताः ।
मोहाद्गृहीत्वासद्ग्राहान्प्रवर्तन्तेऽशुचिव्रताः ॥ १६.१० ॥
*kāmam āśritya duṣpūraṁ dambha-māna-madānvitāḥ,*
*mohād gṛhītvā sad-grāhān pravartante'śucivratāḥ. (16.10)*

(*kāmam+āśritya duṣpūram*) Filled with insatiable desires, (*dambha*) false perception of the only custodianship of dharma, (*māna*) pride, and (*mada*) arrogance; (*grahitvā*) observing (*asad-grāhān*) evil conduct (*mohād*) due to delusion; they [materialists] (*pravartante*) act (*aśuchi-vratāḥ*) with ulterior motives.

चिन्तामपरिमेयां च प्रलयान्तामुपाश्रिताः ।
कामोपभोगपरमा एतावदिति निश्चिताः ॥ १६.११ ॥
*cintām aparimeyāṁ ca pralayāntām upāśritāḥ,*
*kāmopabhoga-paramā etāvaditi niścitāḥ. (16.11)*

(*upāśritāḥ*) Engrossed in (*aparimeyāṁ*) innumerable

(*chintāṁ*) anxiety (*pralayāntām*) that can end only with death, they have (*etāvad iti*) only the (*niśchitāḥ*) consideration that (*kāma+upabhoga+paramā*) the sensual gratification is the highest goal of their life.

आशापाशशतैर्बद्धा: कामक्रोधपरायणा: ।
ईहन्ते कामभोगार्थमन्यायेनार्थसंचयान् ॥ १६.१२ ॥
*āśā-pāśa-śatair baddhāḥ kāma-krodha-parāyaṇāḥ,*
*īhante kāma-bhogārtham anyāyenārtha-sañcayān. (16.12)*

(*baddhāḥ*) Bound by (*pāśa-śataiḥ*) hundreds of fetters of (*āśā*) desire and (*parāyaṇāḥ*) enslaved by (*kāma*) lust and (*krodha*) anger; (*īhante*) they strive to hoard (*artha-sañchayān*) wealth (*anyāyena*) by unlawful means for the (*kāma-bhogārtham*) fulfilment of desires.

इदमद्य मया लब्धमिमं प्राप्स्ये मनोरथम् ।
इदमस्तीदमपि मे भविष्यति पुनर्धनम् ॥ १६.१३ ॥
*Idam adya mayā labdhamimaṁ prāpsye manoratham,*
*Idam astīdam api me bhaviṣyati punar dhanam. (16.13)*

[They think that] (*idam*) this has been (*labdham*) gained (*mayā*) by them (*adya*) today, (*prāpsye*) I shall obtain (*imam*) this also (*manoratham*) to fulfil my desire, (*idam asti*) this is theirs and (*idam api dhanam*) that property (*bhaviṣyati*) will (*punaḥ*) also be (*me*) theirs in the future.

असौ मया हत: शत्रुर्हनिष्ये चापरानपि ।
ईश्वरोऽहमहं भोगी सिद्धोऽहं बलवान्सुखी ॥ १६.१४ ॥
*asau mayā hataḥ śatrur-haniṣye cāparān api,*
*īśvaro'ham ahaṁ bhogī siddho'haṁ balavān sukhi. (16.14)*

(*asau*) That (*śatruḥ*) enemy has been (*hataḥ*) slain by (*mayā*) me, and (*haniṣye*) I shall slay (*aparān*) others (*api*) also. (*Īśvaraḥ ahaṁ*) I am the Lord. (*aham*) I am the only (*bhogī*) enjoyer of material comforts. (*aham siddhaḥ*) I am successful, (*balavān*) powerful, and (*sukhī*) happy.

आढ्योऽभिजनवानस्मि कोऽन्योस्ति सदृशो मया।
यक्षये दास्यामि मोदिष्य इत्यज्ञानविमोहिता: ॥ १६.१५ ॥
*āḍhyo'bhijanavān asmi ko'nyo'sti sadṛśo mayā,*
*yakṣye dāsyāmi modiṣya ityajñāna-vimohitāḥ. (16.15)*

(*āḍhyaḥ*) I am rich and (abhijanvān asmi) born in a noble family. (ko anyaḥ asti)) No one is (*sadṛśaḥ*) parallel (*mayā*) to me. (*yakṣaye*) I will perform Yajña, (*dāsyāmi*) I will give charity, and (*modiṣye*) will rejoice. (*iti*) Thus they (*vimohitāḥ*) stay deluded (*ajñān*) by false notions.

अनेकचित्तविभ्रान्ता मोहजालसमावृता:।
प्रसक्ता: कामभोगेषु पतन्ति नरकेऽशुचौ ॥ १६.१६ ॥
*aneka-citta-vibhrāntā moha-jāla-samāvṛtāḥ,*
*prasaktāḥ kāma-bhogeṣu patanti narake'śucau. (16.16)*

(*Vibhrāntāḥ*) Bewildered by (*aneka-chitta*) many fancies; (*samāvṛtāḥ*) entangled (*mohajāla*) in the net of delusion; (*prasaktāḥ*) addicted to (*kāmabhogeṣu*) the enjoyment of sensual pleasures; (*patanti*) they fall (*narake*) into lower species (*aśuchau*) which are loathsome.

आत्मसंभाविता: स्तब्धा धनमानमदान्विता:।
यजन्ते नामयज्ञैस्ते दम्भेनाविधिपूर्वकम् ॥ १६.१७ ॥
*ātma-sambhāvitāḥ stabdhā dhana-māna-madānvitāḥ,*
*yajante nāma-yajñaiste dambhenāvidhi-pūrvakam. (16.17)*

(*ātma+sambhāvitāḥ*) Suffering from a self-grandiosity, (*stabdhāḥ*) stubborn, (*anvitāḥ*) filled with (*dhana*) pride of wealth and (*mada*) arrogance; (*te*) they (*yajante*) perform yajña (*nāma-yajñaiḥ*) only for the name's sake, (*dambhena*) to show that they are custodian of dharma (*avidhi-pūrvakam*) without knowledge of the proper procedure.

अहंकारं बलं दर्पं कामं क्रोधं च संश्रिता: ।
मामात्मपरदेहेषु प्रद्विषन्तोऽभ्यसूयका: ॥ १६.१८ ॥
*ahaṅkāraṁ balaṁ darpaṁ kāmaṁ krodhaṁ ca sañśritāḥ,*
*māmātma-para-deheṣu pradviṣanto'bhyasūyakāḥ. (16.18)*

(*Sañśritāḥ*) Clinging to (*ahaṅkāram*) egoism, (*balam*) power, (*darpam*) arrogance, (*kāmam*) lust, (*cha*) and (*krodham*) anger; (*pradviṣantaḥ*) they violate the command of (*māma*) Brahman (*ātma+paradeheṣu*) located in their bodies and others, and (*abhi+asūyakāḥ*) criticize those who are endowed with good qualities and follow the path of dharma.

तानहं द्विषत: क्रुरान्संसारेषु नराधमान् ।
क्षिपाम्यजस्रमशुभानासुरीष्वेव योनिषु ॥ १६.१९ ॥
*tānahaṁ dviṣataḥ krūrān sansāreṣu narādhamān,*
*kṣipāmyajasram aśubhānāsurīṣveva yoniṣu. (16.19)*

(*Aham*) Brahman (*kṣipāmi*) throws (*kṣipram*) immediately (*tān*) these (*dviṣantaḥ*) opposer of good path and good persons, (*krurān*) cruel, and (*narādhamān*) mean people (*sansāreṣu*) of the world into (*āsrīṣu eva yoniṣu*) āsura species [birds, animals, and insects] only which are (*aśubhān*) engaged in cruel and low level of karmas.

आसुरीं योनिमापन्ना मूढा जन्मनिजन्मनि ।
मामप्राप्यैव कौन्तेय ततो यान्त्यधमां गतिम् ॥ १६.२० ॥
*āsurīṁ yonim āpannā mūḍhā janmani janmani,*
*mām aprāpyaiva kaunteya tato yāntyadhamāṁ gatim. (16.20)*

हे कुंती पुत्र अर्जुन, (अपन्न:) (आसुरिम्) निम्न (योनिम) योनियों (मूढ़ा:) में प्रवेश करते हुए, जो भ्रमित लोग अच्छे और बुरे कर्मों के बीच अंतर करने में सक्षम नहीं हैं, उन्हें (माम्) मुझ द्वारा दिखाया गया अच्छा मार्ग (अप्राप्य) कभी नहीं मिलता है। दोबारा मानव जीवन पाने से पहले वे (तत:) और पेड़-पौधों की सबसे निचली योनी (अधमाम् गतिम्) को (यांति) प्राप्त करते हैं।

O son of Kunti, (*āpannāḥ*) entering into the (*āsurīm*) lower (*yonim*) species (*mūḍhāḥ*), the deluded ones who are not able to distinguish between good and bad actions (*aprāpya*) never find (*māma*) the good path shown by me. They continue (*yānti*) to sink (*tataḥ*) further down to (*adhamām gatim*), the lowest species of trees and plants, before getting human life again.

## Three Gates of Naraka

त्रिविधं नरकस्येदं द्वारं नाशनमात्मनः ।
कामः क्रोधस्तथा लोभस्तस्मादेतत्त्रयं त्यजेत् ॥ १६.२१ ॥
*trividhaṁ narakasyedaṁ dvāraṁ nāśanam ātmanaḥ,*
*kāmaḥ krodhas tathā lobhas tasmād etat-trayaṁ tyajet. (16.21)*

(कामः) वासना, (क्रोधः) अपमानित या दुर्व्यवहार किए जाने पर उत्तेजित हो जाना, और (लोभः) भौतिक चीजों को जमा करने का लालच - (त्रिविधम्) ये तीन द्वार हैं जो नरक (मनुष्य से निचली योनियों) की ओर खुलते हैं। (आत्मानः नाशनम्) ये आत्मा को निम्न योनि में पतन की ओर ले जाते हैं। (तस्मात्) अतः (त्यजेत्) इन तीनों को (एतत् त्रयम्) त्याग दें।

श्री कृष्ण कहना चाहते हैं कि काम, क्रोध और लालच मनुष्य के निम्न योनियों —पशु, पक्षी, कीड़े, पौधे आदि में जन्म का कारण बनते हैं। यहाँ, 'नरक' का अर्थ निम्न योनियाँ है।

(*kāmaḥ*) Lust, (*krodhaḥ*) to get provocative on being humiliated or abused, and (*lobhaḥ*) greed for hoarding material things (*trividham*). These three gates open towards the Naraka (species lower than human beings). (*ātmanaḥ nāśanam*) They lead to the downfall of the soul to the lower species. (*Tasmāt*) Therefore, (*tyajet*) give up (*etat trayam*) all these three.

Śri Krishna wants to say that the presence of lust, anger, and greed are signs of the downfall of human beings into lower beings - animals, birds, insects, plants, etc. Here, Naraka means lower species.

एतैर्विमुक्तः कौन्तेय तमोद्वारैस्त्रिभिर्नरः ।
आचरत्यात्मनः श्रेयस्ततो याति परां गतिम् ॥ १६.२२ ॥
*etair-vimuktaḥ kaunteya tamodvārais tribhir naraḥ,*
*ācaratyātmanaḥ śreyas tato yāti parāṁ gatim. (16.22)*

(कौन्तेय) हे कुंती पुत्र अर्जुन, जो नरक (पशु पक्षी आदि निचली योनियों ) में ले जाने वाले इन (त्रिभिः) तीन (तमो-द्वारैः) तमोगुणी द्वारों से (विमुक्तः) छुटकारा पा लेता है और जो (आत्मानः श्रेयः) अपने सर्वोत्तम उत्थान के लिए (आचरति) प्रयास करता है; वही (याति) परम लक्ष्य [मोक्ष] को प्राप्त करता है।

One who (*vimuktaḥ*) gets rid of (*etaiḥ*) these (*tribhiḥ*) three (*tamo-dvāraiḥ*) tamoguṇa dominant gates of Naraka [lower species], (*Kaunteya*) O son of Kunti, and (*ācharati*) attempts what is (*ātmanaḥ śreyaḥ*) best for his upliftment; he only (*yāti*) attains the (*paramāṁ gatim*) supreme goal.

यः शास्त्रविधिमुत्सृज्य वर्तते कामकारतः ।
न स सिद्धिमवाप्नोति न सुखं न परां गतिम् ॥ १६.२३ ॥
*yaḥ śāstra-vidhim-utasṛjya vartate kāma-kārataḥ,*
*na sa siddhim avāpnoti na sukhaṁ na parāṁ gatim. (16.23)*

(यः) जो (शास्त्र-विधिम्) शास्त्रों के आदेशों का पालन (उत्सृज्य) नहीं करता और (कामकारतः) अपनी इच्छा के अनुसार कार्य (वर्तते) करता है, (सः) वह (सिद्धि) जीवन के लक्ष्य [मोक्ष] को प्राप्त करने की योग्यता (अवाप्नोति) प्राप्त (न) नहीं करता तथा (न) न ही (सुखम) सुख और न (परम) सर्वोच्च (गतिम्) लक्ष्य अर्थात् मोक्ष को प्राप्त कर सकता है।

(*yaḥ*) One (*utsṛjya*) who does not follow (*śāstra-vidhim*) the injunctions of scriptures and (*vartate*) acts (*kāmakārataḥ*) according to his whims and desires, (*saḥ*) he (*na*) neither (*avāpnoti*) attains (*siddhi*) qualification or merit for achieving the goal of life [*mokṣa*], (*na*) nor (*sukham*) happiness (*na*) nor (*parāṁ*) the supreme (*gatim*) goal.

तस्माच्छास्त्रं प्रमाणं ते कार्याकार्यव्यवस्थितौ ।

ज्ञात्वा शास्त्रविधानोक्तं कर्म कर्तुमिहार्हसि ॥ १६.२४ ॥
*tasmāc-chāstraṁ pramāṇaṁ te kāryākārya-vyavasthitau,*
*jñātvā śāstra-vidhānoktaṁ karma kartum-ihārhasi. (16.24)*

(तस्मात्) इसलिए, (शास्त्र) शास्त्र (ते) आपका (प्रमाणम्) मार्गदर्शक (व्यवस्थितौ) है जो यह निर्धारित करता है कि (कार्य) क्या किया जाना चाहिए और (अकार्य) क्या नहीं किया जाना चाहिए। (शास्त्र-विधान + उक्तम्) शास्त्रों के आदेशों को (ज्ञात्वा) जानने के बाद, आप (इह) अपने क्षेत्र में अपना कर्तव्य कर सकते हैं।

(*tasmāt*) Therefore, (*Śāstra*) the Śāstra is (*te*) your (*pramāṇam*) guide (*vyavasthitau*) in determining (*kārya*) what should be done and (*akārya*) what not. (*Jñātvā*) Having known (*Śāstra-vidhāna+uktaṁ*) the injunctions of Śāstras, you (*kartum*) can perform (*karma*) your duty (*iha*) here [in a field where you are required to do your duty].

ॐ तत्सदिति श्रीमद् भगवद्गीतासूपनिषत्सु ब्रह्मविद्यायां योगशास्त्रे श्रीकृष्णार्जुनसंवादे दैवासुरसंपद्विभागयोगोनाम षोडशोऽध्याय: ॥१६ ॥

Here ends the 16th chapter, named Daiva-Āsura-Śampad-Vibhāga Yoga in the *Bhagvadgitā*, dealing with the Brahmavidyā as propounded in the Upaniṣad and Yogaśāstra in the form of dialogue between Śri Krishna and Arjuna.

# अथ सप्तदशोऽध्याय:

## श्रद्धात्रयविभागयोग:

# Chapter 17

[Threefold Human tendency or Attitude]

In this chapter, Śri Krishna tells Arjuna about the three natural personality types— Sātvika, Rājasika, and Tāmasika. Based on the nature of one's personality, an individual will have respect for different things. A Sātvika personality type will have respect for knowledge and spiritualism. A Rājasika personality type will have respect for materialism. The money-hoarding tendency and desire for materialistic comforts is materialism. Today, we come across many so-called Godfathers hoarding money in the name of spiritualism, yoga, and devotionalism. They spend that public money for their own luxury, comfort, fun and amusements, not in the public interest. They do not hand over their legacy to others in the future. Their vast empire collapses at their own collapse. It is Rājasika tendency. A Tāmasika personality type will have respect for dead bodies. Burying the dead and their worship or glorification like mummies of Egyptian Pyramids is all Tāmasika tendency. The different personality types have different likings for food. For example, the juicy foods that promote longevity, intelligence, strength, physical and mental health, happiness, and cheerfulness, which are nutritious (long-lasting), wholesome, and agreeable - are liked by the Sāttvika personality type persons. Foods that are bitter, sour, salty, very hot, pungent, dry, and burning, which cause pain, grief, worries, and disease - are liked by Rājasika persons. The foods liked by Tāmasika persons are tin foods, half-cooked, tasteless, rotten, preserved with the help of preservatives and freezers for many days, stale, refuses, and impure [such as meat and alcohol]. Similarly, the nature of Yajña, Dāna [donations], and Tapa [austerity] done by three personality types have been defined as three types. One can mould oneself into different personality types by changing food habits, likings, etc.

अर्जुन उवाच

Arjuna said

ये शास्त्रविधिमुत्सृज्य यजन्ते श्रद्धयान्विताः ।
तेषां निष्ठा तु का कृष्ण सत्त्वमाहो रजस्तमः ॥ १७.१ ॥

*ye śāstra-vidhim utsṛjya yajante śradhayānvitāḥ,*
*teṣāṁ niṣṭhā tu kā kṛṣṇa sattvam āho rajas tamaḥ. (17.01)*

(*kā*) What is the (*niṣṭhā*) position (*teṣām*) of (*ye*) those (*yajante*) who perform spiritual practices (*śraddhayānvitāḥ*) with śraddhā [positive attitude] (*utsṛjya*) but fail to follow the (*śāstra-vidhim*) scriptural injunctions, (*Kṛṣṇa*) O Krishna? Is it (*sattvam*) Sāttvika, (*rajas*) Rājasika, or (*tamaḥ*) Tāmasika?

श्री कृष्ण उवाच

Śri Krishna said

त्रिविधा भवति श्रद्धा देहिनां सा स्वभावजा ।
सात्त्विकी राजसी चैव तामसी चेति तां शृणु ॥ १७.२ ॥

*trividhā bhavati śraddhā dehināṁ sā svabhāvajā,*
*sāttvikī rājasī caiva tāmasī ceti tāṁ śṛṇu. (17.02)*

Śri Krishna said— (*śraddhā*) Tendencies (*dehinām*) of embodied souls, (*sā svabhāvajā*) born of their sanskāras, (*bhavati*) is (*trividhā*) of three types— (*sāttvikī*) Sāttvika, (*rājasī*) Rājasika, (*cha+eva*) and (*tāmasī*) Tāmasika. (*śṛṇu*) Hear (*tāṁ*) that from Me.

**Note:** The innate nature of an individual is governed

by sanskāras of good or bad deeds performed by an individual in the past life.

सत्त्वानुरूपा सर्वस्य श्रद्धा भवति भारत।
श्रद्धामयोऽयं पुरुषो यो यच्छ्रद्धः स एव सः ॥ १७.३ ॥
*sattvānurūpā sarvasya śraddhā bhavati bhārata,*
*śraddhāmayo'yaṁ puruṣo yo yacchradddhaḥ sa eva saḥ. (17.03)*

(*Bharata*) O descendant of Bharatas (*śraddhā*), the attitude (*sarvasya*) of each individual (*sattva+anurūpā*) depends upon his/her sanskāras [information stored in mind]. (*ayaṁ puruṣaḥ*) The personality of an individual (*śraddhāmayaḥ*) is shaped by his/her tendency. In fact, (*yaḥ yat śraddhaḥ*) an individual's tendency or attitude (*saḥ eva saḥ*) reflects in his personality.

यजन्ते सात्त्विका देवान्यक्षरक्षांसि राजसाः।
प्रेतान्भूतगणांश्चान्ये यजन्ते तामसा जनाः ॥ १७.४ ॥
*yajante sāttvikā devān yakṣa-rakṣānsi rājasāḥ,*
*pretān bhūta-gaṇāñś cānye yajante tāmasā janāḥ. (17.04)*

The persons with sāttvika sanskāras (*yajante*) pray for divinity; persons with the rājasika sanskāras for (*yakṣa*) hoarding and (*rakṣānsi*) preserving materialistic things, and the persons with tāmasika sanskāras (*yajante*) pray for (*pretān*) dead bodies and (*bhūtagaṇān*) creatures of lower species like animals, birds, insects, plants, trees (*cha anye*) and other lifeless things or objects.

अशास्त्रविहितं घोरं तप्यन्ते ये तपो जनाः।
दम्भाहंकारसंयुक्ताः कामरागबलान्विताः ॥ १७.५ ॥
*aśāstra-vihitaṁ ghoraṁ tapyante ye tapo janāḥ,*
*dambhāhaṅkāra-sañyuktāḥ kāma-rāga-balānvitāḥ. (17.05)*

(*ye*) Those who (*tapyante*) practice (*ghoram*) severe (*tapaḥ*) austerities (*aśāstra-vihitam*) without following the guidelines of scriptures, (*dambha+ahaṅkāra+yuktāḥ*) for pomp and show, and (*anvitāḥ*) impelled by (*kāma*) lust, and (*rāga*) attachment;

कर्शयन्तः शरीरस्थं भूतग्राममचेतसः ।
मां चैवान्तःशरीरस्थं तान्विद्ध्यासुरनिश्चयान् ॥ १७.६ ॥
*karśayantaḥ śarīrasthaṁ bhūta-grāmam-acetasaḥ,*
*māṁ caivāntaḥ śarīrasthaṁ tān viddhyāsura-niścayān.* (17.06)

(*achetasaḥ*) Senselessly (*karśayantaḥ*) torturing (*bhūtagrāmam*) his/her five senses, motor organs and (*mām*) the soul (*antaḥ+śarīrastham*) in the body; (*viddhi*) know (*tān*) these ignorant persons to be of (*asura+niśchayān*) āsurī [materialistic] nature.

आहारस्त्वपि सर्वस्य त्रिविधो भवति प्रियः ।
यज्ञस्तपस्तथा दानं तेषां भेदमिमं शृणु ॥ १७.७ ॥
*āhārastvapi sarvasya trividho bhavati priyaḥ,*
*yajñas tapas tathā dānaṁ teṣāṁ bhedam imaṁ śṛṇu.*(17.07)

(*āhāraḥ*) The food (*priyaḥ*) liked (*sarvasya*) by all (*bhavati*) is also of (*trividhaḥ*) three types. So are the yajña, tapa [austerity], and dāna [charity]. Now (*śṛṇu*) hear the (*bhedam*) distinction (*imam*) amongst them.

आयुःसत्त्वबलारोग्यसुखप्रीतिविवर्धनाः ।
रस्याः स्निग्धाः स्थिरा हृद्या आहाराः सात्त्विकप्रियाः ॥ १७.८ ॥
*āyuḥ-sattva-balārogya sukha-prīti-vivardhanāḥ,*
*rasyāḥ snigdhāḥ sthirā hṛdyā āhārāḥ sāttvika-priyāḥ.* (17.08)

(*rasyāḥ*) The juicy (*āhārāḥ*) foods that (*vivardhanāḥ*) promote (*āyuḥ*) longevity, (*sattva*) intelligence, (*bala*) strength, (*ārogya*) physical and mental health, (*sukha*) spiritual happiness, and (*prīti*) cheerfulness; which are (*sthirāḥ*) long-lasting, (*snigdhāḥ*) not dried up, and (*hṛdyā*) tasty – are (*sāttvika-priyāḥ*) dear to the sāttvika persons.

कट्वम्ललवणात्युष्णतीक्ष्णरूक्षविदाहिनः ।

आहारा राजसस्येष्टा दुःखशोकामयप्रदाः ॥ १७.९ ॥
*kaṭvamla-lavaṇātyuṣṇa tīkṣṇa-rūkṣa-vidāhinaḥ,*
*āhārā rājasasyeṣṭā duḥkha-śokāmaya-pradāḥ. (17.09)*

(*āhārāḥ*) Foods that are (*kaṭu*) bitter, (*amla*) sour, (*lavaṇa*) salty, (*atyuṣṇa*) excessively hot, (*tīkṣṇa*) pungent, (*rukṣa*) dry, and (*vidāhinaḥ*) burning; which (pradāḥ) cause (diḥkha) pain, (śoka) grief, and (*āmayaḥ*) diseases – *(rājasasya iṣṭāḥ)* are liked by rājasika persons.

यातयामं गतरसं पूति पर्युषितं च यत्।
उच्छिष्टमपि चामेध्यं भोजनं तामसप्रियम्॥ १७.१० ॥
*yāta-yāmaṁ gata-rasaṁ pūti paryuṣitaṁ ca yat,*
*ucchiṣṭam api cāmedhyaṁ bhojanaṁ tāmasa-priyam. (17.10)*

(*Bhojanam*) The foods (*tāmasa-priyam*) liked by tāmasika persons are: (*yātayāmam*) half-cooked (*gatarasam*) those have lost their flavour or sap, (*pūti*) stinking [foul-smelling], (*paryuṣitam*) stale, (*uccchhiṣṭam*) refuses, and (*amedhyam*) impure [which cannot be used in yajña].

अफलाकाङ्क्षिभिर्यज्ञो विधिदृष्टो य इज्यते।
यष्टव्यमेवेति मनः समाधाय स सात्त्विकः॥ १७.११ ॥
*aphalākāṅkṣibhiryajño vidhi-dṛsto ya ijyate,*
*yaṣṭavyam eveti manaḥ samādhāya sa sāttvikaḥ. (17.11)*

(*yajñaḥ*) Yajña, (*yaḥ*) which is (*ijyate*) performed (*vidhidṛṣṭaḥ*) according to the ordinances of the scriptures, (*aphalākāṅkṣī*) without any vested interest and (*yaṣṭavyam+eva+iti manaḥ samādhāya*) with firm belief as a duty, is Sāttvika Yajña.

अभिसंधाय तु फलं दम्भार्थमपि चैव यत्।
इज्यते भरतश्रेष्ठ तं यज्ञं विद्धि राजसम्॥ १७.१२ ॥
*abhisandhāya tu phalaṁ dambhārtham api caiva yat,*
*ijyate bharataśreṣtha taṁ yajñaṁ viddhi rājasam. (17.12)*

(*yat*) Yajña, which is (*ijyate*) performed with (*abhisandhāya phalam*) a vested interest, (*cha+eva*) only (*dambhārtham*) for the show, (*viddhi*) know (*tam yajñam*) that to be (*rājasam*) Rājasika one, (*Bharata-śreṣṭha*) O Best among the descendants of Bharatas.

विधिहीनमसृष्टान्नं मन्त्रहीनमदक्षिणम्।
श्रद्धाविरहितं यज्ञं तामसं परिचक्षते॥ १७.१३॥
*vidhi-hīnam asṛṣṭānnaṁ mantra-hīnam adakṣiṇam,*
*śraddhā-virahitaṁ yajñaṁ tāmasaṁ paricakṣate. (17.13)*

Yajña performed (*vidhihīnam*) without the scriptural ordinance, (*asṛṣṭānnam*) devoid of food offering, (*mantrahīnam*) mantra, (*śradhhā-virahitam*) faith, and (*adakṣiṇam*) desired results is (*parichakṣate*) said to be (*tāmasam*) Tāmasika Yajña.

देवद्विजगुरुप्राज्ञपूजनं शौचमार्जवम्।
ब्रह्मचर्यमहिंसा च शारीरं तप उच्यते॥ १७.१४॥
*deva-dvija-guru-prājña-pūjanaṁ śāucam-ārjavam,*
*brahmacaryam-ahinsā ca śārīraṁ tapa ucyate. (17.14)*

(*Pūjanam*) The respect for Devas [divine persons], (*dvija*) scholars (*guru*) mother, father, āchārya, (*prājña*) wise persons, and (*śaucham*) observance of purity, (*ārjavam*) straightforwardness, (*brahmacharyam*) celibacy, and (*ahiṁsā*) nonviolence – these are (*uchyate*) said to be (*tapa*) the austerity of the (*śārīram*) physical body.

अनुद्वेगकरं वाक्यं सत्यं प्रियहितं च यत्।
स्वाध्यायाभ्यसनं चैव वाङ्मयं तप उच्यते॥ १७.१५॥
*anudvegakaraṁ vākyaṁ satyaṁ priyahitaṁ ca yat,*
*svādhyāyābhyasanaṁ caiva vāṅmayaṁ tapa ucyate. (17.15)*

(*vākyam*) Speech (*unudvegakaram*) that does not agitate the listeners, that which is (*satyam*) truthful, (*priya*) pleasant, (*hitam*) beneficial, and (*svādhyāya+abhyasanam*) the practice of regular studies of scriptures is (*uchyate*) called the (*tapa*) austerity of (*vāṅmayam*) speech.

मनः प्रसादः सौम्यत्वं मौनमात्मविनिग्रहः ।
भावसंशुद्धिरित्येतत्तपो मानसमुच्यते ॥ १७.१६ ॥
*manaḥ-prasādaḥ saumyatvaṁ maunam ātma-vinigrahaḥ,*
*bhāva-saṅśuddhir ityetat tapo mānasam ucyate. (17.16)*

The (*prasādaḥ*) serenity of (*manaḥ*) mind, (*saumyatvam*) gentleness, (*maunam*) silence, (*ātma-vinigrahaḥ*) self-restraint, and the (*saṅśuddhiḥ*) purity of (*bhāva*) thought is called the (*tapaḥ*) austerity of (*mānasam*) mind.

श्रद्धया परया तप्तं तपस्तत्त्रिविधं नरैः ।
अफलाकाङ्क्षिभिर्युक्तैः सात्त्विकं परिचक्षते ॥ १७.१७ ॥
*śraddhayā parayā taptaṁ tapas tat trividhaṁ naraiḥ,*
*aphalākāṅkṣibhir yuktaiḥ sāttvikaṁ paricakṣate. (17.17)*

(*trividham*) Threefold (*tapaḥ*) austerity [of thought, speech, and body] (taptam) practised (*naraiḥ*) by people with (*parayā*) supreme (*śraddhayā*) devotion, (*aphala+ākāṅkṣibhiḥ+yuktaiḥ*) without a vested interest, is (*parichakṣate*) said to be (*sāttvikam*) sāttvika austerity.

सत्कारमानपूजार्थं तपो दम्भेन चैव यत् ।
क्रियते तदिह प्रोक्तं राजसं चलमध्रुवम् ॥ १७.१८ ॥
*satkāra-māna-pūjārthaṁ tapo dambhena caiva yat,*
*kriyate tadiha proktaṁ rājasaṁ calam adhruvam. (17.18)*

(*tapaḥ*) Austerity done (*satkār-māna-pūjārtham*) for gaining respect, honour, reverence, (*cha+eva*) also (*kriyate*) done (*dambhena*) for showing that you can only do it, is (*proktam*) said to be (*rājasam*) rājasika. It is (*chalam*) transitory and (*adhruvam*) unstable.

मूढग्राहेणात्मनो यत्पीडया क्रियते तपः ।

परस्योत्सादनार्थं वा तत्तामसमुदाहृतम् ॥ १७.१९ ॥
*mūḍha-grāheṇātmano yat pīḍayā kriyate tapaḥ,*
*parasyotsādanārthaṁ vā tat tāmasam-udāhṛtam. (17.19)*

(*Tapaḥ*) Austerity (*kriyate*) performed (*mūḍha-grāheṇa*) without proper understanding, or (*yat*) that (*ātmanaḥ pīḍayā*) with self-torture, (vā) or (*utsādanārtham*) for harming (*parasya*) others, is (*udāhṛtam*) declared as (*tāmasam*) tāmasika.

दातव्यमिति यद्दानं दीयतेऽनुपकारिणे ।
देशे काले च पात्रे च तद्दानं सात्त्विकं स्मृतम् ॥ १७.२० ॥
*dātavyam iti yaddānaṁ dīyate'nupakāriṇe,*
*deśe kāle ca pātre ca taddānaṁ sāttvikaṁ smṛtam. (17.20)*

(*yat+dānam*) Charity (*dīyate*) done (*dātavyam iti)* with a sense of duty (*pātre*) to a deserving person (*anupakāriṇe*) who is not able to repay for it, (*deśe*) at the right place (*kāle*) and time is (*smṛtam*) called (*sāttvikaṁ*) a sāttvika charity.

यत्तु प्रत्युपकारार्थं फलमुद्दिश्य वा पुनः ।
दीयते च परिक्लिष्टं तद्दानं राजसं स्मृतम् ॥ १७.२१ ॥
*yattu pratyupakārārthaṁ phalam uddiśya vā punaḥ,*
*dīyate ca parikliṣṭaṁ taddānaṁ rājasaṁ smṛtam. (17.21)*

Charity which has been (*dīyate*) done (*pratypakārārtham*) to get something in return, (*vā*) or (*phalam uddiśya*) with the view to get reward (*punaḥ*) in future or the next life (*cha*) or (*parikliśṭam*) with regret is (*smṛtam*) called (*rājasam*) rājasika charity.

अदेशकाले यद्दानमपात्रेभ्यश्च दीयते ।
असत्कृतमवज्ञातं तत्तामसमुदाहृतम् ॥ १७.२२ ॥
*adeśa-kāle yaddānam-apātrebhyaśca dīyate,*
*asatkṛtam avajñātaṁ tat tāmasam udāhṛtam. (17.22)*

A charity that is (*dīyate*) done (*adeśa-kāle*) at a wrong

place and time, (*apātrebhyaḥ*) to undeserving persons, (*asatkṛtam*) without respect or (*avajñātam*) with contempt, is (*udāhṛtam*) said to be (*tāmasam*) tāmasika charity.

ॐ तत्सदिति निर्देशो ब्रह्मणस्त्रिविधः स्मृतः ।
ब्राह्मणास्तेन वेदाश्च यज्ञाश्च विहिताः पुरा ॥ १७.२३ ॥
*oṁ tat-sad-iti nirdeśo brahmaṇastri-vidhaḥ smṛtaḥ,*
*brāhmaṇāstena vedāśca yajñāśca vihitāḥ purā. (17.23)*

"Oṁ Tat Sat" is (*smṛtaḥ*) said to be (*trividhaḥ*) the threefold (*nirdeśaḥ*) designation of (*Brahmaṇaḥ*) Brahman. (*purā)* In ancient times (*Brāmaṇāśḥ*), the Brāhmaṇa texts were written, (*vedaścha*) Vedas were chanted (cha), and (*yajñāḥ*) the performance of Yajñas was (*vihitāḥ*) done (*tena*) with the chanting of this designation [Oṁ Tat Sat].

तस्मादोमित्युदाहृत्य यज्ञदानतपःक्रियाः ।
प्रवर्तन्ते विधानोक्ताः सततं ब्रह्मवादिनाम् ॥ १७.२४ ॥
*tasmād om ityudāhṛtya yajña-dāna-tapaḥ-kriyāḥ,*
*pravartante vidhānoktāḥ satataṁ brahma-vādinām. (17.24)*

Here the implication of 'Om' is mentioned.

(*tasmāt*) Therefore, (*kriyāḥ*) the acts of (*yajña*) the yajña, (*dāna*) charity, and (*tapaḥ*) austerity (*pravartante*) performed by (*brahmavādinām*) Brahmavādins [high spirited yogis] (*vidhāna+uktāḥ*) in accordance with the ordinance of scriptures (*satatam*) always commenced (*udāhṛtya*) with the utterance of (*Om iti)* "Om".

तदित्यनभिसंधाय फलं यज्ञतपःक्रियाः ।
दानक्रियाश्च विविधाः क्रियन्ते मोक्षकाङ्क्षिभिः ॥ १७.२५ ॥
*tad ityanabhisandhāya phalaṁ yajña-tapaḥ-kriyāḥ,*
*dānakriyāś ca vividhāḥ kriyante mokṣa-kāṅkṣibhiḥ. (17.25)*

Here the implication of 'Tat' is mentioned.

(*Vividhāḥ*) Various types of (*yajña*) yajñas, (*tapaḥ kriyā*) acts of austerity (*dāna-kriyāścha*) and charity are (*kriyante*) performed (*mokṣa-kāṅkṣibhiḥ*) by the seekers of mokṣa by uttering (*Tat iti)* "Tat" (or He is all) (*anabhisandhāya*) without seeking a (*phalam*) reward.

सद्भावे साधुभावे च सदित्येतत्प्रयुज्यते।
प्रशस्ते कर्मणि तथा सच्छब्दः पार्थ युज्यते॥ १७.२६॥
*sadbhāve sādhubhāve ca sad ityetat prayujyate,*
*praśaste karmaṇi tathā sacchabdaḥ pārtha yujyate. (17.26)*

Finally, the implication of 'Sat' is mentioned.

(*Sat+ityetat*) 'Sat' is (*prayujyate*) used (*sad-bhāve*) in the sense of ever-existence and (*sādhu-bhāve*) goodness. (*sachchhabdaḥ*) The word "Sat" is also (*yujyate*) used (*praśaste*) for an auspicious (*karmaṇi)* act, (*Pārtha*) O Son of Kunti.

यज्ञे तपसि दाने च स्थितिः सदिति चोच्यते।
कर्म चैव तदर्थीयं सदित्येवाभिधीयते॥ १७.२७॥
*yajñe tapasi dāne ca sthitiḥ sad iti cocyate,*
*karma caiva tadarthīyaṁ sad ityevābhidhīyate. (17.27)*

(*sthitiḥ*) Act of yajña, charity, and austerity is also called Sat. (*karma*) Any action (*tadarthīyaṁ*) related to the Supreme is (*ityeva*) indeed termed as 'Sat'.

अश्रद्धया हुतं दत्तं तपस्तप्तं कृतं च यत्।
असदित्युच्यते पार्थ न च तत्प्रेत्य नो इह॥ १७.२८॥
*aśraddhayā hutaṁ dattaṁ tapas-taptaṁ kṛtaṁ ca yat,*
*asad ityucyate pārtha na ca tat pretya no iha. (17.28)*

Whatever is (*kṛtam*) done (*aśraddhayā*) with negative attitude; whether it is (*hutaṁ*) yajña, (*dattaṁ*) charity, (*tapaḥ taptam*) austerity, (*cha*) or (*yat*) any other (*kṛtam*) act; is (*uchyate*) called 'asat'. (*tat*) It has (*naḥ*) no value (*iha*) here (*cha*) or (*pretya*) hereafter, (*Pārtha*) O son of

Pṛthā.

ॐ तत्सदिति श्रीमद् भगवद्गीतासूपनिषत्सु ब्रह्मविद्यायां योगशास्त्रे श्रीकृष्णार्जुनसंवादे श्रद्धात्रयविभागयोगोनाम सप्तदशोऽध्याय: ॥१७ ॥

Here ends the 17th chapter, named Śraddhātraya-vibhāga yoga in the *Bhagvadgitā*, dealing with the Brahmavidyā as propounded in the Upaniṣad and Yogaśāstra in the form of dialogue between Śri Krishna and Arjuna.

# अथाष्टादशोऽध्याय:

## मोक्षसंन्यासयोग:

# Chapter 18

[Mokṣa through Renunciation of Kāmya Karmas]

In this chapter, Śri Krishna tells how to achieve mokṣa through renunciation. Renunciation never means the renunciation of karmas. However, renunciation means to do karmas without any selfish interest or motive. Arjuna is fighting the war not to get dominion over the country but to get the nation rid of the undeserving and cruel king who does not leg behind to outrage the modesty of even his sister-in-law if given an opportunity, who does not apply his own mind and wit and is constantly being guided by a misguided lot, Śakunī, from abroad. A person who believes in flattery, surrounded by backbiters and never applies his mind is not worthy to be a good administrator. This chapter defines the five causative factors leading to the accomplishment of an action. He classifies the nature of karma [action], karttā [doer] as Sāttvika, Rājasika, and Tāmasika. Śri Krishna also defines wisdom as Sāttvika, Rājasika, and Tāmasika, depending upon its power to decipher acts worthy to be done and worthy to be abandoned.

अर्जुन उवाच

Arjuna said

संन्यासस्य महाबाहो तत्त्वमिच्छामि वेदितुम्।
त्यागस्य च हृषीकेश पृथक्केशिनिषूदन॥ १८.१॥

*Saṁnyāsasya mahābāho tattvam icchāmi veditum,*
*tyāgasya ca hṛṣīkeśa pṛathak keśi-niṣūdana.* (18.01)

Arjuna said— I wish to know the nature of Saṁnyāsa and Tyāga and the difference between the two, O Krishna.

श्री कृष्ण उवाच
Śri Krishna said

काम्यानां कर्मणां न्यासं संन्यासं कवयो विदुः ।
सर्वकर्मफलत्यागं प्राहुस्त्यागं विचक्षणाः ॥ १८.२ ॥
*kāmyānāṁ karmaṇāṁ nyāsaṁ Saṁnyāsaṁ kavayo viduḥ,*
*sarva-karma-phala-tyāgaṁ prāhus-tyāgaṁ vicakṣaṇāḥ.(18.02)*

Śri Krishna said— The sages define Saṁnyāsa as the renunciation of Kāmya Karmas [acts performed with selfish interest or desire]. The Wisemen define Tyāga as the renunciation of fruits of all sorts of actions [even Nitya Karmas]. (See also 5.1, 5.5, and 6.1).

त्याज्यं दोषवदित्येके कर्म प्राहुर्मनीषिणः ।
यज्ञदानतपःकर्म न त्याज्यमिति चापरे ॥ १८.३ ॥
*tyājyaṁ doṣavad ityeke karma prāhur manīṣiṇaḥ,*
*yajña-dāna-tapaḥ-karma na tyājyam iti cāpare. (18.03)*

Some philosophers say that all works need to be given up, because all these actions are full of doṣa [cause of bondage] or should be given up like the doṣas [afflictions] of affection [rāga], dveṣa [hatred] etc., while others say that acts of yajña, charity, and austerity should not be abandoned, as they are nitya karmas.

निश्चयं श्रृणु मे तत्र त्यागे भरतसत्तम ।
त्यागो हि पुरुषव्याघ्र त्रिविधः सम्प्रकीर्तितः ॥ १८.४ ॥
*niścayaṁ śṛṇu me tatra tyāge bharatasattama,*
*tyāgo hi puruṣa-vyāghra trividhaḥ samprakīrtitaḥ. (18.04)*

O Best among Bharatas, listen to my conclusion about Tyāga. Tyāga is said to be of three types— sāttvika, rājasika, and tāmasika.

यज्ञदानतपःकर्म न त्याज्यं कार्यमेव तत्।
यज्ञो दानं तपश्चैव पावनानि मनीषिणाम्॥ १८.५॥
*yajña-dāna-tapaḥ karma na tyājayaṁ kāryam eva tat,*
*yajño dānaṁ tapaś caiva pāvanāni manīṣiṇām. (18.05)*

Acts of yajña, charity, and austerity should not be abandoned but must be performed since all these actions purify even the wise men.

एतान्यपि तु कर्माणि सङ्गं त्यक्त्वा फलानि च।
कर्तव्यानीति मे पार्थ निश्चितं मतमुत्तमम्॥ १८.६॥
*etānyapi tu karmāṇi saṅgaṁ tyaktvā phalāni ca,*
*kartavyānīti me pārtha niścitaṁ matam uttamam. (18.06)*

These nitya karmas of yajña, dāna and tapa also should be performed without any attachment and desire of fruits. This is my final opinion, O Son of Pṛthā.

Śri Krishna wants to say that a person should perform nitya karmas also without any selfish motive behind them. If they are done with selfish motive, they will come in the category of kāmya karmas.

नियतस्य तु संन्यासः कर्मणो नोपपद्यते।
मोहात्तस्य परित्यागस्तामसः परिकीर्तितः॥ १८.७॥
*niyatasya tu Saṁnyāsaḥ karmaṇo nopapadyate,*
*mohāttasya parityāgaḥ tāmasaḥ parikīrtitaḥ. (18.07)*

The renunciation of (*niyatasya*) nitya [obligatory] karmas is not proper. *(parityāgasya)* The abandonment of (*tasya*) nitya karmas *(mohāt)* due to delusion is (*parikīrtitaḥ*) declared to be (*tāmasaḥ*) tāmasika tyāga. Here, delusion is associated with a tāmasika tendency.

दुःखमित्येव यत्कर्म कायक्लेशभयात्त्यजेत्।
स कृत्वा राजसं त्यागं नैव त्यागफलं लभेत्॥ १८.८॥
*duḥkham ityeva yat karma kāya-kleśa-bhayāt tyajet,*
*sa kṛtvā rājasaṁ tyāgaṁ naiva tyāgaphalaṁ labhet. (18.08)*

One who (*tyajet*) abandons (*yatkarma*) karma or duty (*ityeva*) merely because it is (*kāya-kleśa bhayāt*) troublesome to physical body, (*saḥ*) he (*na*) does not (*labhet*) get the (*tyāga-phalam*) benefit of tyāga, since such a (tyāgam) tyāga is (*rājasam*) rājasika in nature.

कार्यमित्येव यत्कर्म नियतं क्रियतेऽर्जुन।
सङ्गं त्यक्त्वा फलं चैव स त्यागः सात्त्विको मतः॥ १८.९॥
*Kāryam ityeva yat karma niyataṁ kriyate'rjuna,*
*Saṅgaṁ tyaktvā phalaṁ caiva sa tyāgaḥ sāttviko'mataḥ. (18.09)*

(*yatkarma niyatam*) When nitya karmas are (*kriyate*) performed (*kāryam ityeva*), as obligatory karmas (*tyaktvā*) without (*saṅgam*) any attachment (*cha+eva*) and (phalam) selfish desire or motive, (*saḥ*) it is regarded as (*sāttvikaḥ tyāgaḥ*) sāttvika tyāga, (Arjuna) O Arjuna!

न द्वेष्ट्यकुशलं कर्म कुशले नानुषज्जते।
त्यागी सत्त्वसमाविष्टो मेधावी छिन्नसंशयः॥ १८.१०॥
*na dveṣṭyakuśalaṁ karma kuśale nānuṣajjate,*
*tyāgī sattva-samāviṣto mesdhāvī chinna-sañśayaḥ. (18.10)*

One who (*na*) neither (*dveṣṭi*) hates a (*akuśalam karma*) disagreeable kāmya karmas, (*na*) nor with some motive is (*anuṣajjate*) attached to (*kuśale*) agreeable nitya karmas, he/she is (*tyāgī*) a renunciant (*sattva-samāviṣṭaḥ*) sāttvika, (*medhāvī*) wise, and (*chhinna-sañśayaḥ*) free from all doubts.

Note: Kāmya karmas cause bondage, and nitya karmas if performed without selfish motives and attachment, are helpful in mokṣa.

What are nitya karmas? All karmas necessary for sustaining life, yajña, dāna, tapa, and inculcation of dharma—are nitya karmas.

न हि देहभृता शक्यं त्यक्तुं कर्माण्यशेषतः।

यस्तु कर्मफलत्यागी स त्यागीत्यभिधीयते ॥ १८.११ ॥
*na hi dehabhṛtā śakyaṁ tyaktuṁ karmāṇyaśeṣataḥ.*
*yastu karma-phala-tyāgī sa tyāgītyabhidhīyate. (18.11)*

It is (*na*) not (*śakyam*) possible for (*dehabhṛtā*) an ignorant human being who takes his body for the soul to (*aśeṣataḥ*) completely (*tyaktum*) abandon karmas. Therefore, (*yaḥ*), the one who (*karma-phala-tyāgī*) does not perform karmas with some motive or seeking some personal benefit, is (*abhidhīyate*) considered to be a (*tyāgī*) real tyāgī (or renunciant).

Note: Here, two types of seekers are described.

1. *Dehabhṛt* are those who take their body for the soul. Such seekers cannot abandon kāmya karmas completely. The only way for them is to do all karmas without being attached to them and seeking some benefit or fulfilment of some desire by doing them. If they can do so, they will be called tyāgī.

2. The second seeker type is *Adehabhṛt*, who can identify their true nature [that they are pure spiritual element or ātman] and seek mokṣa. They can completely abandon kāmya karmas and minimize the nitya karmas [without attachment and personal motive]. They are called saṁnyāsīs.

अनिष्टमिष्टं मिश्रं च त्रिविधं कर्मणः फलम्।
भवत्यत्यागिनां प्रेत्य न तु संन्यासिनां क्वचित्॥ १८.१२ ॥
*aniṣṭam iṣṭaṁ miśraṁ ca trividhaṁ karmaṇaḥ phalam,*
*bhavatyatyāgināṁ pretya na tu sannyāsināṁ kvacit. (18.12)*

Every act has three types of fruits - (*aniṣṭam*) leading to lower species of animals, birds, plants, etc, (*iṣṭam*) leading to divinity or liberation and (*miśram*) mixed one maintaining a *status quo* of human species. These fruits are received by those who are not tyāgīs in the technical terms defined above and not by saṁnyāsīs.

पंचमानि महाबाहो कारणानि निबोध मे।
साङ्ख्ये कृतान्ते प्रोक्तानि सिद्धये सर्वकर्मणाम्॥ १८.१३॥
*pañcamāni mahābāho kāraṇāni nibodha me,*
*Sāṅkhye kṛtānte proktāni siddhaye sarva-karmaṇām. (18.13)*

Learn from me, O Arjuna, the five causative factors, as described in the Sāṅkhya doctrine by the end of Satyayuga. They play a lead role behind the accomplishment of all karmas. That is, no action can be accomplished if any one of the five causative factors is missing.

Note: The above verse of the *Bhagvadgītā* tells clearly that the Sāṅkhya system originated by the end of Satyayuga, i.e. 216,5125 years ago [as of 2023].

अधिष्ठानं तथा कर्ता करणं च पृथग्विधम्।
विविधाश्च पृथक् चेष्टा दैवं चैवात्र पंचमम्॥ १८.१४॥
*adhiṣthānaṁ tathā kartā karaṇaṁ ca pṛthagvidham,*
*vividhāśca pṛthak ceṣtā daivaṁ caivātra pañcamam. (18.14)*

Those causative factors are:

1. **Adhiṣṭhāna [The Base]**: Without a proper base, no action can be performed. The physical body is the base of ātman [soul] for doing any action. A soul devoid of the physical body can do no action. That is why it has been observed: *śariram ādyaṁ khalu dharma-sādhanam.* The physical body is required first for doing any act of dharma.

2. **Kartā [The Doer]**: No action can be performed without a doer. The body itself is the doer [in living beings].

3. **Karaṇam [Sense or motor organs]**: Our sense and motor organs are used to perform various actions by the body. A body devoid of these organs [means] cannot perform any action.

4. **Cheṣṭā [Plan and its execution]**: No work can be accomplished without proper plan and its execution [efforts]. Various efforts in the body are materialized due to the functioning of vital airs like prāṇa, apāna, etc.

5. **Daiva [Sanskāras of past life]**: Daiva is the fifth causative factor. Daiva means tendency as per sanskāras accumulated in previous lives.

Śri Krishna wants to say that without all five factors being at our disposal, no action can be accomplished.

शरीरवाङ्मनोभिर्यत्कर्म प्रारभते नरः ।
न्याय्यं वा विपरीतं वा पंचैते तस्य हेतवः ॥ १८.१५ ॥
*śarira-vāṅmanobhir-yat karma prārabhate naraḥ,*
*nyāyyaṁ vā viparītaṁ va pañcaite tasya hetavaḥ. (18.15)*

Whatever action, whether right or wrong, just or unjust, is performed with the help of the body, speech, and mind, are caused by the above-mentioned five factors.

तत्रैवं सति कर्तारमात्मानं केवलं तु यः ।
पश्यत्यकृतबुद्धित्वान्न स पश्यति दुर्मतिः ॥ १८.१६ ॥
*tatraivaṁ sati kartāram ātmānaṁ kevalaṁ tu yaḥ,*
*paśyatyakṛta-buddhitvān na sa paśyati durmatiḥ. (18.16)*

(*tatra evaṁ sati*) This being the case, (*durmatiḥ*) a person with downgraded buddhi [intellect] considers ātman united with the above five factors and (*paśyati*) takes it granted (*kartāram*) for the agent [doer]. (*akṛta-budhitvāt*) Due to impurity in buddhi, (*saḥ*) he (*na paśyati)* does not understand the reality.

यस्य नाहंकृतो भावो बुद्धिर्यस्य न लिप्यते ।
हत्वाऽपि स इमाँल्लोकान्न हन्ति न निबध्यते ॥ १८.१७ ॥
*yasya nāhaṅkṛto bhāvo buddhir yasya na lipyate,*
*hatvāpi sa imān llokān na hanti na nibadhyate. (18.17)*

The one who is free from the notion of doership and whose mind is not disturbed by good or bad results of action, he even after slaying these people, neither be held responsible for slaying nor is he affected by the act of killing.

ज्ञानं ज्ञेयं परिज्ञाता त्रिविधा कर्मचोदना ।
करणं कर्म कर्तेति त्रिविधः कर्मसंग्रहः ॥ १८.१८ ॥
*jñānaṁ jñeyaṁ parijñātā trividhā karma-codanā,*
*karaṇaṁ karma karteti trividhaḥ karma-saṅgrahaḥ. (18.18)*

(*karmachodanā)* Karmas [actions] are initiated [to abandon or gain something] when (*jñānam*) knowledge, (*jñeyam*) object to be known and (*parijñātā*) knower — (*trividhā*) all three come together. [When the knower knows something, he/she will become interested or disinterested in the object. Should he/she become interested, he/she would try to achieve it; otherwise, he/she would try to get rid of it. In both cases, the action will be initiated].

(*karma-saṅgrahaḥ*) All karmas [actions] are accomplished with the help of (*trividhaḥ*) three factors— (*karaṇam*) means of karmas like sense organs, motor organs and mind; (*karma*) action to be initiated by the doer; and (*kartā iti*) the doer [body] itself, who puts all means of karmas [sense organs and motor organs] into action.

ज्ञानं कर्म च कर्ता च त्रिधैव गुणभेदतः ।
प्रोच्यते गुणसङ्ख्याने यथावच्छृणु तान्यपि ॥ १८.१९ ॥
*jñānaṁ karma ca kartā ca tridhaiva guṇa-bhedataḥ,*

*procyate guṇasaṅkhayāne yathāvacchṛṇu tānyapi. (18.19)*

(*jñānam*) knowledge, (*karma*) action, (*cha*) and (*kartā*) doer (*prochyate*) are said to be of (*tridhā+eva*) three types (*guṇa-bhedataḥ*) as per three types of guṇas [sattva, rajas, and tamas] in (*guṇa-saṅkhyāne*) in Sāṅkhya Darśana. (*śṛṇu*) Hear now (*api)* also (*tāni*) them.

## Nature of Sāttvika Jñāna

सर्वभूतेषु येनैकं भावमव्ययमीक्षते।
अविभक्तं विभक्तेषु तज्ज्ञानं विद्धि सात्त्विकम्॥ १८.२०॥
*sarvabhūteṣu yenaikaṁ bhāvam avyayamīkṣate,*
*avibhaktaṁ vibhakteṣu taj jñānaṁ viddhi sāttvikam.(18.20)*

(*yena*) Knowledge by which (*īkṣate*) one sees (*ekam*) single (*avyayam*) unchangeable (*bhāvam*) Supreme power (*sarvabhūteṣu*) in all animate and inanimate things prevalent (*vibhakteṣu*) in their various divided bodies (*avibhaktam*) as undivided; (*tat jñānam*) such knowledge is (*viddhi)* considered to be (*sāttvikam*) sāttvika.

## Nature of Rājasika Jñāna

पृथक्त्वेन तु यज्ज्ञानं नानाभावान्पृथग्विधान्।
वेत्ति सर्वेषु भूतेषु तज्ज्ञानं विद्धि राजसम्॥ १८.२१॥
*pṛthak-tvena tu yaj-jñānaṁ nānā-bhāvān pṛthag-vidhān,*
*vetti sarveṣu bhuteṣu taj-jñānaṁ viddhi rājasam. (18.21)*

(*yat jñānam*) Knowledge by which one (*vetti)* sees (*sarveṣu bhūteṣu*) all animate beings and inanimate things as (*nānā)* various *(pṛthagvidhān)* separate *(bhāvān*) entities (*pṛthaktvena*) independant of Brahman [without being pervaded by Brahman], (*viddhi*) consider (*tat jñānam*) that knowledge (*rājasam*) to be rājasika.

## Nature of Tāmasika Jñāna

यत्तु कृत्स्नवदेकस्मिन्कार्ये सक्तमहैतुकम्।

अतत्त्वार्थवदल्पं च तत्तामसमुदाहृतम् ॥ १८.२२ ॥

*yattu kṛatsnavad ekasmin kārye saktam ahaitukam.*
*atattvārtha-vad alpaṁ ca tat tāmasam udāhṛtam. (18.22)*

(*yat*) Knowledge by which one (*saktam*) delimits the (*kṛtsnavat*) All-pervading [Omnipresent] Brahman to (*ekasmin kārye*) one single effect such as a human being or a mūrti made of stone or wood, and which is (*ahaitukam*) irrational [not based upon reasoning], (*atattvārtha-vad)* devoid of truth, and (*alpam*) worthless; (*tat)* such knowledge is (*udāhṛtam*) declared to be (*tāmasam*) tāmasika.

## Mūrti Pūjā and the Concept of Human-God is Tāmasika

Here, Śri Krishna clearly declares that considering a human being as God and idolatry or Mūrtipūjā is tāmasika worship. Generally, an idolater or human worshipper confines God to a particular icon or idol or human form he worships and not beyond that. This fact has also been corroborated by Ādi Śaṅkarāchārya in his commentary of the *Bhagavad Gītā* in connection with the śloka under reference. He says:

एकस्मिन् कार्ये (देहे बहिः वा प्रतिमादौ) सक्तम् (एतावान् एव आत्मा ईश्वरो वा न अतः परम् अस्ति इति यथा नग्नक्षपणकादीनां शरीरानुवर्ती देहपरिमाणो जीव ईश्वरो वा पाषाणदार्वामात्र इति एवम् एकस्मिन् कार्ये सक्तम्) ।

*ēkasmin kārye (dehe bahiḥ vā pratimādau) saktam (ētāvān ēva ātmā īśvaro vā na ataḥ param asti iti yathā nagnakṣapaṇakādīnāṁ śarīrānuvartī dehaparimāṇo jīva īśvaro vā pāṣāṇadārvāmātra iti ēvam ēkasmin kārye saktam).*

[Meaning] Delimiting All-pervading Brahman into

one single effect means delimiting Him into a body or some (*pratimā*) mūrti. Only this human form or mūrti is Brahman or Īśvara and nothing is beyond it. Just as Digambara Jains consider the measurement of Īśvara or ātmā equal to the human body or idolators think that Brahman is limited to a particular mūrti made up of stone or wood.

## Nature of Sāttvika Karma

नियतं सङ्गरहितमरागद्वेषत: कृतम् ।
अफलप्रेप्सुना कर्म यत्तत्सात्त्विकमुच्यते ॥ १८.२३ ॥
*niyataṁ saṅga-rahitama rāga-dveṣataḥ kṛtam,*
*Aphal-aprepsunā karma yat tat sāttvikaṁ ucyate. (18.23)*

(*niyatam*) Nitya (karma) karmas (*kṛtam*) performed (*arāga+dveṣataḥ*) without likes, dislikes, and (*saṅga-rahitam*) attachment by the (*aphala-prepsunā*) one who does not desire fruit is (*uchyate*) said to be (*sāttvikam*) sāttvika.

## Nature of Rājasika Karma

यत्तु कामेप्सुना कर्म साहंकारेण वा पुन: ।
क्रियते बहुलायासं तद्राजसमुदाहृतम् ॥ १८.२४ ॥
*yattu kāmepsunā karma sāhaṅkāreṇa vā punaḥ,*
*kriyate bahulāyāsaṁ tad rājasam udāhṛtam. (18.24)*

(*kāmepsunā*) Kāmya (*karma*) karma (*kriyate*) performed (*sa+ahaṅkāreṇa*) with the notion of doership, (*vā punaḥ*) and (*bahulāyāsam*) with too much effort; is (*udāhṛtam*) declared (*rājasam*) to be rājasika.

## Nature of Tāmasika Karma

अनुबन्धं क्षयं हिंसामनपेक्ष्य च पौरुषम् ।
मोहादारभ्यते कर्म यत्तत्तामसमुच्यते ॥ १८.२५ ॥
*anubandhaṁ kṣayaṁ hinsām anapekṣya ca pauruṣam,*
*mohād ārabhyate karma yat tat tāmasam ucyate. (18.25)*

(*karma*) Action (*ārabhyate*) undertaken (*mohāt*) without knowing truth; (*anapekṣya*) disregarding (*anubandham*) consequences, (*kṣayam*) loss, or (*hinsām*) injury to other beings, as well as (*pauruṣam*) one's own ability, is said to be tāmasika action.

## Nature of Sāttvika Kartā

मुक्तसङ्गोऽनहंवादी धृत्युत्साहसमन्वितः ।
सिद्ध्यसिद्ध्योर्निर्विकारः कर्ता सात्त्विक उच्यते ॥ १८.२६ ॥
*mukta-saṅgo'nahaṁvādī dhṛtyutsāha-samanvitaḥ,*
*siddhyasiddhyor nirvikāraḥ kartā sāttvika ucyate. (18.26)*

The doer who is (*muktasaṅgaḥ*) free from attachment and (*anahaṁ-vādī*) does not claim doership, (*samanvitaḥ*) endowed with (*dhṛti*) self-restraint and (*utsāha*) enthusiasm, and (*nirvikāraḥ*) unperturbed in (*siddhi-asiddhayoḥ*) success or failure is (*uchyate*) called (*sāttvika*) sāttvika.

## Nature of Rājasika Kartā

रागी कर्मफलप्रेप्सुर्लुब्धो हिंसात्मकोऽशुचिः ।
हर्षशोकान्वितः कर्ता राजसः परिकीर्तितः ॥ १८.२७ ॥
*rāgī karma-phala-prepsur-lubdho hinsātmako'śuciḥ,*
*harṣa-śokānvitaḥ kartā rājasaḥ parikīrtitaḥ. (18.27)*

(*kartā*) The doer who is (*rāgī*) passionate (*karma-phala prepsuḥ*) performs kāmya karmas, (*lubdhaḥ*) have eyes on others' property, (*hiṁsātmakaḥ*) violent, (*aśuchi*) impure, and is (*harṣa-śoka-anvitaḥ*) affected by joy and sorrow; (*prikīrtitaḥ*) is proclaimed to be (*rājasaḥ*) rājasika.

## Nature of Tāmasika Kartā

अयुक्तः प्राकृतः स्तब्धः शठो नैष्कृतिकोऽलसः ।
विषादी दीर्घसूत्री च कर्ता तामस उच्यते ॥ १८.२८ ॥
*ayuktaḥ prākṛtaḥ stabdhaḥ śaṭho' naiṣkṛtiko'lasaḥ,*

*viṣādī dīrghasūtrī ca kartā tāmasa ucyate. (18.28)*

(*ayuktaḥ*) Whose mind has not settled in samādhi, (*prākṛtaḥ*) who is without sanskāras of moral, ethical values and education, (*stabdhaḥ*) stubborn, (*śaṭhaḥ*) deceitful, (*naiṣkṛtikaḥ*) ready to destroy others' job, (*alasaḥ*) not ready to do his duty, (*viṣādī)* depressed, and (*dīrgha-sūtrī)* procrastinating [dilly delaying matters]; such a (*kartā)* doer is (*uchyate*) called (*tāmasaḥ*) tāmasika.

## Divisions of Buddhi

बुद्धेर्भेदं धृतेश्चैव गुणतस्त्रिविधं श्रृणु।
प्रोच्यमानमशेषेण पृथक्त्वेन धनंजय॥ १८.२९॥

*buddher bhedaṁ dhṛteś caiva guṇatas trividhaṁ śṛṇu,*
*procyamānam-aśeṣeṇa pṛthaktvena dhanañjaya. (18.29)*

(*śṛṇu*) Now hear the (*trividhaṁ*) threefold (*bhedam*) division (*buddheḥ*) of Buddhi and (*dhṛteḥ*) self-restraint based on guṇas, (*prochyamānam*) as explained by me (*aśeṣeṇa*) fully and (*pṛthaktvena*) separately, O Dhanañjaya.

## Sāttvika Buddhi

प्रवृत्तिं च निवृत्तिं च कार्याकार्ये भयाभये।
बन्धं मोक्षं च या वेत्ति बुद्धिः सा पार्थ सात्त्विकी॥ १८.३०॥

*pravṛttiṁ ca nivṛttiṁ ca kāryākārye bhayābhaye,*
*bandhaṁ mokṣaṁ ca yā vetti buddhiḥ sā pārtha sāttvikī. (18.30)*

(*Pārtha*) O Son of Pṛthā, Buddhi (*yā*) which (*vetti*) knows *(pravṛttim)* that embracing the path of kāmya karmas leads to bondage, and *(nivṛttiṁ)* their renunciation leads to mokṣa; (*kārya-akārye*) that knows that the karmas prescribed in Śāstra are worth doing and prohibited karmas worth abandoning; similarly (*bhaya-abhaye*) the Buddhi that identifies the causes of visible and invisible fear as well as fearlessness and knows the causes of (*bandham*) bondage and (*mokṣam*) liberation, is sāttvika.

## Rājasika Buddhi

यया धर्ममधर्मं च कार्यं चाकार्यमेव च।
अयथावत्प्रजानाति बुद्धिः सा पार्थ राजसी॥ १८.३१॥
*yayā dharmam adharmaṁ ca kāryaṁ cākāryameva ca,*
*ayathāvat prajānāti buddhiḥ sā pārtha rājasī. (18.31)*

(*yayā*) The Buddhi by which (*ayathāvat prajānāti*) one cannot distinguish between (*dharma*) values and duties prescribed by Śāstra and (*adharma*) values and duties prohibited by Śāstra; between (*kāryam*) actions worth doing as per Śāstra (*eva cha*) and (*akāryam*) worth abandoning as per Śāstra; (*sā*) that (*buddhiḥ*) Buddhi is (*rājasī)* rājasika, (*Pārtha*) O son of Pṛthā.

## Tāmasīka Buddhi

अधर्मं धर्ममिति या मन्यते तमसावृता।
सर्वार्थान्विपरीतांश्च बुद्धिः सा पार्थ तामसी॥ १८.३२॥
*adharmaṁ dharmam iti yā manyate tamasāvṛtā,*
*sarvārthān viparītāñś ca buddhiḥ sā pārtha tāmasī. (18.32)*

(*Pārtha*) O son of Pṛthā, (*buddhiḥ*) the Buddhi (*tamas+āvṛttā*) obscured by tamoguṇa, (*manyate*) accepts (*adharmaṁ*) adharma (*iti)* as (*dharmam*) dharma and perceives (*sarvarthān*) everything (*viparītāṁścha*) from an opposite angle; (*sā)* that is (*tāmasī*) tāmasika Buddhi.

## Sāttvika Dhṛti (Dhāraṇā)

धृत्या यया धारयते मनःप्राणेन्द्रियक्रियाः।
योगेनाव्यभिचारिण्या धृतिः सा पार्थ सात्त्विकी॥ १८.३३॥
*dhṛtyā yayā dhārayate manaḥ-prāṇendriya-kriyāḥ,*
*yogenāvyabhicāriṇyā dhṛtiḥ sā pārtha sāttvikī. (18.33)*

When (*kriyāḥ*) tendencies of (*manaḥ*) mind, (*prāṇa*) prāṇas and (*indriyāḥ*) sense organs conforming to the Śāstra (dhārayate) become the subject of (*yayā dhṛtyā)* focus of mind [concentration] achieved through (*avyabhichāriṇyā)* constant (*yogena*) practice of yoga, (sā) that (*dhṛtiḥ*) concentration is (*sāttvikī)* sāttvika, (*Pārtha*) O son of Pṛthā.

## Rājasika Dhṛti (Dhāraṇā)

यया तु धर्मकामार्थान्धृत्या धारयतेऽर्जुन।
प्रसङ्गेन फलाकाङ्क्षी धृतिः सा पार्थ राजसी॥ १८.३४॥
*yayā tu dharma-kāmārthān dhṛtyā dhārayate'rjuna,*
*prasaṅgena phalākāṅkṣī dhṛtiḥ sā pārtha rājasī. (18.34)*

When (*yayā dhṛtyā*) mind is (*dhārayate*) focused on (*dharma*) dharma, (*kāma*) kāma and (*artha*) artha (*prasaṅgena*) with (*phalākāṅkṣī*) a selfish motive, (*sā)* that (*dhṛti*) dhāraṇā [focus of mind or concentration], (Pārtha) O Arjuna is (*rājasī*) rājasika.

## Tāmasika Dhṛti (Dhāraṇā)

यया स्वप्नं भयं शोकं विषादं मदमेव च।
न विमुंचति दुर्मेधा धृतिः सा पार्थ तामसी॥ १८.३५॥
*yayā svapnaṁ bhayaṁ śokaṁ viṣādaṁ madameva ca,*
*na vimuñcati durmedhā dhṛtiḥ sā pārtha tāmasī. (18.35)*

(*yayā*) When Dhāraṇā [focus of mind] of a stupid person (*na*) does not (*vimuñchati*) give up (*svapnam*) sleep, (*bhayam*) fear, (*śokam*) grief, (*viṣādam*) despair, and (*madam*) arrogance, (*sā)* that (*dhṛti)* dhāraṇā [focus of mind/concentration] is called tāmasika, O Arjuna.

## Types of Sukha (Pleasure)

सुखं त्विदानीं त्रिविधं शृणु मे भरतर्षभ।
अभ्यासाद्रमते यत्र दुःखान्तं च निगच्छति॥ १८.३६॥
*sukhaṁ tvidānīṁ trividhaṁ śṛṇu me bharatarṣabha,*

*abhyāsād ramate yatra duḥkhāntaṁ ca nigacchati. (18.36)*

Moreover, (*idānīm*) now (*śṛṇu*) listen (*me*) from me, (*Bharatarṣabha*) O Best among Bharatas, about the (*trividham*) threefold (*sukham*) pleasure. (*yatra*) The pleasure which, once saught, gives one (*ramate*) enjoyment (*abhyāsāt*) repeatedly and (*nigachchhati)* results in (*duḥkhāntam*) cessation of sorrow.

## Sāttvika Sukha (Pleasure)

यत्तदग्रे विषमिव परिणामेऽमृतोपमम्।
तत्सुखं सात्त्विकं प्रोक्तमात्मबुद्धिप्रसादजम्॥ १८.३७॥
*yat tad agre viṣam iva pariṇāme'mṛtopamam,*
*tatsukhaṁ sāttvikaṁ proktam ātma-buddhi-prasādajam. (18.37)*

(*yat*) Such a pleasure originated (*prasādajam*) as a result of (*ātmabuddhi)* self-experience [self-realisation], achieved through knowledge, detachment, concentration and samādhi, (*agre*) commences with (*viṣam+iva*) hardships but (pariṇāme) culminates into (*amṛtopamam*) nectar of happiness at the end. (*tat sukham*) This pleasure (*proktam*) is called as (*sāttvikam*) sāttvika one.

## Rājasika Sukha (Pleasure)

विषयेन्द्रियसंयोगाद्यत्तदग्रेऽमृतोपमम्।
परिणामे विषमिव तत्सुखं राजसं स्मृतम्॥ १८.३८॥
*viṣayendriya-saṁyogād yat tad agre'mṛtopamam,*
*pariṇāme viṣamiva tatsukhaṁ rājasaṁ smṛtam. (18.38)*

On the other hand, pleasure originated (*sañyogāt*) from the contact of (*viṣaya-indriya*) sense organs with their stimuli [or say sensory pleasures] (*agre*) starts with (*amṛtopamam*) an ecstatic feeling, but (*pariṇāme*) culminates into (*viṣam+iva*) hardship at the end; (*tatsukham*) such pleasure is (*smṛtam*) called (*rājasam*) rājasika one. (See also 5.22)

## Tāmasika Sukha (Pleasure)

यदग्रे चानुबन्धे च सुखं मोहनमात्मनः।
निद्रालस्यप्रमादोत्थं तत्तामसमुदाहृतम्॥ १८.३९॥

*yad agre cānubandhe ca sukhaṁ mohanam ātmanaḥ,*
*nidrālasya pramādotthaṁ tat tāmasam udāhṛtam. (18.39)*

(*sukham*) The pleasure (*yat*) that (*mohanam*) deludes a person [creates confusion about a reality] (*agre*) in the beginning and (*cha*) even (*anubandhe*) in the end; which is (*uttham*) consequent upon (*nidrā*) sleep, (*ālasya*) laziness, and (*pramāda*) negligence, intoxication or madness; (*tat*) such pleasure is (*udāhṛtam*) called (*tāmasam*) tāmasika one.

## The Universality of Three Guṇas

न तदस्ति पृथिव्यां वा दिवि देवेषु वा पुनः।
सत्त्वं प्रकृतिजैर्मुक्तं यदेभिः स्यात्त्रिभिर्गुणैः॥ १८.४०॥

*na tad asti pṛthivyāṁ vā divi deveṣu vā punaḥ.*
*sattvaṁ prakṛtijāir muktaṁ yad ebhiḥ syāt tribhir guṇaiḥ.*

(*na tat+asti*) There is no (*sattvam*) living being or non-living thing, (*pṛthivyām*) either on the earth (*vā*) or (*divi*) in space or (*deveṣu*) in any universe, (*yat*) that is (*muktam*) free from (*ebhiḥ*) these (*tribhiḥ*) three (*guṇaiḥ*) guṇas (*prakṛtijaiḥ*) of prakṛti.

Note: Here ends the teachings of Vedas, Smṛtis, which needs to be followed by those who want to achieve Puruṣārtha (four goals of human life prescribed in the Śāstras.

Now, the division of Professions/Karmas based upon guṇās born of one's sanskāras is suggested.

## Division of Professions/Karmas based upon Three Guṇas

ब्राह्मणक्षत्रियविशां शूद्राणां च परंतप।
कर्माणि प्रविभक्तानि स्वभावप्रभवैर्गुणैः॥ १८.४१॥
*brāhmaṇa-kṣatriya-viśāṁ śūdrāṇāṁ ca parantapa,*
*karmāṇi pravibhaktāni svabhāva-prabhavair-guṇaiḥ. (18.41)*

(*pravibhaktāni)* The division of (*karmāṇi)* professions into the four categories of (*brahmaṇa-kṣatriya-viśām*) Brāhmaṇa, Kṣatriya, Vaiśya, (*cha*) and (*śudrāṇām*) Śudra -- is done based upon the (*guṇaiḥ*) sattva, rajas and tamas guṇas (*prabhavaiḥ*) born of (*svabhāva*) sanskāras inherited from the past life by human beings. (See also 4.13)

Note: There is a difference between the Varṇa and caste systems. Varṇa system is a Vedic concept, whereas the caste system is the mediaeval period concept. Varṇa system was based upon the sattva, rajas and tamas guṇas born of sanskāras of past life and not based upon birth. Sanskāras of past life are the leading cause of sattva, rajas, and tamas guṇas' dominance in the present life. Nobody can be Brahmaṇa, Kṣatriya, Vaiśya, and Śudra because he is born to Brahmaṇa, Kṣatriya, Vaiśya, and Śudra parents. However, a person can be called Brāhmaṇa, Kṣatriya, Vaiśya and Śudra depending upon the karma/profession he pursued based upon the guṇas born of his/her sanskāras. Brāhmaṇa personality types are born of sattva guṇa. Kṣatriya personality types are born of sattva guṇa mixed with rajoguṇa. Vaiṣya personality types are born of rajoguṇa mixed with tamoguṇa. Similarly, Śudra personality types are born of tamoguṇa mixed with rajoguṇa.

The caste system developed very late in India under

the influence of foreign invaders. Caste is considered to be a birthright. A person of Brāhamaṇa caste does not necessarily belong to the Brāhmaṇa varṇa. Śri Krishna emphasizes upon the Varṇa system instead of the caste system.

## Sanskāra-born Karmas of Brāhmaṇa

शमो दमस्तप: शौचं क्षान्तिरार्जवमेव च।
ज्ञानं विज्ञानमास्तिक्यं ब्रह्मकर्म स्वभावजम्॥ १८.४२॥
*śamo damas tapaḥ śāucaṁ kṣāntir ārjavam eva ca.*
*jñānaṁ vijñānam āstikyaṁ brahma-karma svabhāvajam. (18.42)*

(*śama*) Withdrawal of sense-organs from the attraction to the outside world, (*dama*) withdrawal of the mind from the attraction to the outside world, (*tapa*) three types of austerity— austerity of mind, body and speech, (*śaucha*) purity—internal and external, (*kṣāntiḥ*) tolerance, patience, (ārjavam) simplicity, honesty, (*jñānam*) true knowledge, (*vijñānam*) realisation of truth [experiencing the truth], and (*āstikyam*) positive attitude or faith in the statements of scriptures is the (*brāhmaṇa-karma*) karma/profession of a Brāhmaṇa (*svabhāvajam*) born of sattva guṇa of previous life sanskāras.

## Sanskāra-born Karmas of Kṣatriya

शौर्यं तेजो धृतिर्दाक्ष्यं युद्धे चाप्यपलायनम्।
दानमीश्वरभावश्च क्षात्रं कर्म स्वभावजम्॥ १८.४३॥
*śauryaṁ tejo dhṛtir dākṣyaṁ yuddhe cāpyapalāyanam,*
*dānamīśvarabhāvaś ca kṣātraṁ karma svabhāvajam.(18.43)*

(*śauryam*) Heroism, (*tejaḥ*) domineering, (*dhṛtim*) power of concentration, (*dākṣyam*) quick action and efficiency in dealing with emergent circumstances (*apalāyanam*) not fleeing (*yuddhe*) from a battle, (*dānam*) making charity of charitable things, (*cha*) and (*īśvara-bhāvaḥ*) administrative skills are (*kṣātra-karmas*) karmas of Kṣatrīya (*svabhāvajam*) born of rajoguṇa mixed with sattva guṇa of previous life sanskāras.

## Sanskāra-born Karmas of Vaiśya and Śudra

कृषिगौरक्ष्यवाणिज्यं वैश्यकर्म स्वभावजम्।
परिचर्यात्मकं कर्म शूद्रस्यापि स्वभावजम्॥ १८.४४॥

*kṛṣi-gaurakṣya-vāṇijyaṁ vaiśya-karma svabhāvajam,*
*paricaryātmakaṁ karma śūdrasyāpi svabhāvajam. (18.44)*

(*kṛṣiḥ*) Cultivation, production (*gaurakṣyam*), cattle rearing, (*vāṇijyam*), trade and commerce are (*vaiśya-karma*) karmas of Vaiśya (*svabhāvajam*) born of rajoguṇa mixed with tamoguṇa of previous life sanskāras. (*paricharyātmakam*) The service-providing act is the (*karma*) karma (*śudrasya*) of Śudra (*svabhāvajam*) born of tamoguṇa mixed with rajoguṇa of previous life sanskāras.

## How to Attain Self-realisation by doing Karmas According to one's Sanskāras of Birth

स्वे स्वे कर्मण्यभिरत: संसिद्धिं लभते नर:।
स्वकर्मनिरत: सिद्धिं यथा विन्दति तच्छृणु॥ १८.४५॥

*sve sve karmaṇyabhirataḥ sansiddhiṁ labhate naraḥ,*
*svakarma-nirataḥ siddhiṁ yathā vindati tacchṛṇu. (18.45)*

(*naraḥ*) A person (*abhirataḥ*), by doing the (*karmaṇi*) karmas (*sve sve*) conforming to his/her sanskāras gets his/her sanskāras exhausted and (*labhate*) can attain (*sansiddhim*) success in making his/her sense organs and body efficient towards the attainment of self-knowledge. (*śṛṇu*) Hear, (*yathā*) how (*vindati*) one can attain (*siddhim*) success in making his/her sense organs and body efficient towards the attainment of self-knowledge (*sva-karma-nirataḥ*) while being engaged in the work suitable to his/her sanskāras.

यतः प्रवृत्तिर्भूतानां येन सर्वमिदं ततम्।
स्वकर्मणा तमभ्यर्च्य सिद्धिं विन्दति मानवः॥ १८.४६॥
*yataḥ pravṛttir bhūtānāṁ yena sarvam idaṁ tatam,*
*svakarmaṇā tam abhyarcya siddhiṁ vindati mānavaḥ.(18.46)*

(*yataḥ*) He, by Whom (*bhūtānam*) all beings (*pravṛtti*) are originated and made active; and (*yena*) by whom (*idam sarvam*) this entire universe is (*tatam*) pervaded; (*mānavaḥ*) everybody (vindati) can achieve (*siddhim*) success in making his/her sense organs and body efficient towards the attainment self-knowledge (*sva-karmaṇā*) by dedicating his/her karmas (*abhyarchya*) as a service to (*tam*) Him [Brahman]. (See also 9.27, 12.10)

श्रेयान्स्वधर्मो विगुणः परधर्मात्स्वनुष्ठितात्।
स्वभावनियतं कर्म कुर्वन्नाप्नोति किल्बिषम्॥ १८.४७॥
*śreyān svadharmo viguṇaḥ para-dharmāt svanuṣṭhitāt,*
*svabhāva-niyataṁ karma kurvannāpnoti kilbiṣam. (18.47)*

Living (*svadharmaḥ*) one's own dharma [sanskāras], (*viguṇaḥ*) howsoever inferior [causing downfall] it is, is (*śreyān*) far better than (*su+anuśṭhitāt*) beautifully living other's (dharma [sanskāras]. A person (*kurvan*) doing the (*karma*) karma [job] (*svabhāva-niyatam*) suitable to his sanskāras [dharma] (*na*) does not (*āpnoti*) experience (*kilbiṣam*) downfall. (See also 3.35)

Note: While doing so, a person can exhaust his previous life sanskāras and receive their fruits. By that time, he will develop efficiency in withdrawing his mind from the external world and making his body and sense organs efficient enough to attain self-realisation. So, even if your karmas are backed by those of a śudra-sanskāras, you can exhaust them and move up the ladder in next life by accumulating good sanskāras in the current life.

सहजं कर्म कौन्तेय सदोषमपि न त्यजेत्।

सर्वारम्भा हि दोषेण धूमेनाग्निरिवावृताः ॥ १८.४८ ॥
*sahajaṁ karma kaunteya sadoṣam api na tyajet,*
*sarvārambhā hi doṣeṇa dhūmenāgnir ivāvṛtāḥ. (18.48)*

(*karma*) Work (*sahajam*) suitable to one's sanskāras [dharma] of birth, (*api*) even though (*sadoṣam*) appear consisting of doṣas [factors causing the downfall of a human being], (*na*) should not be (*tyajet*) abandoned; (*hi*) because all karmas have content of three guṇās [and so far as the content of three guṇas is there, nothing can be devoid of doṣa]. This condition is (*iva*) similar to the (*agniḥ*) fire (*āvṛtāḥ*) enveloped (*dhūmena*) by smoke.

असक्तबुद्धिः सर्वत्र जितात्मा विगतस्पृहः ।
नैष्कर्म्यसिद्धिं परमां संन्यासेनाधिगच्छति ॥ १८.४९ ॥
*asakta-buddhiḥ sarvatra jitātmā vigataspṛhaḥ,*
*naiṣkamrya-siddhiṁ paramāṁ sannyāsenādhigacchati. (18.49)*

(*asakta-buddhiḥ*) A seeker whose mind is always free from (*sarvatra*) all attachments like son, wife, etc., (*jitātmā*) who has subdued the mind and senses, (*vigataspṛhaḥ*) who has no desire of body, life and enjoyments of material things and who (*adhigachchhati*) attains a (*paramām*) supreme state of (*naiṣkarmya siddhi*) Naiṣkarmya siddhi, [a state where one has abandoned kāmya karmas and performs nitya-karmas without any selfish motive] (*saṁnyāsena*) through renunciation of kāmya karmas.

Note: Saṁnyāsa is the renunciation of kāmya karmas after proper visualization, which helps a seeker in liberation. A seeker's action is targeted towards the goal of liberation. Once his goal is achieved, he is not required to do any action or put in any other effort.

सिद्धिं प्राप्तो यथा ब्रह्म तथाप्नोति निबोध मे।
समासेनैव कौन्तेय निष्ठा ज्ञानस्य या परा॥ १८.५०॥
*siddhiṁ prāpto yathā brahma tathāpnoti nibodha me.*
*Samāsenaiva kaunteya niṣṭhā hā jñānasya yā parā. (18.50)*

(*prāptaḥ*) Having achieved (*siddhim*) success in making his/her sense organs and body efficient towards the attainment of self-realisation by dedicating his/her karmas as a service to God, (*nibodha*) know (*me*) from me (*samāsena*) briefly (tathā) the method of (*āpnoti*) realisation of (*Brahma*) Brahman after self-realisation, (*Kaunteya*) O son of Kunti. (*yā*) This Brahma realisation is (*parā niṣṭhā*) the climax of (*jñānasya*) knowledge [realisation]. The knowledge ends with knowledge of Brahman, as nothing is left to be known after that, and that is called Vedānta [end of the Veda].

Note: Ātmajñāna (Self-realisation) and Brahma-jñāna (Brahma-realisation) are two different things. Brahma-jñāna (Brahma-realisation) is achieved, followed by Ātmajñāna (Self-realisation).

बुद्ध्या विशुद्धया युक्तो धृत्यात्मानं नियम्य च।
शब्दादीन्विषयांस्त्यक्त्वा रागद्वेषौ व्युदस्य च॥ १८.५१॥
*buddhyā viśuddhayā yukto dhṛtyātmānaṁ niyamya ca,*
*śabdādīn viṣayān styaktvā rāga-dveṣau vyudasya ca. (18.51)*

(*yuktaḥ*) Endowed with (*viśuddhayā*) purified (*buddhyā*) buddhi [buddhi uncoloured with the sanskāras of material world], (*niyamya*) controlling (*ātmānam*) the mind (*dhṛtyā*) by dhārāṇā [focussing it on ātman], (*tyaktvā*) turning away from the (*viṣyān*) stimuli of sense organs (*śabda-ādīn*) like sound, etc. (*cha*) and (*vyudasya*) setting aside (*rāga*) likes and (*dveṣa*) dislikes; and

विविक्तसेवी लघवाशी यतवाक्कायमानसः।

ध्यानयोगपरो नित्यं वैराग्यं समुपाश्रित: ॥ १८.५२ ॥
*vivikta-sevī laghvāśī yata-vāk-kāya-mānasaḥ,*
*dhyāna-yoga-paro nityaṁ vairāgyaṁ samupāśritaḥ. (18.52)*

(*vivikta-sevī)* Living in solitude, (*laghu+āśī)* eating lightly, (*yat*) controlling the (*vāk*) speech, (*kāya*) body and sense organs, (*mānasaḥ*) and mind; (*paraḥ*) ever absorbed (*nityam*) always in (*dhyāna-yoga*) prolonged focus of mind at one point [in this case, dhyāna yoga means prolonged focus of mind on one's own ātman], and (*samupāśritaḥ*) resorting to (*vairāgyam*) detachment.

अहंकारं बलं दर्पं कामं क्रोधं परिग्रहम्।
विमुच्य निर्मम: शान्तो ब्रह्मभूयाय कल्पते ॥ १८.५३ ॥
*ahaṅkāraṁ balaṁ darpaṁ kāmaṁ krodhaṁ parigraham,*
*vimucya nirmamaḥ śānto brahmbhūyāya kalpate. (18.53)*

(*vimuchya*) Relinquishing (*ahaṅkāram*) the notion of doership, (*balam*) obsession for sensual pleasures, (*darpam*) arrogance, *(kāmam)* desires, *(krodham)* intolerance, *(parigraham)* tendency of hoarding and *(nirmamaḥ)* devoid of the notion of 'I', 'my', 'me'; *(śāntaḥ)* having attained peace; *(kalpate)* one becomes fit (*brahmabhūyāya*) for attaining oneness with Brahman.

ब्रह्मभूत: प्रसन्नात्मा न शोचति न काङ्क्षति।
सम: सर्वेषु भूतेषु मद्भक्तिं लभते पराम्॥ १८.५४ ॥
*brahma-bhūtaḥ prasnnātmā na śocati na kāṅakṣati,*
*samaḥ sarveṣu bhūteṣu mad-bhaktiṁ labhate parām.(18.54)*

(*Brahmabhūtaḥ*) Who has attained self-realisation, (*prasannātmā)* who has achieved spiritual serenity and who (*na*) neither *(śochati)* grieves for any material loss (*na*) nor *(kāṅkṣati)* desires to gain material things; who (*samaḥ*) feels the pleasure and pain of (*sarveṣu bhūteṣu*) all animate beings as with regard to himself, he (*labhate*) attains (*parām*) highest (*madbhaktim*) proximity to

Brahman.

भक्त्या मामभिजानाति यावान्यश्चास्मि तत्त्वतः ।
ततो मां तत्त्वतो ज्ञात्वा विशते तदनंतरम् ॥ १८.५५ ॥
*bhaktyā mām-abhijānāti yāvān yaś cāsmi tattvataḥ,*
*tato māṁ tattvato jñātvā viśate tad anantaram. (18.55)*

(*bhaktyā*) By proximity to Brahman, (*abhijānāti*) one knows (*māma*) Him *(cha)* and *(yāvān, yaś asmi)* whatever His expanse is. (*tataḥ jñātvā*) Having known *(mām)* Brahman (*tattvataḥ*) in true sense, (*tadanantaram*) one (*viśate*) enters into him [attains mokṣa]. (See also 5.19).

सर्वकर्माण्यपि सदा कुर्वाणो मद्व्यपाश्रयः ।
मत्प्रसादादवाप्नोति शाश्वतं पदमव्ययम् ॥ १८.५६ ॥
*sarva-karmāṇyapi sadā kurvāṇo madvyapāśrayaḥ,*
*matprasādād avāpnoti śāśvataṁ padam avyayam. (18.56)*

One (*avāpnoti*) attains (*śāśvataṁ*) the eternal (*avyayam*) imperishable (*padam*) abode (*api*) even after (*kurvāṇaḥ*) doing (*sarvāṇi karmāṇi*) all types of karmas including kāmya karmas (*madvyapāśrayaḥ*) if one dedicates them to Brahman as his servant.

चेतसा सर्वकर्माणि मयि संन्यस्य मत्परः ।
बुद्धियोगमुपाश्रित्य मच्चित्तः सततं भव ॥ १८.५७ ॥
*cetasā sarva-karmāṇi mayi sannyasya matparaḥ,*
*buddhi-yogam upāśritya maccittaḥ satataṁ bhava. (18.57)*

(*chetasā*) Mentally (*saṁnyasya*) dedicate (*sarvakarmāṇi*) all actions—either having visible or invisible fruits (*mayi*) unto Brahman and (*matparaḥ*) devote yourself entirely to Brahman. Applying the method of Buddhi-yoga [keeping the mind unconcerned about material gain or loss], you should have Brahman constantly in your mind.

मच्चित्तः सर्वदुर्गाणि मत्प्रसादात्तरिष्यसि ।

अथ चेत्त्वमहंकारान्न श्रोष्यसि विनङ्क्ष्यसि ॥ १८.५८ ॥
*maccittaḥ sarva durgāṇi mat-prasādāt tariṣyasi,*
*atha cet tvam ahaṅkārān na śroṣyasi vinaṅkṣyasi. (18.58)*

(*macchitaḥ*) Keeping Brahman in mind (*tariṣyati*), you will overcome (*sarva-durgāṇi*) all difficulties (*matprasādāt*) by His grace. (*Atha*) But, (*chet*) if (*na*) you do not (*śroṣyasi*) listen to me [Krishna] (*ahaṅkārāt*) due to the ego that you know everything, (*vinaṅkṣyasi*) you will be destroyed.

यदहंकारमाश्रित्य न योत्स्य इति मन्यसे ।
मिथ्यैष व्यवसायस्ते प्रकृतिस्त्वां नियोक्ष्यति ॥ १८.५९ ॥
*yad ahaṅkāram āśritya na yotsya iti manyase,*
*mithyaiṣa vyavasāyas te prakṛtis-tvāṁ niyokṣyati. (18.59)*

(*āśritya*) Entrenched in (*ahaṅkāram*) egoism, (*iti)* if (*manyase*) you think that you will (*na*) not (*yotsya*) fight war; (*vyavasāyaḥ*) this resolve (*te*) of yours is (*mithyā+eṣa*) vain, as the (*tvām*) your (*prakṛtiḥ*) sanskāras (*niyokṣyati*) will compel you [to fight the war].

स्वभावजेन कौन्तेय निबद्धः स्वेन कर्मणा ।
कर्तुं नेच्छसि यन्मोहात्करिष्यस्यवशोऽपि तत् ॥ १८.६० ॥
*svabhāvajena kaunteya nibaddhaḥ svena karmaṇā,*
*kartuṁ necchasi yan mohāt kariṣyasyavaśo'pi tat. (18.60)*

You are (*nibaddhaḥ*) bound to (*svena*) your (*karmaṇā*) karma of kṣatriya (*svabhāvajena*) by your sanskāras. If you *(na)* do not (*icchasi)* wish to (*kartum*) fight *(yat)* it (*mohāt*) due to ignorance, (*kariṣyasi*) you will helplessly do (*tat*) it, (*Kaunteya*) O Son of Kunti.

ईश्वरः सर्वभूतानां हृद्देशेऽर्जुन तिष्ठति ।
भ्रामयन्सर्वभूतानि यन्त्रारूढानि मायया ॥ १८.६१ ॥
*īśvaraḥ sarvabhūtānāṁ hṛddeśe'rjuna tiṣṭhati,*
*bhrāmayan sarvabhūtāni yantrārūḍhāni māyayā. (18.61)*

(*Īśvaraḥ*) The God (*tiṣṭhati*) abides in the (*hṛdeśe*) heart (*sarva-bhūtānām*) of all beings, (*Arhuna*) O Arjuna, (*bhrāmayan*) causing (*sarva-bhūtāni*) all beings to travel from one body to another body (*yantra-āruḍhāni)* like puppets mounted on a machine (*māyayā)* according to their sanskāras.

तमेव शरणं गच्छ सर्वभावेन भारत।
तत्प्रसादात्परां शान्तिं स्थानं प्राप्स्यसि शाश्वतम्॥ १८.६२॥
*tameva śaraṇaṁ gaccha sarvabhāvena bhārata,*
*tatprasādāt-parāṁ śāntiṁ sthānaṁ prāpsyasi śāśvatam. (18.62)*

(*gacchha*) Seek (*śaraṇam*) refuge (*tam*) in Him (*eva*) alone, (*sarvabhāvena*) by all means, (*Bhārata*) O Arjuna. (*tat+prasādāt*) By His grace, (*prāpsyasi*) you shall attain (*parām*) supreme (*śāntim*) peace and (*śāśvatam*) the eternal (*sthānam*) abode of mokṣa.

इति ते ज्ञानमाख्यातं गुह्याद्गुह्यतरं मया।
विमृश्यैतदशेषेण यथेच्छसि तथा कुरु॥ १८.६३॥
*iti te jñānam ākhyātaṁ guhyād guhyataraṁ mayā,*
*vimṛśyaitad aśeṣeṇa yathecchasi tathā kuru. (18.63)*

(*iti*) Thus (*jñānam*) the knowledge that is (*guhyāt-guhyataram*) most secret (*ākhyātam*) has been explained to (*te*) you (*mayā*) by me. Having (*aśeṣeṇa*) fully (*vimṛśya*) reflected (*etad*) on it, (*kuru*) do (*yathā*) as (*icchhasi*) you wish.

**Here ends the Upadeśa [teaching]**

सर्वगुह्यतमं भूयः श्रृणु मे परमं वचः।
इष्टोऽसि मे दृढमिति ततो वक्ष्यामि ते हितम्॥ १८.६४॥
*Sarva-guhyatamaṁ bhūyaḥ śṛṇu me paramaṁ vacaḥ,*
*Iṣṭo'si me dṛḍham iti tato vakṣyāmi te hitam. (18.64)*

(*śṛṇu*) Listen (*bhuyaḥ*) again to (*me*) my (*paramam*) most important (*vachaḥ*) words, (*sarva-guhyatamam*) most secret of all. (*iti)* Since you are (*dṛḍham*) very (*iśṭaḥ asi)* dear to (*me*) me, (*tataḥ*) therefore, (*vakṣyāmi*) I shall tell this for (*te*) your (*hitam*) benefit.

मन्मना भव मद्भक्तो मद्याजी मां नमस्कुरु।
मामेवैष्यसि सत्यं ते प्रतिजाने प्रियोऽसि मे॥ १८.६५॥
*manmanā bhava mad-bhakto mad-yājī māṁ namaskuru,*
*mām evaiṣyasi satyaṁ te pratijāne priyo'si me. (18.65)*

(*manmanā bhava*) Fix your mind on what I say, (*madbhaktaḥ*) have full faith in me, (*madyājī)* do what I say and (*namaskuru*) thank (*mām*) me for my advice, (*eṣyasi)* you shall (*eva*) certainly reach (*mām*) my stage of liberation following my advice. (*pratijāne*) I promise this (*satyam*) actually to you because (*asi*) you are (*priyaḥ*) very dear to (*me*) me.

सर्वधर्मान्परित्यज्य मामेकं शरणं व्रज।
अहं त्वा सर्वपापेभ्यो मोक्षयिष्यामि मा शुचः॥ १८.६६॥
*sarva-adharmān parityajya mām ekaṁ śaraṇaṁ vraja,*
*ahaṁ tvā sarva pāpebhyo mokṣayiṣyāmi mā śucaḥ. (18.66)*

(*parityajya*) Renunciating (*sarva-dharmān*) all karmas based upon sanskāras, (*mām+ekam śaraṇam vraja*) completely act according to me. (*ahaṁ*) I shall (*mokṣayiṣyāmi*) liberate you from (*sarva-pāpebhyaḥ*) all acts leading to your downfall. (*mā śuchaḥ*) You need not to grieve.

इदं ते नातपस्काय नाभक्ताय कदाचन।
न चाशुश्रूषवे वाच्यं न च मां योऽभ्यसूयति॥ १८.६७॥
*idaṁ te nātapaskāya nābhaktāya kadācana,*
*na cāśuśrūṣave vācyaṁ na ca māṁ yo'bhyasūyati. (18.67)*

(*idam*) This knowledge is given (*te*) to you for your benefit to cut off the bondage of the birth and death cycle. It (*na vāchyam*) should never be spoken *(atapaskāya)* to one who is devoid of austerity, (*na+abhaktāya*) who is without dedication and devotion for attaining Brahman, (*na cha aśuśrūṣave*) who does not desire to listen, or (*yaḥ*) who (*abhyasūyati*) criticizes me.

य इदं परमं गुह्यं मद्भक्तेष्वभिधास्यति।
भक्तिं मयि परां कृत्वा मामेवैष्यत्यसंशयः॥ १८.६८॥
*ya idaṁ paramaṁ guhyaṁ mad-bhakteṣvabhidhāsyati,*
*bhaktiṁ mayi parāṁ kṛtvā mām eva-iṣyatyasañśayaḥ.(18.68)*

The one who (*abhidhāsyati*) shall propagate this (*paramam*) supreme (*guhyam*) secret knowledge (*madbhakteṣu*) amongst my followers, he shall be considered as (*kṛtvā*) having rendered the (*parām*) highest (*bhaktim*) job of (*mayi*) mine. (*eṣyati*) Such a person becomes famous (*mām*) as me, (*asañśayaḥ*) there is no doubt about it.

न च तस्मान्मनुष्येषु कश्चिन्मे प्रियकृत्तमः।
भविता न च मे तस्मादन्यः प्रियतरो भुवि॥ १८.६९॥
*na ca tasmān-manuṣyeṣu kaścin me priyakṛttamaḥ,*
*bhavitā na ca me tasmādanyaḥ priyataro bhuvi. (18.69)*

The one who propagates this knowledge, (*na cha kaśchit)* no other person (manuśyeṣu) among men than him (*priyakṛttamaḥ*) performs dearer job (*me*) of mine, (*cha*) and so (*na*) no one (*bhuvi*) on the earth (*bhavitā*) shall do (*priyataraḥ*) more dear job of mine (*tasmāt anyaḥ*) than him.

अध्येष्यते च य इमं धर्म्यं संवादमावयोः।
ज्ञानयज्ञेन तेनाहमिष्टः स्यामिति मे मतिः॥ १८.७०॥
*adhyeṣyate ca ya imaṁ dharmyaṁ saṁvādam āvayoḥ,*
*jñāna-yajñena tenāham iṣṭaḥ syām iti me matiḥ. (18.70)*

(Cha) And (*yaḥ*) who (*adhyeṣyate*) shall study (*imam*) this (*saṁvādam*) dialogue (*āvayoḥ*) of ours *(dharmyam)* reflecting on dharma, *(aham)* I *(syāma)* shall be *(iṣṭaḥ)* honoured *(tena)* by him *(jñāna-yajñena)* through this jñāna-yajña.

श्रद्धावाननसूयश्च शृणुयादपि यो नरः।
सोऽपि मुक्तः शुभाँल्लोकान्प्राप्नुयात्पुण्यकर्मणाम्॥ १८.७१॥
*śraddhāvān anasūyaś ca śṛṇuyād api yo naraḥ,*
*so'pi muktaḥ śubhānllokān*
*prāpnuyāt puṇya-karmaṇām. (18.71)*

(*yaḥ naraḥ*) Whoever (*śṛṇuyāt api*) listens to this with (*śraddhāvān*) positive attitude (*cha*) and (*anasūyaścha*) without envy, (*saḥ api*) he will also be (*muktaḥ*) free from all confusions of what to do and what not and (*prāpnuyāt*) attains (*śubhān lokān*) good families of yogis and agnihotris, etc. in the next life due to his good karmas.

## Question to Arjuna to know the effect of Teaching

कच्चिदेतच्छ्रुतं पार्थ त्वयैकाग्रेण चेतसा।
कच्चिदज्ञानसम्मोहः प्रनष्टस्ते धनंजय॥ १८.७२॥
*kaccid etacchrutaṁ pārtha tvayaikāgreṇa cetasā.*
*kaccid ajñāna-sammohaḥ praṇaṣṭas te dhanañjaya. (18.72)*

*(Pārtha!)* O Arjuna, (*kacchit*) did (*tvayā*) you (*śrutam*) listen to this (*ekāgreṇa*) with a concentrated (*chetasā*) mind? (*kacchit*) Has (*te*) your (*sammohaḥ*) delusion [lost power of discrimination between real and unreal things]*(ajñān)* born of ignorance (*pranaṣṭaḥ*) been destroyed? *(Dhanañjaya!)* O Arjuna.

अर्जुन उवाच
Arjuna said

नष्टो मोहः स्मृतिर्लब्धा त्वत्प्रसादान्मयाऽच्युत।
स्थितोऽस्मि गतसंदेहः करिष्ये वचनं तव॥ १८.७३॥

*naṣṭo mohaḥ smṛtir-labdhā tvat prasādān mayācyuta,*
*sthito'smi gata-sandehaḥ kariṣye vacanaṁ tava. (18.73)*

Arjuna said— (*tvat prasādāt*) By your grace, (*naṣṭaḥ mohaḥ*) my delusion is over, (*smṛtiḥ labdhāḥ*) I have regained my power of discrimination between real and unreal things, (*sthitaḥ asmi*) I am now at your disposal, (*gatasandehaḥ*) free from all doubts. (*kariṣye tava vachanam*) I shall act according to your instructions.

संजय उवाच

Sañjaya said

इत्यहं वासुदेवस्य पार्थस्य च महात्मनः ।
संवादमिममश्रौषमद्भुतं रोमहर्षणम् ॥ १८.७४ ॥
*ityahaṁ vāsudevasya pārthasya ca mahātmanaḥ,*
*saṁvādam imam aśrauṣam adbhutaṁ roma-harṣaṇam. (18.74)*

Sañjaya said to Dhṛtarāṣṭra— (*iti+aham*) Thus I (*aśrauṣam*) heard (*imam*) this (*roma-harṣaṇam*) thrilling (*saṁvādam*) dialogue between the (*mahātmanaḥ*) great (*Vāsudevasya*) Śri Krishna (*cha*) and (*Pārthasya*) Arjuna.

व्यासप्रसादाच्छ्रुतवानेतद्गुह्यमहं परम् ।
योगं योगेश्वरात्कृष्णात्साक्षात्कथयतः स्वयम् ॥ १८.७५ ॥
*vyāsa-prasādāc-chrutavān etada guhyam ahaṁ param,*
*yogaṁ yogeśvarāt kṛṣṇāt sākṣāt kathayataḥ svayam. (18.75)*

(*Vyāsa-prasādāt*) By the grace of sage Vyāsa, (*aham*) I (*śrutavān*) heard (*etat*) this (*param*) most (*guhyam*) secret and (*yogam*) supreme yoga (*sākṣāt*) directly from (*yogeśvara Kṛṣṇāt*) Yogeśvara Krishna (*kathayataḥ*) speaking (*svayam*) himself to Arjuna.

राजन्संस्मृत्य संस्मृत्य संवादमिममद्भुतम् ।
केशवार्जुनयोः पुण्यं हृष्यामि च मुहुर्मुहुः ॥ १८.७६ ॥
*rājan sansmṛtya sansmṛtya saṁvādam imam adbhutam,*
*keśavārjunayoḥ puṇyaṁ hṛṣyāmi ca muhur-muhuḥ. (18.76)*

(Rājan) O King, (*sansmṛtya-sansmṛtya*) by repeated remembrance of (*imam*) this (*adbhutam*) marvelous, (*puṇyam*) beneficial (*saṁvādam*) dialogue (*Keśavārjunayoḥ*) between Śri Krishna and Arjuna, (*hṛṣyāmi*) I am thrilled (*muhurmuhuḥ*) at every moment; and

तच्च संस्मृत्य संस्मृत्य रूपमत्यद्भुतं हरेः ।
विस्मयो मे महान्राजन्हृष्यामि च पुनः पुनः ॥ १८.७७ ॥
*tacca sansmṛtya sansmṛtya rūpam-atyadbhutaṁ hareḥ,*
*vismayo me mahān rājan hṛṣyāmi ca punaḥ punaḥ. (18.77)*

(*sansmṛtya-sansmṛtya*) Recollecting again and again, (*Rājan*) O King, (*tat+cha*) that (*adbhutam*) marvelous (*rūpam*) stature of Śri Krishna, I am greatly amazed and I rejoice over and over again.

यत्र योगेश्वरः कृष्णो यत्र पार्थो धनुर्धरः ।
तत्र श्रीर्विजयो भूतिर्ध्रुवा नीतिर्मतिर्मम ॥ १८.७८ ॥
*yatra yogeśvaraḥ kṛṣṇo yatra pārtho dhanurdharaḥ,*
*tatra śrīrvijayo bhūtiḥ dhruvā nītir-matir-mama. (18.78)*

(*yatra*) Where there is (*Yogeśvaraḥ Kṛṣṇaḥ*) Yogeśvara Krishna; and (*yatra*) where there is (*Pārthaḥ*) Arjuna, (*dhanuardharaḥ*) the expert of Dhanurveda; (*tatra*) there will be (*śrīḥ*) everlasting prosperity, (*vijayaḥ*) victory, (*bhūtiḥ*) expansion of happiness, (*dhruvā nitiḥ*) firm policy. This is (*mama*) my [Sañjaya's] (*matiḥ*) conviction.

ॐ तत्सदिति श्रीमद् भगवद्गीतासूपनिषत्सु ब्रह्मविद्यायां योगशास्त्रे श्रीकृष्णार्जुनसंवादे मोक्षसंन्यासयोगोनाम अथाष्टादशोऽध्यायः ॥१८ ॥

Here ends the 18th chapter named Mokṣa Saṁnyāsa Yoga in the *Bhagvadgitā* dealing with the Brahmavidyā as propounded in the Upaniṣad and Yogaśāstra in the form of dialogue between Śri Krishna and Arjuna.

www.ingramcontent.com/pod-product-compliance
Lightning Source LLC
Chambersburg PA
CBHW051341040426
42453CB00007B/359